- **Helen Musick** (Chapter 4) is an instructor in youth ministry at Asbury Seminary in Kentucky, coauthor of the *Girls* and *Guys* curriculums (Youth Specialties), and a member of Youth Specialties' The CORE™ training team.

- **Chap Clark** (Chapter 5) is associate professor of youth, family and culture at Fuller Theological Seminary, and is a team leader of The Community, a new community outreach ministry in La Crescenta, California. His books include *The Youth Worker's Handbook to Family Ministry* and *Daughters and Dads*.

- **Marv Penner** (Chapter 6) chairs the youth and family ministry department—and directs the Canadian Center for Adolescent Research—at Briercrest Bible College and Seminary in Saskatchewan, Canada. He's author of *Creative Bible Lessons in 1 & 2 Corinthians* (Youth Specialties) and a member of member of Youth Specialties' The CORE™ training team.

- **Rick Warren** (Chapter 7) is founding pastor of Saddleback Church, one of America's largest congregations, and author of the best-selling *The Purpose-Driven® Church*. He also founded pastors.com, an online community for ministers on the Internet.

- **Jana L. Sundene** (Chapter 8) is assistant professor of Bible and Christian education at Trinity International University's College of Arts and Sciences. Before assuming her position at Trinity in 1990, Sundene was associate director of youth at Willow Creek Community Church. She coauthored "Speaking to High School Students" with Dan Webster for *The Complete Book of Youth Ministry*.

- **Bo Boshers** (Chapter 9) is executive director of student ministry at the Willow Creek Association, a best-selling author (*Reaching Kids Most Ministries Miss*, *Doing Life with God*, and others), and a world-renowned speaker.

- **Duffy Robbins** (Chapter 10) is associate professor of youth ministry at Eastern University outside Philadelphia, author of several books, including *The Ministry of Nurture*, and a member of Youth Specialties' The CORE™ training team.

- **Tony Campolo** (Chapter 11) is a beloved, passionate communicator, professor of sociology at Eastern University outside Philadelphia, and author of many books, including *It's Friday, but Sunday's Coming* and *Revolution and Renewal*.

- **Richard Ross** (Chapter 12) is founder of True Love Waits and a youth ministry professor at Southwestern Baptist Theological Seminary. He has written or compiled 16 books on youth ministry, many of which have been classroom texts in Southern Baptist colleges and seminaries.

before you dig in

As I was writing this book, a friend asked, "Doug, can you even *remember* your first two years of youth ministry?" I smiled and replied, "Yes. But fortunately this book doesn't have anything to do with my actual first two years. If it did, it would be short, discouraging, and not very helpful."

Your First Two Years of Youth Ministry isn't about copying Doug Fields' first two years; it's about making good choices so you'll survive and become a healthy youth worker for the long haul, no matter what your role—volunteer or lead youth worker.

Because of many years I've spent in the youth ministry trenches, I'm confident that I know youth ministry and youth workers—but I surely don't have all the answers. Still I've experienced enough youth ministry and heard enough of the questions that I believe I can help you, regardless of your status. I wrote this book to both volunteers *and* to leaders of youth ministries (paid or volunteer). I've approached the tone of this book to mirror real conversations you and I might share, as if we were sitting together at a restaurant and talking about youth ministry. Now, I realize that no book can answer your every question, but because I've poured a lot of my life into these pages to help you survive and thrive in your calling, I'm sure this book will prepare you to forge your own path and direction as you love students and point them toward Jesus.

But before you dig in, here are a few important points I want you to know:

1. Without a clear understanding of the big picture in youth ministry, your actions will become desperate moves, and you'll be easily defeated. These chapters were written to help you better understand some of the key truths, constants, and nuances of youth ministry, and to give you practical ideas on how to succeed in your calling.

2. Don't rush through this book. Take your time, interact with the chapters, and make this resource one of your youth ministry friends. Consider reading it with another youth ministry friend and dialogue over some of the questions at the end of each chapter. Then go to my Web site and offer your comments about each chapter and read some of the other responses and questions that others are asking. (www.dougfields.com)

3. Most of the learning I've picked up over the years has come through failures. Yes, I've failed a lot! But I have a richer education because of those failures. In these pages I try to protect you from some potential failures, but I know you'll experience plenty of your own, regardless of what I suggest. (Just remember that your failures should be educational!)

4. If you're a volunteer and the leader of your ministry has given you a copy of this book, consider yourself a *blessed* leader—someone wants you to win! If you're the leader of the ministry, try to get this book into the hands of your volunteers, because when they win, you win. Ideally you should try to read this book before you start your paid or volunteer position. But even if you're already in "the game," the book will still help you immeasurably.

5. This book is very different from my last book, *Purpose-Driven® Youth Ministry* (PDYM). When I was writing this one, a lot of friends asked about those differences. Aside from length (PDYM is 400-plus pages), *Your First Two Years in Youth Ministry* is about making you a better youth worker while PDYM is about building a better youth ministry. PDYM helps you think about and organize your ministry. While I summarize a lot of key

elements of *PDYM* in Chapter 10, *Your First Two Years in Youth Ministry* is primarily about emotional survival so you'll be around long enough to organize your ministry. If you must choose one book to read first, I suggest you read this book first—then pick up *PDYM* and read that one.

6. This book is very different from most other youth ministry books you've seen. It's not a how-to manual—it's a heart-to-heart talk. It's story sharing. It's truth telling. And not only have I opened my heart and poured myself into these pages, others have done so as well. You'll find their voices—some known, some unknown—in a multitude of sidebars in each chapter. All the contributors help to make this book your most complete companion to getting through your first two years of youth ministry.

7. Learning to be a healthy youth worker isn't as easy as some make it sound. So enjoy the process, learn along the way, and together let's give God the glory for using flawed people like us to point students to Jesus.

My Story

I don't presume you as a reader will or should care about my story. But the editors believe that some notes from my youth ministry journey might help put a little more flesh and bone on the pages and help bridge the gap between the practical and the personal. (Seriously, for all I care, you can jump right into Chapter 1 and skip the rest of this…or, if you're the curious type, you can read on and find out where some of this book came from.)

I started my youth ministry journey in 1979 while I was just a junior in high school at my home church, Orange (California) Presbyterian. My youth pastor, Jim Burns, saw a quality and potential in me that I didn't see in myself—leadership. So he gave me the opportunity to lead a small group of junior high students at our church. Then I was given some teaching responsibilities, and eventually I played a major role on the junior high leadership team until I graduated from high school in 1981. During those two years, my mentors were very affirming toward me, and I sensed God leading me into youth ministry. And I had no idea that the journey I began as a 17-year-old would lead me to one day write a book for people who were beginning in youth ministry, just like I was!

I had no training. But I did love God, and some great adult models poured their lives into mine and pointed me to Jesus. I just wanted to be like them.

For the next several years I worked as an intern with Jim at a church plant called South Coast Community Church (now Mariners Church) in Southern California. During this time, I finished college (BA, Vanguard University) and seminary (M. Div., Fuller Seminary) to supplement my practical experience. Then in 1985, Jim "cut the cord" and left me on my own to run the youth ministry after he moved on to start a national youth ministry organization. While I was eager to take the lead, I had no idea how much the point person of a ministry went through! I had always been protected, and now the protection was gone; I was faced with lots of failure (and lots of learning).

It was during the next several years that I developed most of my youth ministry philosophies and practices. I worked with some incredible leaders and volunteers and experienced some of the greatest memories of my life. While I was at South Coast, my pastor, Tim Timmons, encouraged me to write and speak. Like Jim, he saw something in me that I didn't see in myself—the ability to communicate and create resources that help students and volunteers. He would always say, "You've got to be creating tools, Doug. People need tools. How can what you're doing here be used to help other churches?" He helped me to develop a heart for other youth workers. It was also in 1985 that Youth Specialties offered me the opportunity to train youth workers on a national level. I didn't see myself as a trainer—they did. (Again, more people seeing things in my life that I didn't see.) I still can't believe they let a 24-year-old teach other youth workers!

And what being in front of other youth workers forced me to do is really think through and translate youth ministry ideas into tangible handles that could be implemented by volunteers in all types of youth ministry settings and sizes. As I write this book, I continue in my relationship with Youth Specialties—a relationship for which I'm very thankful.

In 1992 I became the interim pastor to students at Saddleback Church in Lake Forest, California. I planned to be at Saddleback only long enough for them to find a full-time youth pastor, and then I would refocus on my plans to continue writing and speaking. I'd heard great things about Saddleback (since my other church was only 15 miles away), and I knew it would be a great place to do youth ministry for whomever

your first two years in youth ministry

a personal and practical guide to starting right

Doug Fields

ZONDERVAN™

WWW.ZONDERVAN.COM

Youth Specialties

www.youthspecialties.com

Youth Specialties

Your First Two Years in Youth Ministry: A Personal and Practical Guide to Starting Right
Copyright © 2002 by Doug Fields

Youth Specialties Books, 300 S. Pierce St., El Cajon, CA 92020, are published by Zondervan, 5300 Patterson Ave. S.E., Grand Rapids, MI 49530.

Library of Congress Cataloging-in-Publication Data
Fields, Doug. 1962—
    Your first two years in youth ministry : a personal and practical guide to starting right / Doug Fields.
        p. cm.
    ISBN-10: 0-310-24045-X
    ISBN-13: 978-0-310-24045-7
  1. Church group work with youth. I. Title.
    BV4447 .F545 2002
    259'.23—dc21

                                                                                        2002004941

Web site addresses listed in this book were current at the time of publication. Please contact Youth Specialties via e-mail (YS@YouthSpecialties.com) to report URLs that are no longer operational and replacement URLs if available.

The names within have been changed where appropriate.

Edited by Vicki Newby and Dave Urbanski
Cover and Interior design by Joshua Dunford/BURNKIT
Photography by Joshua Dunford
Printed in the United States of America

HB 08.13.2020

dedication

This book is dedicated to my incredible family—Cathy, Torie, Cody, and Cassie. I love being your husband and dad. My life is richer because of each of you. You make me smile, laugh, and long to be with you when I'm not. Thank you for your commitment to youth workers by supporting my ministry with your love and sacrifice.

contents

acknowledgments

The writing of this book spanned two years, countless hours, and immeasurable support from so many new and old friends. These people asked about my progress, prayed for my inspiration, and hung out with my family during times when I had to write. I want to say thank you for your friendship and for the gracious roles you played in my life and in this book. My thanks go to...

- The student ministry staff at Saddleback Church, whose names are always my answer to the question, "What do you love most about your job?"

- Linda Kaye, Deb Pflieger, Paul Alexander, Andy Brazelton, and Susan Pope—my staff at www.dougfields.com who serve God and youth workers by turning my books, tapes, and videos into helpful resources. You are such a gift to me and other youth workers.

- Lynne Ellis, Gregg Farah, and Matt McGill—who served me faithfully by helping me outline chapters and craft words that I could have never come up with myself. This is a better book because of you.

- Katie Brazelton, Mary McNeil, and Susan Reinhardt—who read every word of my early drafts and cleaned up the manuscript so the editors thought I knew what I was doing. Your many hours of love touched me deeply.

- Dennis Beckner, my assistant—who helped with everything from typing, research, editing, and keeping me alive. Thank you for your above-and-beyond-the-call attitude and hard work.

- Dave Ambrose, Kurt Johnston, Billy Fray, and Duffy Robbins—who read my final draft and challenged my thinking, added comments, and breathed life into each chapter. I'm honored by your friendship and the gift of time you gave this book.

- Vicki Newby, Mark Oestreicher, and Dave Urbanski—my Youth Specialties friends who embraced my ideas and applied their brilliant minds to make this a better book than the one I turned in. Thank you for believing in this project and in me.

- Brian Farmer and John-Michael McGinnis—two youth worker friends who graciously let me use material from their e-mails.

- Deanna Davis, Jeanette Fatigati, Chris Garten, Cynthia Hammork, Brad Hartke, Heather Kaiser, Neely McQueen, Linda Vujnov, and Tami Wright—youth ministry volunteers who took the time to think of illustrations and anecdotes I could share.

- Jim Burns, Steve Gerali, Mike Yaconelli, Helen Musick, Chap Clark, Marv Penner, Rick Warren, Jana Sundene, Bo Boshers, Duffy Robbins, Tony Campolo, and Richard Ross are ministry veterans and experts who were gracious enough to add their insight to this project. I was blown away that you did this—thank you.

- Kurt Johnston, Cathy Fields, Matt McGill, Andy Brazelton, Kathleen Hamer, Lynne Ellis, Brad Johnson, Jim McNeff, Ryan Holladay, Greg & Linda Vujnov, and Jeff Maguire—for being some of my favorite people on this earth and adding your voices to these chapters. I loved your contributions, and I think readers will, too.

- Glen Kreun, my friend and "boss" at Saddleback Church—who has faithfully served the Lord for decades and models servanthood and longevity to me. Thank you for your belief and support.

- And, finally, to the volunteer youth workers throughout the world who give so much to love students and reflect Jesus—you amaze me with your commitment and inspire me to be a faithful youth worker.

essay writer profiles

- **Jim Burns** (Chapter 1) is president of YouthBuilders, an organization that provides resources for youth workers, young people, and parents, the author of more than 50 books—including *How to Be a Happy, Healthy Family*—as well as Doug Fields' former high school youth pastor.

- **Steve Gerali** (Chapter 2) draws from more than 20 years of youth ministry experience with preteens and adolescents. This author and speaker is now serving in the youth ministry departments at Judson College and Northern Baptist Theological Seminary, both in Illinois.

- **Mike Yaconelli** (Chapter 3) is a youth ministry pioneer, engaging speaker, coowner of Youth Specialties, Inc., pastor of a small church in Yreka, California, and author of numerous books, including *Messy Spirituality: God's Annoying Love for Imperfect People* and *Dangerous Wonder: The Adventure of Childlike Faith*.

God had in mind to lead full-time. I just had no idea about the ride that God had in store for me. Within just a few months I'd fallen in love with the church and the students—and "life on the road" as a speaker lost its allure rather quickly! The interim title was quickly dropped, and I've been there ever since. Still, if you had asked me in 1992, "Do you think you'll ever experience youth ministry like you did at South Coast during the '80s?" I would have said, "No way! In my wildest dreams I can't imagine a better experience than I had at South Coast!"

Well, I've since learned to dream a little bigger—because my present youth ministry is much stronger than my last one ever was. At Saddleback I was given the chance to start over and rebuild a youth ministry—to take everything I'd learned in my first dozen years and start over with more experience, wisdom, and spiritual health. I can't imagine doing youth ministry anywhere else. I love my church, the community, our volunteer leaders, the students, families, and the staff. It isn't close to perfect, but it's a place where I feel God's blessing on my leadership, gifts, and faithfulness.

As I write this, I'm convinced that my best years of youth ministry are ahead of me, and I look forward to many more chances to learn and grow. In addition, my pastor and friend, Rick Warren, believes in me enough to let me help train church leaders all over the world through what we call Purpose Driven Church conferences; in them we discuss ways to fulfill the biblical purposes of evangelism, worship, discipleship, ministry, and fellowship.

All that brings me to the present and these words you're reading (if you're the curious type, that is). Please know that I've been praying for you—I prayed for the heart of each person who reads this book. My specific prayer is that you will be helped, encouraged, and refreshed as you move ahead in the wonderful journey of youth ministry. Get started, read Chapter 1, and then prayerfully consider the commitments of health I've identified. I look forward to hearing from you, and if our paths ever cross, let's rejoice over God's goodness and your ability to last longer in this profession than two years!

Your friend and partner in youth ministry,
Doug Fields

where do i start?

committing to the essentials

In 1979 I was a rookie youth worker with no idea what I was doing. I took teenagers to R-rated movies; I had a Jacuzzi party in the baptismal because a 12-year-old thought it would be fun; I yelled at a group of parents; I taught a 15-year-old to drive using the church van, and I almost got arrested for having underage students in an over-21 club. Thankfully, a lot has changed, but it's been an eventful ride ever since.

As I write this, I'm still working with students in the church, and I love to talk about youth ministry, especially with new youth workers! Every day that I worked on this book, I thought and prayed especially for you. If you're just starting out, you're my favorite type of youth worker to help! (If you've been in the trenches for a few—or many—years, I love you too, and I'm confident you'll find help and encouragement in these pages.) I'm thrilled to play a role in your youth ministry journey. Whether you're a paid staff member or a volunteer, the principles and ideas in this book are written to help you survive and thrive as you work with teenagers.

Youth Ministry as a Marathon

One of my life goals (that I haven't accomplished yet) is to run a marathon. I've run several shorter races, but the 26.2 mile monster has eluded me so far. I watch them on TV, eagerly anticipating the day I finish a marathon.

> I can't believe I just admitted that I watch marathons on TV!

Have you ever watched a marathon? They're inspiring. When I look into the eyes of the runners, I see two types of expressions. Standing behind the starting line, the seasoned marathoners are focused, mentally preparing for the task before them. They know what it takes to complete a race of this caliber, so they stretch to prepare their bodies, run in place to warm their muscles, and close their eyes to visualize the race's hills and mile markers. The vets know what's ahead. This isn't a party; it's abuse. And since they have to endure pain over the next several hours, the task is to run efficiently. Their bodies have even instructed their faces not to smile or to express any form of joy. Veteran runners know what they're doing.

The other runners are rookies. This is a fun group to watch. They typically stick together, taking in all the action from the free race T-shirts to the vendors selling running gear to the maps locating the portable toilets on the route. The rookies are excited, feeling good, smiling, bantering with others, enjoying the pre-race hype. Little do they know that their valuable adrenaline is being wasted long before the one-mile mark. Their actions are to be expected; after all, this is an exciting time, but it's also deceptive.

How so?

Watch the race from an elevated viewpoint. At the start, a mass of humanity moves forward as one group, bunched closely together, seemingly inseparable, until the second or third mile when the crowd begins to thin. By mile 10, some have decided to walk and are tempted to stop and watch a matinee. By mile 15, many are eating lunch early. After mile 20, only those who are the most prepared have a realistic chance of finishing well. Finishing is not only a matter of the body, but the emotions and the mind.

Running a marathon is a fitting picture of youth ministry. It's not an easy task within the church. If it were, we'd have more youth workers than ushers. Youth ministry is filled with long, tiring, often unrewarding, complex, unique, intense, humorous, joy-filled, and painful experiences. Many within the body of Christ have entered the youth ministry marathon, but many quit before long, having lost joy and satisfaction. They're wounded and weary.

The Race before Us

I desperately want you to last in your ministry to students. Longevity in our field is uncommon. This is both unfortunate for the individuals who leave and tragic for the health of the church. The longer you work in youth ministry, the easier it becomes, and the better you minister to students. Quick departures have a lot to do with inadequate preparation and unrealistic expectations. But, like running, setting the proper pace assures long-term results and your ability to finish strong.

As I wrote this book, I kept two verses taped to my computer that served as the foundation for my writing. I want to share them with you.

And let us run with endurance the race that God has set before us. (Hebrews 12:1)

Youth ministry—like the Christian life—is a race that requires both training and endurance. Fortunately, our endurance and strength increase as we run the race and follow the course God has set out for us. Our success in the youth ministry race has a lot to do with developing a big-picture perspective. Check out the second verse:

Because of you I will weep and wail; I will go about barefoot and naked. I will howl like a jackal and moan like an owl. (Micah 1:8)

Oh wait…that's not the right verse. Here it is:

But I will not do this all in one year because the land would become a wilderness, and the wild animals would become too many to control. I will drive them out a little at a time until your population has increased enough to fill the land. (Exodus 23:29-30)

The wild animal reference shouldn't be viewed as synonymous with the students in your group, but this verse accurately portrays a youth worker's world. The Exodus passage describes God's plan for the *gradual* conquest of Canaan. God didn't want to overwhelm Israel by giving them the Promised Land in one day. Besides, knowing Israel wasn't completely prepared, God put together a journey that allowed them to develop their faith and confidence as they learned to depend on him.

This biblical principle applies to your youth ministry. God won't give you everything at once. The foundation of your ministry is strengthened as you develop faith, skills, leadership, experience, character, disciplines, and passion.

Where Do I Start?

Whenever you pull out this book to read a chapter, I'd love for you to imagine that you and I are at your favorite informal restaurant, meeting again to talk about you and youth ministry. The goal of the meeting is for me to coach you during your first years as a youth worker. You're filled with questions, enthusiasm, ideas, hopes, fears, dreams, and prayers for your new ministry. I'm there because I heard you have a passion for God, a humble heart, a love for students, an eagerness to learn, and—hey, let's be honest—because you offered to pay. But who really cares about the food? This is a great setting for a heart-to-heart discussion about youth ministry!

The questions you're asking during our time together have been asked by most youth workers over the years. The number one question I'm asked after I teach a seminar or after someone has finished reading my book, *Purpose-Driven® Youth Ministry*, is, "Where do I start?"

While many beginning youth workers would love for me to hand them a checklist of the exact steps to take, it's an impossible request. Since every church is unique, each youth worker complex, all students different, the steps you'll need to take won't be the same as the next youth worker's.

Even with the variety of youth workers who will read this book, some commitments are relevant to all youth workers regardless of denomination, church size, and country they live in. In this chapter, I've identified 10 commitments I'd like for you, as a new youth worker, to prayerfully consider making. They can serve as a foundation for your effectiveness, health, and happiness in youth ministry. Copy the summary on pages 21 and 22, post it in a visible place, and allow the commitments to influence you during your next several months in the trenches.

Doug's Top 10 Youth Ministry Commitments

// 1. I will move slowly.

Speed often leads to pain. When we first moved into our home, I teased my wife about her cautious parking habit. While it was a tight fit in our garage, it seemed to take her an absurd amount of time to pull into her space. One day when I was parking her car, I confidently and arrogantly zipped into the garage much faster than she did (I'm sure I shaved 10-15 seconds off of her time), but I also caused over $250 in damage as I broke off the side mirror. My teasing halted immediately, and this experience led to a teaching principle…for my children, of course: what looks to be quick and easy may need to be approached slowly and carefully. The principle applies to youth ministry.

It's safe to assume you want to make some changes at your church during your first two years. Great! But these changes probably don't need to be implemented right away. With confidence, I can guarantee that even the changes that appear to be no-brainers cause pain for someone. If you're a volunteer, immediately suggesting changes may communicate a divisive or critical attitude to the lead youth worker. If you're the lead youth worker, fast changes can appear arrogant or reveal a maverick's personality to your church.

Instead of making immediate changes, keep a record of all potential changes as soon as you think of them. This allows you to give them prayerful consideration. Hang on to your list. Continue to be a critical thinker in the arena to which God has called you, but realize you don't have to apply all (or any) of the ideas that come to you. Slow down. If you're in this for the long haul, what's the rush? Hurried changes are often perceived as lacking thought. (I've committed an entire chapter to making the change process successful. See Chapter 11.)

When I arrived at Saddleback Church in 1992, I told my pastor that it would take at least five years for us to begin to see a healthy, balanced, volunteer-laden, vibrant ministry. This wasn't an arbitrary figure. I had come to Saddleback Church after spending 11 years in youth ministry at another church. I knew there's no such thing as a just-add-water approach.

Remember, God didn't move the Israelites into the Promised Land overnight, and he's not expecting you to change your church within your first two years. Relax. Prepare your own heart before you change your church. Remember, Jesus took 30 years to prepare for three years of ministry (and he had that God-thing going for him).

// 2. I will regularly check my motives and evaluate my heart.

God honors pure motives, and the more you check yours, the stronger your leadership and decision-making will be. If your motives are pure, you'll persevere, reproduce student ministers, be productive, and contribute effectively, all while having fun. Most conflicts arise from unclear, mixed, or impure motives. If you don't personally evaluate your motives, others will—and if they're not pure, the impurity will be exposed.

I've learned that to check my motives, I must continually ask questions about myself:

- Why do I want to lead this ministry?
- Why do I want to teach this material?
- What's my motive for saying yes to that request?
- Why do I *really* want to change this program?
- When do I let people know I don't have a clue about what I'm doing?

You may think of other questions you need to ask yourself. It's good for you to evaluate your motives so you can lead with integrity.

In my early years, I wanted to cancel a student-run praise and worship night. Nothing was wrong with the program, and most people would have considered it a fairly successful night for students. I told people I wanted to cancel it because it wasn't growing and it was taking students out another night of the week (both good reasons). When I held the mirror up to examine my motives, I saw that my motives were to be noticed, to develop my credibility, and to highlight my speaking gifts (which weren't being seen because students were running the program). I used excuses as a smokescreen to cover my real agenda. My entire plan reeked of bad motives. Thankfully I didn't cancel the program, but I did see my ugly, dark side that was close to the surface and very real.

To keep your motives right, commit yourself to an honest and regular evaluation of your heart, the source of your spiritual growth and leadership. (I have written an entire chapter about your heart's condition. See Chapter 3.)

I've made my own pledge to never do any training if I can't talk about the spiritual life of a leader. Unfortunately, I spent my first several years in youth ministry creating

(A VOICE FROM THE TRENCHES)

I was 25, married with a child, and fresh out of seminary. My first, full-time youth ministry position was at a medium-size church in my hometown.

I thought seminary had prepared me pretty well for the things I would face. I mean, I spent several years in part-time youth ministry and felt ready to take on any challenge. I worked with the pastor as the only other paid, full-time staff member. One particular week, the pastor went out of town on vacation. I would get to do the radio program, preach, and perform all the duties that go with it. I was ecstatic.

Until the phone call.

A member of our church committed suicide. He was in his 40s, with a wife and eight-year-old son. I was asked to go to his house and minister there. I have to admit it was one of the few times in my life that I had no idea what to do—much less say.

On my way to the house, I prayed, asking God for guidance. Basically I just didn't want to make things worse. The scene was beyond explanation; I had never been exposed to anything resembling this. I prayed with his wife, quoted a variety of Scriptures—but somehow it seemed very inadequate. So then I just did what I could. I washed dishes, made food, played with their eight-year-old boy.

And I learned a very valuable lesson that day: A minister is a minister and needs to be prepared for any and all situations. I knew all the youth stuff, had all the youth experience, yet I couldn't minister outside of my element. I realized that day there's more to being a youth *minister* than just working with youth. I have gone on to take counseling courses and even worked with a counselor for a year to gain the experience necessary should I ever be presented with this kind of ministry opportunity again.

—*Larry Darnell, associate pastor youth and college, Adventure Baptist Church, Tallahassee, Florida*

fancy programs, inventing wild games, and growing the group to head-turning numbers, all on my own power. I was the antithesis of John 15 where Jesus tells us to be connected to the Father in order to bear fruit. I was connected to youth ministry books and magazines instead of God and his Word. Believe me, I'm a different man today and a much better youth worker because of my heart's connection. I don't have the energy that I did in 1979, but my church doesn't have the spiritually immature leader my previous church once had—I've learned to give myself regular heart check-ups since then.

// 3. I will steer clear of the numbers game.

You don't need to be in youth ministry long before you hear this famous question: "How many kids are in your group?" I've heard it asked more times than I want to admit. Now I feel embarrassed for the person who asks this question. It feeds into the myth that bigger is better and that the value of your leadership is based on how many students you have. Here's my fleshly response to this carnal question: "Who cares?"

Please commit during your beginning years to not engage in the numbers game. Don't join the group of youth workers who erroneously base their value on how many students attend a particular event. This is not a basis for determining value.

Carol was a great volunteer youth worker who left our youth ministry team because she was "tired." Later when I asked for an exit interview, she admitted that the real reason was because she felt she was ineffective. She had only three girls in her small group while the other female leaders had at least twice as many. Even as a volunteer small group leader, she felt the pressure to grow.

Truthfully, Carol was a great small group leader, and if she had had more students in her group she wouldn't have had enough time to adequately care for them. She played the numbers game, and at the end of the game, our ministry lost, Carol lost, and those three girls lost. The numbers game is a losing game! Don't be fooled into becoming a loser!

Throwing out numbers can be exciting or debilitating depending on who you're talking to. Bigger isn't better; healthier is better. Steer clear of churches and youth workers who are driven by numbers, and surround yourself with those who are motivated by serving God faithfully and pursuing health.

What if My Supervisor Is *Really* into Numbers?

First of all, I'd like to say, "I'm sorry." I understand the pressure of numbers, and I hate it. Thankfully some churches use numbers as tools—say, for planning and budgeting—but don't obsess over them. They're more concerned about pursuing health than attendance. But I realize that isn't the case in all churches, and you may feel the pressure of more... bigger... better. Not a fun culture to work in.

To write honestly, I need to say that chances are slim for changing a numbers-driven culture in a short period of time. While people and churches can change, it usually doesn't happen quickly. So what can you do? Here are some thoughts:

1. Understand where the number pressure comes from.

In many churches, the people making decisions are comfortable with a profit-loss mentality. Many church leaders come from the marketplace, and they want to know if they're getting "bang for their buck." That mentality leaks into the church and becomes, "Is the youth worker's salary justified by the number of students we have?" The answer to this isn't always objective, and that's where it becomes ugly. Attendance can be one form of evaluation, but shouldn't be the only form.

The numbers pressure has more history in secular thinking than in it does in biblical examples. But since the church is made up of people, and people are fallible, this type of thinking shouldn't surprise anyone. Regardless of whether you agree with it, it's good to know where these ideas come from.

2. Understand your supervisor.

Have a meeting with your supervisor to ask for her expectations. (Ideally this happens before you begin work. See Chapter 12.) Once you have the expectations, I suggest taking three steps:

1. Put the expectations in writing. Review them with your supervisor to make sure you understand them correctly.

2. If the expectations don't include numbers (and they probably won't), ask whether attendance numbers are related to the expectations, and, if so, what are the numbers expectations?

3. If there are numerical expectations, ask, "What happens if those numbers aren't met?"

3. Learn to communicate in terms of health rather than numbers.

Don't feed others' appetites for numbers by making number statements ("We had so many students there last night.") Instead choose statements that reflect health ("It's exciting to see how students are responding to the Bible study by bringing their friends.") Here are some other actions to take:

- Tell life-change stories. Share the good work God is doing in people's lives.
- Use words like health instead of growth.
- Communicate forward thinking by using terms like reach, build, increase, vision, and change.
- Train the other youth ministry leaders to be more concerned with health than numbers. The more people pursuing health, the better.

Please don't give in to the temptation to inflate numbers so you can stay in favor with your supervisor. You will compromise your integrity if you do. If your ministry is in God's hands, if you're seeking his direction, if you're giving your best effort, that's all you can do. You've got to focus on doing the possible in the best way you know how and trust God for what's beyond your control.

If that isn't good enough for your supervisor, it may be time to ask God to move you in a new direction. Don't be discouraged. Many healthy churches exist and your next ministry opportunity may be at one.

// 4. I will not criticize the past.

It's tempting to talk about the past with contempt to make yourself look better in the present or as an excuse to justify a change. Don't do it! Honor those who went before you in the ministry. Some students will wish you were like their last youth worker. But God didn't make you like that last person. In time the students will move forward.

You may think criticism of the past bolsters your credibility. But if you're working with genuine people—students or adults—they'll see right through you. Only people of weak character are won over by negativity. Your hopes for credibility will only be seen as immaturity in the eyes of authentic people.

Don't give in to the temptation to make your predecessor look bad by highlighting problems you have because of her mistakes. Keep quiet, take notes of what people value about the past, and learn from those who have been at your church longer than you. In doing so, you'll outlast your critics, enhance your character, and model integrity to your students.

Criticizing is easy, but character finds goodness and brings attention to it. Commit to strengthen your character by making others look good.

I think it was Vince Lombardi, the legendary coach and great theologian of the Green Bay Packers, who used to say, "When you have strayed away from the basics, you have gone a long way toward defeat."

Doug does a great job of reminding youth ministry novices and veterans alike to keep the main thing the main thing. The basics of good youth ministry are indeed like the marathon Doug wants to run one day—because life is like a marathon. What I hear Doug saying (and doing) is that so much of our success in youth ministry is in the preparation, focus, perseverance, and commitment to the common sense basics of ministry.

At the end of the Sermon on the Mount (Matthew 7:24ff), Jesus reminds us that wind, rain, and storms will definitely come to all of our lives and ministries. Those who build their houses on the rock will last, and those who build their houses on the sand will crash. It's a very simple illustration; yet it's a great reminder for us to construct a firm foundation in our youth ministries in order to see life-changing results in the kids and families to whom we minister.

Doug and I were sitting together at a youth ministry conference a few years ago, and he turned to me and asked, "Whatever happened to...?" referring to a youth worker who'd ministered to him when he was a student. I sadly answered, "He crashed and burned." Then he asked, "How about...?" I replied, "Gone." Unfortunately, many of the people we talked about that day had burned out, crashed morally, or faded into the past. They had been incredible leaders, too, influencing kids and families in wonderful ways—but they didn't build their lives on the Rock.

They would have benefitted from paying attention to this first chapter, because untended fires soon become raging infernos, then nothing but a pile of ashes.

I was Doug Fields' youth pastor from his last year of junior high until his senior year of high school. (Sorry I didn't make it to your graduation, Doug.) As a freshman in college through his seminary years, he was my intern. *And you think you had problems with your staff!?!* Seriously, during those years, one of the common themes we kept hearing was, "God will often use you in the greatest ways when you are over 40 years old—*if* you stay faithful to your calling."

Back then, turning 40 sounded like a very, very long way off—for me! So you can understand why I couldn't even imagine Doug breaking the 30-year-old barrier! But today, because Doug did stay faithful to his calling, you have in your hands this book—and it's filled with nuggets of truth that, when applied, will help you reach young people, strengthen families, and change lives forever.

–Jim Burns

// 5. I will avoid the comparison trap.

This commitment has a similar result to the numbers game since it can't lead you anywhere good. When you compare you lose. Either you're filled with pride because you're better than another person, or you're dejected because you don't measure up. Both attitudes are wrong and destructive. Comparison places what you know about yourself (or your ministry) against what you don't know about another youth worker (or her ministry). That's not a fair evaluation.

You'll be tempted to compare yourself to others several times during your first two years; you'll wonder if you're going to make it because you're not like someone else. To this day, when I compare myself to another person, I find myself second-guessing my gifts and ministry opportunities. What a depressing position to be in. My prayer is that you steer clear of this temptation early and continually.

We have a wonderful volunteer in our ministry named Li who played the comparison game before she even joined our volunteer team. She was the mom of a student and opened her home

> A trap is so easy to fall into—and so tough to get out of. In youth ministry, we live in a world that's constantly measuring us: *Talented enough? Big enough group? Energetic enough?* I wish youth ministry protected us from the comparison trap, but it's set everywhere—even in church. And I often find myself stepping right into it—and I hate it. Fortunately, I have friends like Doug who love me enough to remind me that God's love for me isn't based on what others are comparing me to (or what I'm comparing myself to)—and that's very freeing.
> —Kurt Johnston

every Wednesday night to host several small groups in several rooms of her home. When we needed an additional small group leader, I approached Li to prayerfully consider the role. She told me that she didn't feel young enough when she compared herself to leaders in their 20s and 30s. She was afraid that none of the students would want to leave the younger leaders to be in a small group with a mom pushing 50.

She committed to pray about the opportunity. Some of the teenagers approached her and said, "We'd like to be in a small group with an older woman who has parented teenagers. We need some wisdom to better understand our parents."

Li was amazed and eagerly jumped at the chance to influence these girls. She later told me, "I can't believe I almost missed this incredible ministry opportunity because I was comparing myself to 20-year-olds. I learned a great lesson."

I can tell you from firsthand experience that nothing is ever as good as it looks from a distance. From outer space, the Earth looks like a peaceful, stress-free place, but up close it's chaotic and dangerous. When you feel tempted to compare yourself to another volunteer, leader, or Bible teacher, stop and focus on God's love for you in that moment. God's love isn't based on how you measure up. He loves you for who you are, not for whom you think you should be more like. Your value as a youth worker must come from God's *unconditional* love for you, or you'll find yourself pursuing the approval of others and trying too hard to earn something from people that God gives freely.

> I don't break this commitment nearly as much as the youth worker down the street!

// 6. I will focus on priorities.

The many demands of youth ministry will keep you busy. But when you're spread too thin, you'll eventually snap. You've got to make a commitment to manage your limited time to go the distance. To do this, you need a healthy understanding of your priorities based on the church's values and expectations. (We'll process this idea from start to finish in Chapter 12).

To help with your priorities you must learn quickly how and when to say no. Without a sense of priorities, you'll say yes to things that deserve a no, and you'll have lost time for those important areas that require your yes. (See page 32 for ideas on time management.)

One reality you'll quickly learn is that youth ministry never ends. More is always waiting to be done, and you'll find yourself wanting to do more. The most difficult decisions you may face are the ones that require saying no to being at more events, meeting with more people, doing more.

Doing more isn't necessarily good youth ministry. Doing the right things, based on your priorities, is good youth ministry regardless of how much time you have available to spend. I'd rather have one youth worker who knows his priorities and does the right thing for 30 minutes a week than have two youth workers who have hours to spend and are aimless with their time. The most effective youth workers are the ones who know how to focus on what's expected of them. People who are spread too thin might be busy, but busyness is not synonymous with effectiveness.

No. No. No. Keep practicing that word!

Develop Time Management Skills

Do whatever it takes to learn time management skills now. Your effectiveness in this area contributes to your success, or your failure in this area will plague you for years.

Here are four realities that confront every youth worker I've ever met:

- You'll be busy!
- You have only 86,400 seconds to live each day.
- You'll struggle in youth ministry if you can't manage your time.
- Plan your time or people will plan it for you.

You can't add more hours, so you need to control the hours you're given. If you're the lead youth worker and you work in a part-time or full-time setting, consider looking at each day as having three blocks of time (21 blocks a week). For example, you might block out your time like this:

> 9 a.m. - 1 p.m.
> 1 p.m. - 5 p.m.
> 5 p.m. - 9 p.m.

How you manage these blocks of time directly influences your success as a youth worker. When are you at your best spiritually, mentally, emotionally, physically? When are you least productive? Complete your most important tasks during your most productive hours.

I'm most alert and productive during the morning block, so I reserve the 9 to 1 p.m. hours for my most crucial thinking and preparation. I use my afternoon hours for people and meetings, since the interactions force me to be alert when I'm more tired.

As you consider your week's 21 blocks of time, make sure you reserve time for yourself, your family, and other important domains of your life outside of ministry. And if you're a full-time youth worker, very rarely should you work during all three blocks, every day. If, for instance, you work blocks 2 and 3 on Wednesday, take block 1 for yourself on Thursday. When you get into the habit of looking at your time in blocks, a week at a time, you can evaluate how you best use your time and plan more efficiently.

Many good books and seminars are available on time management. Ask business-minded people in your church for their current favorites.

// 7. I will pace myself.

Hopefully, you're in youth ministry for a marathon, not a sprint. Right away, you must learn how to stay in shape. Since youth ministry is never finished, and more can always be done, learn to take daily stretches—breathers throughout your day and week so you can be refreshed. Discover places, moments, and people who provide refreshment from the busyness of youth ministry and take your mind away from all that needs to be done.

Because I'm in youth ministry full time, I try to take a daily stretch to clear my mind from youth ministry. It doesn't need to be long, but it does need to be refreshing. My escapes happen when I—

- Coach my kids' sports teams
- Drink diet Pepsi and read the newspaper at Taco Bell
- Play racquetball
- Jog with a friend
- Lift weights
- Relax in the jacuzzi with my wife (or in the church baptismal…kidding!)

These activities slow me down. When I'm out of control and think I need more time in my day, I feel outside of God's will. I know God doesn't plan more for me to do than he's given me time for. The same truth applies to you. Draw up a list of your own ways to get refreshed. (I highly recommend caffeine!)

// 8. I will serve.

This commitment may not impress you as good youth ministry advice, but it's crucial to your long-term effectiveness as a leader. The longer you're in youth ministry, the more likely you'll be in positions where you lead and others follow. That's fine, good, wonderful, and even appealing. But Jesus gave the church a unique model of leadership that requires serving. If you want to be a great youth worker, serve. If you want to be first, be last. If you can't serve, you can't lead, at least not as Christ intended. You're an incredible example of Christ to church leaders, members, and students when you serve. Actually, you're never more like Jesus than when you serve.

This is the part of youth ministry where you'll get God's blessing because you won't get human recognition. This is when you make the extra effort to pick up trash in the Sunday school room, help someone in the church office, carry boxes to the secretary's car, refrain from teasing your pastor about his toupee, give up an hour to help fold church bulletins, and offer transportation to an elderly saint.

These are the tasks that probably aren't included in your job description but should be written on your heart. Jump at the opportunity to serve in the little ways and your youth ministry will benefit because of your character. You can't lose when you serve.

// 9. I will be a learner.

I live by an axiom that's popular in my church: "All leaders are learners. When a leader stops learning, the leader stops leading." Although this attitude requires a constant investment of time and sacrifice, not to mention a diet of humility, it has enhanced my leadership skills as a youth worker. I can only teach what I know, and this truth requires me to keep growing. This habit is especially important to maintaining a decent self-esteem, since many of the teenagers in my church think I don't know anything.

I'm saddened each year at youth ministry conventions when I notice that veteran youth workers choose not to attend the workshop sessions because the material isn't delivered by big-name, general-session speakers. In my experience some of the bright, young, unknown leaders have some of the freshest approaches and newest ideas—ones that offer strong learning opportunities to those of us who're getting wrinkles and losing hair!

Make a commitment today to be an eager, life-long learner. Read. Listen to tapes. Discuss ideas with people you disagree with. Sit at the feet of teachers who are younger and older than you. You'll learn from your mistakes, but a wise leader is proactive and learns from others, too. The fact that you're reading this book shows you value this principle.

// 10. I will pursue contentment.

One of the common themes I hear from new youth workers has to do with discontentment. Typically, they want to see more fruit from their labor and see it faster. They want bigger results and instant rewards and feel abandoned when these don't materialize.

I've learned that when I feel discontent with my ministry situation, every option outside my church seems better. The church down the street looks inviting, that speaking invitation sounds alluring, the opportunity that I said no to last month now appears worthwhile. Each is a symptom of discontentment.

Ministry isn't easy. Your first two years may be the most difficult years you'll ever experience, and our enemy would love to see you ineffective and living in the land of discontentment. One of the most frequent results of discontentment is leaving, walking away from your ministry. When you leave your youth ministry too soon after arriving, you hurt the church. Students stop opening up when adults rotate through their lives. The next leader has to deal with the backlash.

Anika's my neighbor, a 12th grader who's had five different small group leaders at her church. Anika told me she doesn't feel like talking to her small group leaders anymore. She has no confidence they'll stick around. I've tried inviting her to attend one of our small groups, but she has no assurance ours will be any different.

Short-term commitments may be beneficial for the adult, but they damage the student.

If you want to survive, pursue being content with where God has you and the gifts you've been given. Stop looking over your fence into your neighbor's yard, and thank God he's using you where he has you. You've heard the adage, "The grass is greener on the other side"? The truth is, the grass is greener where it's watered. So start watering your own grass.

> When you change ministries, you often simply exchange one set of problems for another.

Discontentment and discouragement are blood relatives. When you have one uninvited guest, you almost always have the other. Since they show up so frequently, I've devoted the entire next chapter to dealing with the problem. And if you and your church are still on a honeymoon, you can come back to the topic later.

The Payoff

These commitments, and others you may think of, form the foundation from which healthy youth ministry can be developed. When we, as youth workers, stack hands over them, we honor our Lord, our church, and our students. Please prayerfully consider committing to these actions and letting them influence you as you work with students, parents, church staff, and volunteers.

I'm happy you've chosen to read this book. I have hope for you and the thousands of men and women who love God and students and who are willing to learn more about youth ministry. Thank you for being open to coaching from a veteran youth worker who's still running the marathon and cheering you on as you enter the race. Because I'm a little further along, I want you to know that, from where I am, the view is better, the terrain is lighter, and the company is incredible. Live by the 10 commitments in this chapter, keep running, and you'll experience the same.

1. I will move slowly.

A simple man believes anything, but a prudent man gives thought to his steps. A wise man fears the Lord and shuns evil, but a fool is hotheaded and reckless. (Proverbs 14:15-16)

2. I will regularly check my motives and evaluate my heart.

Leaders who know their business and care keep a sharp eye out for the shoddy and cheap, for who among us can be trusted to be always diligent and honest? Switching price tags and padding the expense account are two things God hates. Young people eventually reveal by their actions if their motives are on the up and up. Ears that hear and eyes that see—we get our basic equipment from God! (Proverbs 20:8-12, The Message)

3. I will steer clear of the numbers' game.

If a shepherd has one hundred sheep, and one wanders away and is lost, what will he do? Won't he leave the ninety-nine others and go out into the hills to search for the lost one? (Matthew 18:12, NLT)

4. I will not criticize the past.

No, dear brothers and sisters, I am still not all I should be, but I am focusing all my energies on this one thing: Forgetting the past and looking forward to what lies ahead. (Philippians 3:13, NLT)

5. I will avoid the comparison trap.

Be sure to do what you should, for then you will enjoy the personal satisfaction of having done your work well, and you won't need to compare yourself to anyone else. (Galatians 6:4, NLT)

6. I will focus on priorities.

"Teacher, which is the most important commandment in the law of Moses?" Jesus replied, "'You must love the Lord your God with all your heart, all your soul, and all your mind.' This is the first and greatest commandment. A second is equally important: 'Love your neighbor as yourself.'" (Matthew 22:36-40, NLT)

7. I will pace myself.

Patient endurance is what you need now, so you will continue to do God's will. Then you will receive all that he has promised. (Hebrews 10:36, NLT)

8. I will serve.

But among you it is quite different. Anyone wanting to be a leader among you must be your servant. And if you want to be right at the top, you must serve like a slave. Your attitude must be like my own, for I, the Messiah, did not come to be served, but to serve, and to give my life as a ransom for many. (Matthew 20:26-28, LB)

9. I will be a learner.

Learn to be wise, and develop good judgment. Don't forget or turn away from my words. He who walks with the wise grows wise, but a companion of fools suffers harm. (Proverbs 4:5; 13:20, NLT)

10. I will pursue contentment.

I am not telling you this because I need anything. I have learned to be satisfied with the things I have and with everything that happens. (Philippians 4:11, NCV)

The Questions at the End of the Chapter

// For group discussion

- Which commitment is going to be the toughest for you?
- Which commitment offers you the most encouragement?

// For personal reflection

- Do I have a sprint mentality or a marathon mindset when it comes to youth ministry?
- How will it affect the church and/or the student ministry if I quit too soon?
- What is my personal plan to evaluate my motives?
- How can I begin an honest conversation with my supervisor about the "numbers game"?
- What can I do to improve the commitment that I struggle with the most?

// Actions to consider

- Photocopy pages 21 and 22 and keep them in a place where you'll see them every day for the next month.
- Identify one person on your ministry team who personalizes the commitment that you struggle with most and write that person an encouraging letter noting that he or she is a model to you.
- If your ministry team isn't reading this book as a group, find one person on your team to read through it with you and discuss each chapter.

Go to www.dougfields.com and enter your comments under Your First 2 Years: Chapter 1

why do i feel this way?

dealing with discouragement

Discouragement may be the single most powerful feeling that entices great women and men to exit prematurely from youth ministry. If you can learn how to navigate the ebb and flow of discouragement, many years of youth ministry effectiveness can be listed on your life's résumé.

Some of my youth ministry friends who read drafts of this book said, "I'm so excited after reading Chapter 1 that I don't want to think about disappointment already. It seems too abrupt." Exactly! That's the nature of discouragement. You can go from feeling like you're the most effective youth worker on the planet one week to planning your resignation letter the next and wonder, "Why do I feel this way?" You can quickly replace "Where do I start?" with "Is it always this bad?"

If we were meeting face to face, I could see it in your body when you walk into the restaurant: your shoulders slumped, your personality subdued, your lips pursed together, your eyes downcast. (In other words, you'd be expecting me to buy.) Don't worry, I've seen that look before, both in the mirror and on the faces of many other youth workers. When you work with teenagers, it doesn't usually take long to discover these feelings and look this way.

Let's recognize that the task of youth ministry is difficult, the hours are long, and encouragement is minimal. Discouragement is a fairly natural response when put in that perspective. The causes of your discouragement could be any of the following:

- Lack of respect
- Too many calls and e-mails to return
- Marshmallow residue on the church carpet
- Miscommunication and misunderstanding
- Sleep deprivation because of a new baby
- Conflict
- Returning the church van with a dent…caused by pulling into the garage too quickly
- Returning the church van with a dent…caused by the 15-year-old you let drive it
- Criticism
- Conflicting expectations
- No support from the senior pastor
- Minimal support from parents, staff, and volunteers
- Failure to please everyone
- Failure to please anyone
- Body parts scattered around the youth room ("Who's gonna clean up this mess?")
- Verbal abuse
- Students who are difficult to like
- Financial struggles
- Unsupportive spouse
- A failed program
- Your paycheck
- Monday mornings
- A 24-hour lock-in on the calendar
- Youth ministry not valued as highly as other church ministries

Did I mention yours? I've experienced all of these. Some have left scars while others have just stung. Adding them up can influence how you feel about students, ministry, the church, and even God. You catch yourself thinking, "God, if you love me, why is *that kid* in my small group?"

What causes you to be discouraged may be different than what defeats me. Your personal needs combined with your unique ministry experience and church context, as well as the people in your world, all work together to form a potion for discouragement that can't be replicated for other youth workers. If one universal cause of discouragement existed, it would be easy to identify and attack with common action steps. But, since we're all so wonderfully complex and different, I can't present a universal remedy. Discouragement is unique for each youth worker. Basically we're all uniquely messed up. (Hang on. Hope's coming!)

Three Feelings That Will Discourage You on Your Spiritual Journey

- *I'm not worthy:* Comparing your own spirituality to someone else's benefits no one. Judging the other person as less mature than you puffs up your pride. Thinking another is more mature discourages you and leaves you feeling unworthy of God's love and attention. Movement toward God is important, not your position in relationship to others. Go ahead and be "selfish" on this topic by focusing on your spiritual journey and forgetting to measure yourself against others.

- *I feel guilty:* Feeling guilty for missing quiet times is common. The purpose of guilt is to cause repentance and move you closer to God, yet misguided guilt often increases the distance. Every Christian blows it, and guilt is the Holy Spirit's whisper inviting you back to the Cross to bathe in God's grace. When you slack off from your spiritual growth plan, don't go psycho and try to catch up. Just move forward, rest in God's presence, and know God loves you even when you miss your appointments with him. His love is without equal.

- *I feel alone:* There's not a mature Christian alive who hasn't experienced a spiritual rut. At any time, significant numbers of youth workers are tired, burned out, and feeling disconnected from God. Every Christian you know and every spiritual hero you admire has been in the spiritual dumps sometime. The problem isn't limited to the people you know and admire; it's happened since the beginning and will continue until the end. You're definitely not alone. Don't allow feeling alone to drag you down further. Take action using suggestions in this chapter.

My Journey with Discouragement

When I was a teenager, I developed the habit of writing in a journal. Typically, I write my prayers and feelings. Here's an entry written during my first year in youth ministry:

September 15, 1979
I feel so alone. Things are going okay, except I feel like I question my call to ministry every day...even several times a day. Should I just do something else? Or am I simply looking for an escape when things get tough? Jim tells me it's natural to experience confusion and uncertainty in the early years of ministry. But will the investment be worth it? Do I want to pour out my life for these students? Am I willing? Is it wise? Will I make it? I want to be here if it's where God wants me, but, wow...I didn't know it was going to be so dark so fast. I'm tired, lonely, confused, hurting, and in need of something from God that I either can't identify or I'm too tired to care about.

It bothers me to admit this, but the journal entry below isn't much different, and it's written almost 23 years later.

February 4, 2002
I'm feeling better today, but it seems like it has been several weeks that I've been in the pits. I still question if I'm the person for this job anymore. Do I still have it? Does our church need someone different? Better? Younger? With more energy? Less like a parent and more like a friend? Can I still give what it takes? My patience seems to be growing weaker rather than stronger. Things that I should blow off still bother me, and I can't seem to develop thick skin. This week has made me think about why I ever got into ministry. God's call? I hope so. Now I need God's answer and assurance.

I thought it might be fun to flip through my old journals. I envisioned finding pages filled with Diet Pepsi stains, records of my weight, brainstorm sessions, prayers written to God, students' names that would trigger positive memories, and some I wanted to kill (theoretically, of course). I found those, but I also found words of personal pain—lots of them.

Reading the pages of my journals caused me to relive them. To be honest, that was frightening. It's easier—or so it seems—to keep some of those memories in the distant past. Some of those times were difficult, lonely, and scary. When I started out—naïve and inexperienced and easily defeated—the memories were hot and fresh and larger than life.

Instead of confronting my emotions, I hid from them. In public settings I put on a mask and pretended to be the godly, fun, caring, resilient leader everyone expected. When I was alone, though, I feared the quiet, I questioned my abilities, and I searched for answers. Occasionally I even investigated the classified ads. Surely there was another job for me—something easier, less painful, and free of conflict (like being a senior pastor).

Like everyone, I continue to battle negative emotions today, but the battles are less frequent—though still filled with strong emotions. In every war intelligence is key to winning the battles, so let's look at objective truths about discouragement.

> Hang on! Hope's *still* coming!

What's the Truth about Discouragement?

Discouragement is a reality in *all* ministry, not just youth ministry. Where people live, sin exists. Where sin exists, problems abound. Where problems abound, discouragement follows. Count on it! When you say yes to ministry, you also say yes to periods of discouragement. Anyone who doesn't admit to occasional seasons of discouragement owns a timeshare on Fantasy Island. Here are some harsh realities.

// Discouragement is painful.

Christians can be great at hiding their feelings. Have you ever experienced this question and response:

"How are you doing?"

"Fine. Praise the Lord. Couldn't be better!"

Come on! Really? Or is that your socially conditioned Christian response? How can you be fine when that student you've been caring for just gave you the middle finger and hurled four-letter words at you and your mother? You're not fine.

Many churches have become impossible places to reveal your inner self when you're hurt—especially when you're in a leadership position. But just because other leaders aren't transparent doesn't mean they're not in pain. Discouragement hurts. It can dampen your mood, scar your heart, enrage your response to God, affect your objectivity, and hinder your relationships with others.

I can remember being so discouraged after a volunteer meeting that I took a sick *week* immediately following. I was ill, physically hurting, achy, and sore. I couldn't get my leaders to commit to anything, and their apathy seemed to be a statement about my leadership. I took their rejection so personally that I felt like each one of them was saying with their actions, "Doug, you're a loser, not a leader" and then punching me in the stomach. And, as if that weren't discouraging enough, after I came back, no one noticed I was gone!

// Discouragement is untimely.

I have found discouragement's frequency to be the most humbling and sobering truth about youth ministry. In my experience, discouragement appears following success: a powerful retreat, a dynamic outreach event, a life-changing mission trip. Often spiritual highs are followed by discouraging lows.

This predictable chain of events is why I love to read about the prophet Elijah. I relate to him. After standing toe to toe with his enemy and experiencing an incredible weekend retreat when God destroyed 450 prophets of Baal, Elijah experienced a desperate low. Queen Jezebel intimidated him, and he ran for his life. He wanted to die!

Don't you think Elijah would be on a spiritual high? I would! I'd be dancing in the streets waving my bloody sword and talking about how perfect God's timing is. But for some reason Elijah couldn't see beyond the queen's threat to God's power. Come on! God's power versus Jezebel's power? No contest. But in his discouragement, Elijah was caught off guard by emotions and didn't think rationally.

So... who's the Jezebel in your life?

// Discouragement is selfish.

A most repulsive truth is that discouragement is *me*-focused. I get discouraged because of *my* situation, because of what someone said to *me*, because of the way a student treated *me*, because of the way a parent embarrassed *me*, because the leadership team doesn't trust *me*, because the pastor questions *my* leadership. It's self-centered, ugly, and wrong.

Discouraged people like to wallow in their discouragement. They say, "I'm discouraged. I'm going to be discouraged. And no one is going to change how I feel. Leave *me* alone." Ouch. Discouragement continues as long as they're focused on "me."

Let's keep this one short and move on.

// Discouragement is lonely.

I find days (or weeks or months) of discouragement to be a dark time. Discouragement gives birth to despair, dejection, hopelessness, and depression. They all hang on to weight me down. These feelings don't prompt me to throw a party and interact with people.

It's easier to avoid people when we're discouraged than to invite them into our pain. We're taken in by lies like, "I can't let people see me this way," "Others don't want to see me this way," and "I can handle this by myself." I'm lonely because I avoid brothers and sisters in Christ—those I need the most and who are best able to help me. What I need the most, I tend to avoid the most.

Are you depressed now? Before you contemplate ministry suicide or something worse (like putting this book down), let's discover some hope in the midst of discouragement.

> **Differentiating between Discouragement and Depression**
> Be aware that depression can mask itself as discouragement. Some signs of depression include irritability, sadness, exhaustion, low self-image, destructive self-criticism, shame, guilt, and loss of pleasure and fulfillment. If you're experiencing any of these symptoms for more than a couple of months, consult a professional therapist.
> —*Steve Geiali*

"If this is ministry, then I don't want it . . . I'm out!"

I made that statement to a godly mentor and friend when I was a new youth pastor, fresh out of college. When I was in college, I was told there would be discouraging times in ministry—and I knew I could handle discouragement—but I didn't think it would be this intense. I was ready to throw in the towel. I questioned my calling, my abilities, my spirituality (not to mention the spirituality of the church), and much more. Among my thoughts were, "I could make so much more money in a job that could be as fulfilling and less discouraging."

My friend listened to my plight—and had a simple response. "God has called you and equipped you for ministry—stay there!" he said.

After 25 years, I understand and deal with discouragement a little bit better—and I also make my living listening to youth pastors who feel the same emotions. Here are four basic truths I bring up that often help discouraged youth workers cope:

1. Welcome Christ's suffering.

If I'm praying to be like Jesus…if I believe the greatest aim of youth ministry is to reflect Christ…if I truly believe youth ministry is "incarnational," then I must participate with Christ in his suffering. I can't expect to be like Jesus and only experience his joy, peace, wisdom, and power. He'll also let me feel discouragement, frustration, sorrow, and heartache—just like he does.

2. It's okay to question God's calling on my life.

I used to believe that if I questioned God—especially after many years of ministry—I must be really screwed up. But I've come to learn that God uses my questions to refine me. God's Word is clear that he's in the process of completing a great work in each of us. We're great at telling kids the latter, but do we really believe that for ourselves? Our discouragement shapes and develops us. Discouragement makes us more committed to—and dependent on—Jesus.

3. Discouragement isn't necessarily a sign of spiritual incompetence.

Doug rightly points out that those of us in church leadership often believe that we have to have it all together, all the time. But that's when Satan attacks us, whispering that we must be spiritually incompetent if we're discouraged. Not true! I've learned great spiritual lessons from some of the most discouraged men in Scripture. Elijah was so discouraged and felt so alone that he was ready to end his life (1 Kings 18); Jeremiah was faithful to God for years and never saw positive results from his ministry. (No wonder he's known as the weeping prophet!) The list goes on and on: Joseph, David, Esther, Paul. Godly people become discouraged! Don't believe Satan's lie that you're spiritually incompetent. Rather, assess your walk with God and do your best to trust that he'll make you strong in your weaknesses.

4. Keep first things first.

When it comes to our youth ministry jobs, God's only expectation is that we remain faithful to him. And what of results? Numbers? "Fruit"? That's the Holy Spirit's job. No wonder we get discouraged! So often we try to be someone we're not (God) and attempt to control outcomes that we have no control over (kids' spiritual growth). It's easy to buy into a worldly view of "success" and forget that God doesn't need us to help him accomplish anything. It's God who is at work in us—and he controls the results so all the glory goes to him. All we need to do is bow to his sovereign control and be available, useful, and faithful.

—*Steve Gerali*

Hope in the Midst of Discouragement

There *is* hope, and, because the God of the universe is involved, it's plentiful. Light is out there for you. Don't loose sight of the eternal Light in the midst of the temporary darkness. When discouragement hits you, count on God to use that season in your life to increase your ministry effectiveness.

While my visit into my journal wasn't fun, it was insightful, emotional, and eventually encouraging. The encouragement came when I realized that God has been faithful during three decades of youth ministry, continually proving his character and shaping mine. Sure I've refined and sharpened ministry skills, but God has developed and formed me. I'm not the same person I was when I started in youth ministry. (And thankfully I don't dress in 1970s leisure suits anymore.)

Personally, I wish God would use an easier method of maturing us, but for some spiritual reason, discouragement seems to precede effectiveness. God may be using periods of discouragement to take your life and your ministry to a deeper and better place.

Practical Steps to Battle Discouragement

As my journal reveals, the first months of ministry were an overwhelming, disappointing season of life. I'd love to tell you that I only had to gut it out, simply withstanding that initial bout with discouragement...then I experienced 20-plus years of pain-free ministry. I can't write that with integrity. Discouraging thoughts come around from time to time in my life and ministry, but today I'm better equipped to respond to those moments, days, and even weeks.

Here are some truths I've learned. Prayerfully consider and personalize them when your journey takes you to the land of discouragement.

// Be confident that you're not alone.

Everyone deals with some struggle, some issue, some embarrassment, some challenge. So identify the specific issue you're struggling with—or narrow it down to your top 100—and recognize that you're simply a part of the human race! You're *not* the only one struggling with your issue, whatever it is. While it may be painful, it's not unique to

your church or to youth ministry. We're all encouraged when we realize we're not alone in our struggles.

I'm reminded of the power of this truth each month when I send a short devotional
to the youth workers on my Web site e-mail list. Typically, I'll write about some problem, tension, or fear I've experienced during the month. Without exception, when I
share about a painful experience, I'm immediately inundated with responses from youth
workers who are thrilled to hear about my pain because they're experiencing it, too. If
misery loves company, there should be a strong community among today's youth workers.

// Find an experienced, but neutral, mentor.

In Titus 2, Paul encourages older men and older women to be instructors, helpers, and
mentors to younger men and women.

Have you identified a mentor who will love you and encourage you? The ideal
person has ministry experience and understands the youth ministry world you live in.
Look for someone older and wiser, who cares about you and wants to see you succeed.
You may not want this person to be from your church so you can share openly about
your experiences and feelings. Allow time for this relationship to develop.

How to Find a Mentor

I wish the following five ideas for finding a mentor were labeled "Works Every Time." They aren't. Obtaining a mentor relationship can't be reduced to five easy steps. These ideas will help you head in the right direction. They seem to be the most common actions my colleagues have taken to find and keep mentors.

Pray

Don't underestimate the power of prayer and the leading of the Holy Spirit. Ask God to lead you to a mentor. When you find your mentor, be sure to tell the person, "I've been praying for God to lead me to you." Wait until after the person agrees to mentor you before telling her that she was chosen by God for you.

Look

Look at people inside and outside your church. Ask yourself—

- Who impresses me as spiritually mature?
- Who inspires me?
- Who encourages me?
- Who confronts me lovingly?
- Who believes in me?
- Who challenges me?
- Who intrigues me?
- Who do I respect?
- Who has reached some of the goals I've set for myself?
- Who do others speak of highly?
- Who do people go to for advice?

When you gather a few names based on the above questions, watch their lives with the thought of one of them becoming your mentor. As you look, prioritize your list: first choice, second…

Ask

After you've pursued God in prayer and watched lives, it's time to ask. I know firsthand how scary it can be. But when you want to grow and be challenged, it's good—perhaps life-changing—to ask. It's an honor to be asked to be a mentor; you're asking because you respect this person and the life he lives. Choose your top name and go for it.

The person you want for a mentor may be your ideal, but he may be too busy for this type of relationship. When you ask, be aware that you face possible rejection for this— or other—reasons. (But don't let that stop you. Let your potential mentor decide that.)

Being asked to be someone's mentor can seem like an overwhelming responsibility. You can ease the size of your request by knowing exactly what you're looking for. (See the next point.)

Clarify

When asking someone to invest in you, be sure you've thought through what you're asking for. What do you envision for your time together? Do you want to meet once a week or once a month? Do you want to ask your mentor questions or have your mentor teach you? Do you want to read a book together and discuss it? The more specific you are, the more likely you'll receive a realistic response. Make a specific request and see what happens.

Respect

When you meet with your mentor, respect this person's gift of time.

- Don't be late.
- Offer to pay if you meet over a meal.
- Send an occasional thank-you letter.

People are more willing to give their time if they know the recipient values it.

// Find an upbeat friend outside youth ministry.

Just as it's critical to interact with people who share your youth ministry passion, it's equally important to have friends outside youth ministry. Spend time with a friend who makes you laugh, makes you think, challenges you. Someone who feeds you works, too. Your time together could be spent exercising at the gym, discussing books or movies over a cup of coffee, pursing a hobby together—anything but youth ministry. Why? Because, as much as you need a day of Sabbath rest, you need a relationship of Sabbath rest, away from your youth ministry tasks.

> "Is it possible to have friends who aren't teenagers?!"
> —a discouraged youth worker

In my own life, when my entire world is youth ministry, not only do I get discouraged, I find myself not caring anymore. I don't say, "I don't care," but my actions—or inactions—send that message clearly. I once had a crying student phone me, needing to talk, yet I told our receptionist to take a message. (That really hurt my daughter's feelings.) I've had a frightened parent come into the office to talk about her son's drug problem, and I've hidden to avoid the discussion. (That really heart my wife's feelings.) I've allowed my mind to wander during meetings, daydreaming about painting the church van and customizing it, simply because I don't care.

While you might consider my actions inappropriate, they reveal a true portrait of what overflows from a discouraged heart. We all act the same way from time to time. Apathy is the protective response of a discouraged leader.

When I get out and play, talk, travel, gamble (just kidding—I was wondering if you're still reading—I don't really travel) or socialize with friends who don't engage me about youth ministry, I find myself caring again. It's amazing what a few, unique, outside-of-youth-ministry friends can do to the vitality of my spirit.

// Realize that not everyone will understand you and your ministry.

A list of potential complainers can go on a long time: parents, students, church leaders, the administrator, the janitor, people who don't go to your church, the person who waxes your back, the pastor's spouse. Everyone has something to say, input to give, a criticism to cast, and a new vision for you to hear. While it's important to be a listener and a learner, *sometimes* you need to do more enduring than listening. Be polite. Smile. Nod. Move on without regret. Basically, it's difficult for others to completely understand the world of youth ministry until they've lived in it.

Lisha is a wonderful woman in our church who has now "lived it." She's given me a lot of grief over the years about my lousy accounting skills and for failing to follow financial procedures. She has the difficult task of collecting receipts from unorganized people like me. (She's told me a hundred times.) I know I'm supposed to keep my receipts, but in the midst of corralling the students for camp and handling the mini-crises, I forget to ask for them or I misplace them. When I get back to the church I have one of those shame-on-you meetings where I'm scolded about being irresponsible.

Lisha recently went on a mission trip with us. She was in charge of the money for the trip and lost about half of the receipts. (I'm only exaggerating a little.) She's had a change of opinion. I know I shouldn't smile about this, but I've just got to enjoy the irony until she finds another area of my ministry to fault. Lisha is now a wonderful supporter of mine, who recognizes the chaos that happens, and she's much more accepting of what I do—or don't do—because she now *understands*.

Not everyone will be like Lisha. Some won't understand. The only thing you can do is give them your responsibilities for about a year and watch them suffer. Since that isn't likely to happen, be prepared to be misunderstood.

// Take a day off.

No, you didn't get everything done today—or last week—or last month. And, yes, you're really, *really* behind. That's okay! Obviously if you're behind as a result of not showing up to work week after week, that's a problem. But if you're aggravated because some details are getting missed, welcome to ministry! You'll never get everything done. And when you think you have, it's only because you overlooked something. So wipe away the guilt and know we're all behind in our work! If you want to last in ministry longer than six to 18 months, you must grasp the importance of God's command to take a Sabbath rest.

Some days I struggled with this and would sneak a few moments for e-mail or voice mail on my day off. I went into the office for 30 minutes, and it quickly became three hours. Some days I arrogantly said, "I'm too busy to take a day off."

I'm thankful to say those days are over. With my wife's help I discovered going without a Sabbath wasn't worth it. Ultimately who cares if a parent letter goes out on Tuesday instead of Monday? You're wise to find a friend who forces you to have a nonnegotiable day off. Don't skip over this one! The longer you go without some timely breaks, the longer discouragement lingers.

Yes...this applies to volunteers, too!

// Schedule solo time away.

A day off often includes nonministry responsibilities like doing laundry, going to a doctor's appointment, cleaning your house, spending time with your family, visiting with a friend, getting a frontal lobotomy. A solo day, on the other hand, is a *ministry* day that focuses on your heart and your mind. If you're paid by the church, take a monthly workday away from the office to reflect, regroup, and recharge. If you're a volunteer, skip a youth ministry program every once in a while to reflect, regroup, and recharge (just don't skip to watch TV or catch up on laundry).

During the days of Jesus' ministry, solitary time was built in to the ebb and flow of life as he walked everywhere. Considering traveling from one ministry spot to another often consisted of a day's journey, this gave him more than enough time to be alone, to dream about the future, to evaluate his ministry, and simply to enjoy the beauty of creation. Walking must have given him time to recharge his body.

Not many of us walk to our destinations; our mode of travel is automobile. When we're not jockeying for position before the next traffic light, we're often engaging in a cell phone call, listening to a riveting radio talk show, shaving, preparing a Sunday school lesson, or shoving in a late lunch. Today's travel doesn't don't provide much opportunity for reflection—so we have to schedule extended time alone occasionally.

> As I attempt to add thoughts to my husband's book, I feel so overwhelmed, ineffective, and discouraged. After an incredibly busy day, I'm tired and *still* behind! I often feel as though I'm falling short. As a stay-at-home mom, I regularly feel like my home has been hit by a bomb, and the last thing I want to do is stay in it! When I'm not staying at home, my life is driving my kids around and saying "I love you" as they race from the car. And as a volunteer youth worker, I usually feel totally unprepared and ineffective.
>
> I'm about to take some students to Mexico, and I'm not ready. I haven't done a good job of nurturing students for this mission trip, and I don't feel spiritually prepared. Yet I know I must keep going; none of these circumstances are going to change—at least not right now. Yes, I've been here before. Doug and I have ministered together for many years. And fortunately I see Doug put into action the principles he's written about here. Doug gets openly criticized for everything—way more than I ever have. So he takes time out of his busy life to be quiet and journal and think through what God is doing in his discouraging times of ministry. And that really encourages me!
>
> So I know I have to hold on right now. As I cry out to God in all my discouragement, he changes my moans to thanksgiving when I remember he cares for *me*—not how clean my house is, how good my "taxi driving" is, not even how well I minister to students. This truth gives me the hope and strength to keep on going and continue to be the best *me* I can be for *him*.
> —Cathy Fields

// Clear the piles.

At least three times a year, buy some garbage bags and clean up. Get rid of those piles of paper that you plan on reading someday, the 75 sticky notes decorating your desk, last month's mail, and the six half-empty coffee cups. You're more likely to find a bill or the budget you swore you turned in last week than you are to find a check you never cashed, but work through the piles anyway. If this is too difficult for you, give someone permission to clear the piles for you on a day you're gone. (I realize this is virtually impossible for a selection of the population who would rather be kicked in the head than allow someone to throw away your stuff. See *pack rat* in the dictionary.)

While some people work fine when the office is cluttered, most of us find that it leads to chaotic thinking. And discouraged youth workers are easily overwhelmed. Working toward the smallest objective can appear insurmountable, and you'll quickly convince yourself that you're worthless and your efforts are futile.

The prophet Nehemiah was commissioned by God to lead the Israelites in rebuilding the walls of Jerusalem. In the midst of this daunting task, many Israelites were fatigued and discouraged by the work required to fulfill this mission. In Nehemiah 4:10 we read—

> *Then some of the leaders began complaining that the workmen were becoming tired; and there was so much rubble to be removed that we could never get it done by ourselves.*

When some Israelites lost sight of the big picture, the rubble overwhelmed them. Remove some rubble to get rid of those overwhelmed feelings.

// Get some sleep.

Tuck yourself into bed at a decent hour to read, think, journal, and sleep! If you feel it's essential to watch late night TV, put your VCR to work. Let it stay up late, so you can watch your favorite shows at a normal hour. How about turning off your phone's ringer? Simple but effective.

> Trying to figure out how to program your VCR can be discouraging, too.

Psalm 127:2 (NKJV) says it all: "It's vain for you rise up early, to sit up late." You know what happens to a candle that burns on both ends—but the same thing happens to a candle that burns continually on one end. So blow out the flame once in a while and go to bed!

// Begin a discouragement journal.

Go ahead and voice your frustrations, complaints, anger, and the names of students who drive you crazy. And since the subject of this journal is depressing, be creative with it—alphabetize those students who drive you crazy, rank the parents in the order you'd like to kick them out of the church (or somewhere else). Your mentor may listen to a lot of your complaining, but if you unload everything on this person, you'll soon discover your mentor has switched to an unlisted phone number. A journal is a safe place to vent.

Some people might argue that it's important to develop thick skin to allow negative comments to roll off. I agree, but the reality is that those comments don't always roll away. They roll back when you're feeling down. It's good to write about them so you'll have something concrete to reflect on. This helps you see progress as you learn to deal with discouragement. You'll never completely escape discouragement—it rolls in and out like the ocean tide. Your journal functions like a tide chart: it helps you know what to expect when it hits. (Make *sure* no one finds this journal or you could take a few more hits that won't be as refreshing as the ocean tides.)

(A VOICE FROM THE TRENCHES)

I'll never forget the first time I felt discouraged—I reacted like I must have been some kind of youth ministry freak. I *know* my student pastor never felt this way. He always had it together. He was always cool under pressure, always quick with the answer, and he *never* questioned his call—or did he?

But I was in a spot. *How in the world would teenagers ever listen to me if I was feeling discouraged?* I was supposed to be their "rock," but instead I was about as stable as Jell-O. I faked smiles, laughs, and still held my chin high. The only problem was, I knew what was wrong. While others praised my efforts and patted me on the back, I wanted to grab them and shout, "I'm not happy, I'm not excited, and I'm a complete idiot! Please stop trusting me with your students!"

I was discouraged because no matter how hard I tried, I couldn't fix every kid. I knew the textbook answers, but the textbooks were just that. These students were real, tangible human beings—and coming up with the answers around them was a challenge. (Besides, they hadn't read the books, and they didn't know how they were supposed to act.)

I was discouraged because no matter how hard I tried, parents still saw me as a baby-sitter for their teenagers. They gladly forked over their money so their students could go away with me for a weekend, but they looked at me as if I had suddenly grown a second head when I asked them to host a Bible study in their home.

I was discouraged because I didn't view myself as God does—created in his image. I saw myself as a student ministry mess—he saw me as his creation. I wanted to be the best youth worker in town—and he just wanted my obedience.

—*Mike Wilson, minister to middle school students, Two Rivers Baptist Church, Nashville, Tennessee*

// Begin an affirmation file.

When you receive a thank you note or *any sort* of recognition for a job well done (go ahead and reread that last sentence—it will happen…eventually), save it. It's tempting to toss these notes, but don't! Instead, immortalize them by saving them in a file folder or box. After a year you might actually have a few notes and letters to read. After three years, the folder may begin to bulge and after 10 years you'll need a crane to move it.

After several years of throwing away encouraging notes, I promised my wife I would start saving them. Truthfully, I can't remember the last time I ever read my entire affirmation file. Whenever it was, I cried and decided not to read it for a while. But the file still fulfills its purpose because every time I see the bulge in the file cabinet, I smile and thank my wife for her great idea. I know that I have some people who love me.

// Make a personal commitment to last.

This is the ultimate decision—and the most impacting. When you say yes to God and commit to go where he leads and do what he asks, God will use you, in his way and in his timing. If you don't make some of the commitments I described in Chapter 1, you will forever have the balloon of discouragement hovering over your head. A choice as simple as making a commitment to not compare yourself removes the thorn of discouragement that always pricks you when you do compare yourself with another youth worker.

The youth pastor of my adolescence had such a positive influence on me that I tried to be like him, but I never measured up to the standards I imagined he set for me. I developed a frequent, silent desire to quit ministry because I wasn't as good as he was. Eventually God helped me understand that he wanted me to faithfully serve him instead of pursuing my own expectations. I began to experience the blessings that come from being encouraged and from contributing in a positive way.

When you make a commitment to last, you won't be tempted to quit youth ministry each time you're discouraged. Let me share a letter written by my friend Brian.

Doug,

I quit youth ministry yesterday.

I got tired of hearing about how I needed to make sure those youth behave during the worship services like I am the church bouncer.

I got tired of parents who don't live Christian lifestyles and expect me to mold their kids in the few hours a week we have them and then when the kids screw up, the fault is the youth ministry not being deep enough.

I got tired of those kids who play the game of being spiritual, but then live like they have never heard of Jesus.

I got tired of adults who do not have a clue about youth ministry but have an outline of how I should do my job.

I got tired of people not respecting the youth ministry calendar by scheduling the facilities and taking them away from students.

I got tired of people who believe that the way we did church in 1948 worked and that it should still work today.

I got tired of people who have complaints but instead of going to those with whom they have a beef, they make phone calls to gripe to dozens of other people in the congregation.

I got tired of people who do not spend personal time with the Lord (by their own admission) but yet think they should run the church.

I got tired of people who think my wife is also an employee of the church and should be available at all times.

I got tired of people who keep asking when I am going to pastor my own church and become a "real" minister.

I got tired of people who think youth workers can't be trusted and need constant supervision.

I got tired of working late and people thinking that is what I should do.

I got tired of people asking, "What do you do all day when the kids are in school?"

I got tired of all the times that I failed and felt so inadequate to do this job.

Bottom line…I just got tired of being tired all the time!

However, I was smart enough not to tell anyone that I quit. I went home, spent some time with my family (and did not burden them with my quitting), spent some time in prayer, and got a good night's sleep. I am back on the job today. I have read Ephesians 6:13 and am steadfast that I will still remain standing (and not quit).

Those same people who I was tired of yesterday are still in my life, but somehow God has given me grace to love them today. I am grateful for having the best job in the world, the opportunity to be used of God as a conduit for his grace to influence young lives. I am so glad that when I quit on God yesterday, that he refused to quit on me.

Today, I'm making a commitment to last because what God has called me to is too important to quit.

Your friend and (still) fellow youth worker,

Brian

Discouraging words and thoughts come and go, but a loving heavenly Father wants his child to have a new perspective—his perspective—on how to live. Trust him and remember that he is with you on this journey.

The Lord is my shepherd; I have everything I need. He lets me rest in green pastures. He leads me to calm water. He gives me new strength. He leads me on paths that are right for the good of his name. Even if I walk through a very dark valley, I will not be afraid, because you are with me. Your rod and your walking stick comfort me.
(Psalm 23:1-4, NCV)

As you read the next chapter, realize that the depth of your discouragement is minimized by the depth of your spiritual life. When your spiritual life is healthy, the arrows of discouragement only sting instead of piercing and wounding your soul.

Don't skip the next chapter, or I'll be discouraged. (See how easily I can get discouraged?)

The Questions at the End of the Chapter

// For group discussion

- Where do you find yourself most easily discouraged in youth ministry?
- Which suggestion from this chapter can help you respond to your time of discouragement?

// For personal reflection

- Do I have a thoughtful plan for dealing with discouragement? If so, what is it? If not, is it worth thinking through one?
- Over the last year, has my discouragement been painful, untimely, selfish, or lonely?
- Do I have a friend and/or mentor who cares for me beyond youth ministry? If not, how and when can I find one?
- Do I have days throughout my week when I consciously get alone in order to get refreshed? If not, how can I make this a priority?

// Actions to consider

- Begin a journal.
- Find a mentor. Make a list of what you need in a mentor.
- Take a long, hard look at your weekly calendar and make sure there's alone time penciled in.

Go to www.dougfields.com and enter your comments under Your First 2 Years: Chapter 2

how do i stay spiritually fresh?

establishing a heart foundation

I'm a Little League coach for my son's baseball team. (Maybe you heard about Cody on ESPN's Sports Center. His team came in first place this year.) The other coach brings his youngest son, Tate, to practice, and we encourage him to participate with the older boys. He's a nice kid who doesn't hinder our practice. As a matter of fact, he's probably as good as most of the older boys on our team, and he's about the same size.

At any given practice you'll find Tate fielding ground balls, taking batting practice, and even pitching. If you were to observe us from a distance, you wouldn't know Tate wasn't on our team. The only time he's a noticeable outsider is on game days when he's not wearing a uniform. He feels like part of the team during practice, but he lacks any meaningful role during the game. Six days a week he looks the part and the one important day when everyone dresses up, he's left out.

I write about Tate because he does all the right things but has no meaningful influence on the outcome of our season. Tate parallels some youth ministry leaders, men and women who seem to do all the right things on a youth ministry team but have no meaningful impact because of their spiritual lives. When youth workers don't value their spiritual lives, their contributions are sidelined. Hearts that aren't connected to Jesus don't help the youth ministry team. I've met a lot of youth workers who foolishly believe that if they're helping others grow spiritually, they must be growing spiritually, too.

If the typical youth worker were to choose one chapter in this book to skip, it's this one. Looking inward and evaluating the condition of your spiritual life doesn't compare to the fun of working in the ministry. For a few moments, please set aside your youth ministry plans, programs, and responsibilities so you can seriously consider your own spiritual condition. Why? Because it's common for those doing God's work to live with spiritual neglect and fatigue.

> "Can't we just skip to the section about 30 ways to illustrate the Trinity with water balloons and pipe cleaners?"
> —typical youth worker

Without spiritual health, you won't make it in youth ministry. Don't misunderstand: you don't need the knowledge of a Bible scholar or the spiritual disciplines of a monk, but you do need a heart that's tender toward God and open to his leadings. You need to be in love with Jesus.

The spirituality of all the leaders combines to make a difference in a strong ministry. Some youth ministries masquerade spiritual health and survive for a season. They may appear strong from a distance, receiving praise, attracting large numbers of students, and creating flashy programs, but up-close, fruit is noticeably absent. Leaders in this type of ministry are so busy *doing* the work of God, they'll miss the importance of *being* God's people. The discouragement described in the last chapter more readily appears in a spiritually shallow heart. A spiritually healthy heart is more prepared to repel the arrows of discouragement.

Being connected to God on a daily basis is more important than any youth ministry seminar you attend or any book you read. Jesus said, "Abide in me and I'll abide in you, but apart from me you can do nothing." This image of being connected to God in John 15 is the picture I want you to focus on. You must value your spiritual life to survive the youth ministry marathon!

Spirituality...Doing versus Being

God has designed you to be connected to him, the levels of intimacy increasing through the years. Don't allow increasing ministry to decrease your intimacy, and don't let your service exceed your worship. These cause spiritual disconnection. It's not unique for leaders to lead without the right heart connection. Jesus' strongest words were reserved for ministry leaders who had either forgotten or ignored the primacy of their inner world. Jesus clearly communicated where to look for spirituality—inward.

> Blind Pharisee! First clean the inside of the cup and dish, and then the outside also will be clean. (Matthew 23:26)

These leaders had their spirituality inside out. They learned how to look good on the outside, without cleaning any of the ugliness on the inside of their lives. These masters of the exterior failed spirituality basics.

> For I desire mercy, not sacrifice, and acknowledgment of God rather than burnt offerings. (Hosea 6:6)

How often I've fallen into the trap of thinking God wants my sacrifice of time and my offering of hard work, more than he wants my acknowledgment of praise and my pursuit of intimacy with him. Too often I have erroneously equated my spiritual health with my *doing* God's work. Have you done this too?

If I were to ask you over lunch about your spiritual condition, how would you answer? What thoughts immediately come to your mind? I'm embarrassed to admit this, but I often answer with an external focus. Like my pharisaical forefathers, I tend to communicate spiritual connectedness by outward actions. I say, "I'm *doing* well! I'm attending church services, I'm in an accountability small group, and I'm having several quiet times a week."

While externals are easy to quantify, they don't adequately determine my spiritual condition. Let's briefly consider three specific external actions.

■ *Attending church:* Youth workers can attend church with hard hearts and obligatory attitudes. Although attendance may appear growth-motivated, often it's just to check the bulletin for typos, critique the sermon, or be visible to the congregation.

- *Being in a small group:* It's simple to get together and discuss the deep and classical mysteries of the faith without revealing any of your heart, fears, sins, discontent, and confusion. Why talk about your life—and be exposed—when you can talk about the Bible and theology and play it safe?

- *Having a quiet time:* If someone asks you about your quiet time, you might use exclamations like, "Great, insightful, I learned a lot." But what about saying, "I didn't get anything out of it but confusion, more questions, and a sense of dread"? It doesn't sound as spiritual, but maybe the mystery of God and the lack of answers would deepen your faith.

// The greatest thing

I realize true spirituality can be seen through visible activities such as going to church, sharing openly in a small group, and having meaningful quiet times. But spiritual health and Christian behavior don't always exist in a reciprocal relationship. God isn't looking for people who act righteous on the outside but aren't on the inside. God is much more concerned about your *being* than your *doing*. Let's think about what this means by looking at some classic words of Jesus.

Jesus clearly explains the importance of loving God:

> "Teacher, which is the greatest commandment in the Law?" Jesus replied: "'love the Lord your God with all your heart and with all your soul and with all your mind.' This is the first and greatest commandment. And the second is like it: 'Love your neighbor as yourself.'" (Matthew 22:36-39)

The distinction between these two commandments is that one is the greatest and the other is the second greatest. Failing to understand the difference can have devastating effects on your spiritual life because serving in ministry and loving others can become an excuse for not falling more deeply in love with God.

Have you ever heard or said something like—

- I can stop reading the Bible now. I have enough material for tonight's message.
- I don't need to take time for prayer. We'll pray tonight at youth group.
- I'm too tired for time alone with God. I was up late doing ministry.
- I had a rough week at work. I'll skip church this weekend.

Failure to see the difference between loving God and loving others (doing ministry) can result in a ministry-focused life rather than a God-focused life. Does this distinction make sense to you? Your service in youth ministry should never come at the expense of your personal spirituality.

I'm not suggesting you must maintain your spiritual disciplines during youth events. Who can have a meaningful quiet time in the middle of a mission trip or after an all-nighter? Mission trips are hard work and overcoming the effects of an all-nighter can require intensive psychotherapy and heavy medication. Don't feel guilty during those times. Your personal spirituality is greater than the sum of your spiritual disciplines. But your connection to God is more important than spiritual disciplines and can't be measured solely by how many quiet times you've had in the last week.

> "So you're saying it's okay to miss a quiet time?"
> —guilt-ridden youth worker

// The second greatest thing

One commandment is greater than the other, yet they cannot be separated. Faithfulness to the first command (loving God) results in obedience to the second (loving others). However, faithfulness to the second doesn't necessarily lead to authenticity in the first.

Loving God leads to loving others, but "loving" others doesn't necessarily lead to loving God. Without a love for God, youth workers will be ineffective.

// Either…or?

Another implication of the connection between these two commandments is this: the God who has called you to draw near to him is the same God who has called you to serve him. You can do both. You may live with tension, but you don't have to choose between a productive, healthy spiritual life and a productive, healthy ministry. It's not *either…or*. It's *both…and*.

Properly handling this issue is a good litmus test when you're asking yourself whether you should stay in ministry. If you cannot simultaneously minister and remain spiritually healthy, you may need to step away from doing ministry for a season. As a child of God first and a youth worker second, you must be able to effectively answer the question, "How can I remain spiritually healthy while I minister to students?"[1]

[1] If you're the lead youth worker, you must make this a priority for your volunteers. If you're a volunteer who has been given this book, please consider this question seriously. Your lead youth worker wants you to understand the content of this chapter and model it to other leaders on your team.

How Can I Continue to Grow Spiritually?

The only way I know to answer this question is by sharing my own experiences. So I can pass on some warning signs I've come to recognize that indicate I'm in danger of disconnecting spiritually. If I overlook these signs, I'll soon be a light bulb with no source of electricity.

Example: I'm not a car guy. I have friends who know everything about cars. They see a car and say, "That's a Camry. There's a Chevy. What a great looking Sable." (Actually, I can't imagine anyone saying that.) I, on the other hand, can tell it's a car, but not what type unless I'm run over and the emblem is impressed into my forehead.

I don't care much about cars and, because of this, I have no problem allowing mine getting a little messy. It always has clutter inside: soccer ball, briefcase, soda cans. The inside of my car often reflects my life's pace. When I have too much to do, my car gets absolutely no attention. It can be filled with laundry, books, trash, my gym bag, trash, unopened soda cans, tapes, trash, my kids' junk, beach balls, spare body parts, and trash. The mess is now a sign! It warns my family, friends, and me that my life is spinning out of control. I'm too busy, and I'm neglecting areas that I usually respond to.

How about warning signs for the quality of our spiritual lives? Based on evaluating my own life and discussions with youth workers, I've identified some signs that indicate an absence of passion, a hardening of heart, a loss of spiritual growth, and a move toward spiritual disconnection. Let's consider some:

- *Loss of passion:* You no longer get excited about God, his Word, or your ministry. Nothing seems to get you motivated anymore. Life no longer holds any surprises.

- *Physical fatigue:* During the day you're exhausted and every night you fall asleep minutes after your head hits the pillow. You're so tired that you can't stay awake for a few minutes to reflect on your day as you lay in silence.

- *Prayer vacuum:* It's been a long time since you've experienced meaningful prayer. You feel embarrassed that you can go all day without talking to God. And when you do pray, it feels foreign, awkward, or forced.

- *Life is too easy:* Our spiritual journeys usually include tension and temptation. Struggle is a necessary component of a healthy spiritual life, but when life is too easy, it may be evidence that you're ignoring conviction or relying on your strengths and gifts, rather than turning to God to supply you with the power you need.

- *Life is too hard:* Without God's encouragement, direction, and wisdom you find yourself handling life's problems by yourself—something you weren't meant to do.

- *Spiritual skimming:* When your personal spirituality and your youth ministry teaching are at the same depth, you're probably skimming from the top of your spiritual experience. When your teaching is deeper than your spiritual depth, you're treading in pharisaical waters.

- *Relational conflict:* You have tension in your relationships. Minor conflicts go unresolved and bitterness takes root. Your focus is on people rather than God.

- *Loss of awe:* Everything in your life can be explained and understood. God's hand in your life has been neatly wrapped in a little box, and everything makes perfect sense to you.

Are these familiar to you? Have you experienced other warning signs? Once you identify your warning signs, you have a choice: deny them or deal with them.

Denial is the most convenient response, easily justifying the warning sign as "not that bad." If you add comparing yourself to others into the equation (I'm not as bad as that person), more fuel powers the denial.

Since I've already admitted my lack of car savvy, it probably wouldn't surprise you to learn I depend on my dashboard lights to tell me the engine temperature, the fuel level, when the oil needs a change, and when someone is about to fall out of an open door. In the past, I've experimented with how long I might be able to delay my action before actually responding to the warning light. My slow reaction has caused damage to my car, to my body (from pushing the car) and to my wallet (from repair bills). The lesson is simple: see the warning light and take action.

The same truth applies to our spiritual lives. Responding to spiritual warning lights may require sacrifice and will certainly require confession. Sharing your pain with another believer may help you move in the right direction. But you don't simply slip out of this condition.

During my early years of ministry I was a spiritual loser. I knew the Bible because I had attended a Christian college and a seminary, but I treated God's Word as a textbook, not a divine love letter. I forced myself to pray. I taught about depending on God's power rather than experiencing it. I didn't intend to live my life disconnected from God. It just resulted from doing ministry and being ignorant about what was happening in my heart. Thankfully I didn't do anything to disqualify me from ministry, but I wasn't qualified to be a spiritual leader, let alone the main leader of a growing team. I was the poster child for *doing* ministry at the expense of *being* God's person.

The turning point came when I realized I was losing control of the ministry and that my heart was hard and cold to things of God. Instead of pretending I was okay, I fearfully told a friend that I needed to get right with God and that I was feeling alone. I was frightened to admit my spiritual failure, but it was the impetus for the reconnection I desperately needed.

I wish I could have read this chapter during my first years instead of going through a spiritual desert, then writing from experience. But because of my experience, I can confidently challenge you to do what it takes, right now, to get your heart right.

Above all else, guard your heart, for it affects everything you do. (Proverbs 4:23, NLT)

Don't take this admonition lightly. Don't skim it. Don't believe the lie that you'll get over it. Do something soon! It's imperative that you frequently check your spiritual condition and deal with problems at the first sign. If the leaders' spirituality isn't a top

Your relationship with Jesus *is* your youth ministry.

It's that simple.

But I need to add a warning: *Nobody cares.*

Don't get me wrong; the people in your church, the parents of the young people you work with, the staff all "care" about you and your relationship with God. But because they're all busy, the shape of care usually looks like shock and disbelief and anger when you crash and burn at work. Most churches and places that hire us to do youth ministry assume our spirituality. They expect that you'll take the time to work on your soul, that you're spending time alone with God, that you're doing whatever is necessary to stay connected to God. But they don't actively support or pay attention to you and your walk with God; they don't actively, intentionally check to see how you are doing when it comes to being.

Your relationship with Jesus is more than doing stuff like reading your Bible and praying; it's the process of becoming intimate with God. Intimacy with God sounds incredibly spiritual, but the road to intimacy runs against the grain of almost everything I do in youth ministry. It's more than having a quiet time; it's developing a *quiet* life. Intimacy doesn't happen in a day or a week or after reading a book; it happens during a lifetime pursuit, a long-term adventure with Christ.

Let's break it down further:

Doing nothing instead of doing something

We've been hired to do ministry. Those around us want to see results, to "get what they pay for"—and what they pay for is someone like you doing stuff with their kids. Which means you feel the pressure to perform, to do "stuff" to justify your paycheck. But doing stuff is exactly what keeps me from developing my relationship with Jesus. By the time I'm done doing the stuff of youth ministry, I have no energy for Jesus—even to do *nothing* with Jesus! This may be difficult to believe, but doing nothing is the most important decision you can make. If you're going to have an intimate relationship with Jesus, you must spend a designated time every week doing nothing.

Listening to God instead of talking about God

We love to talk about God. In fact, we were hired to talk about God. Youth ministry is centered on our talk about God. "Faith comes by hearing," the Bible says…but intimacy comes by listening. Take time each day to listen to God, to pay attention and notice where God is and what God is doing.

Waiting instead of acting

You've been hired to make things happen. To make progress. To grow the ministry. And we all know what that means: get the program going! Programs take time and require activity—but our relationship with Jesus requires inactivity. It will take a strong will for you to resist activity in favor of inactivity. In other words, you need to set aside regular time when you forget your program and wait on Jesus. Your relationship with Jesus is all about presence instead of program.

Here are some more practical tips that I hope will motivate you to work on your relationship with God.

• *Gently request that each staff meeting include 30 minutes to an hour to focus on Jesus (praying, sharing, listening, reading together).* Trust me, very few church staffs actually spend time together on a weekly basis just being with God.

• *Ask for a spirituality budget so you can buy books and other material that will help you get closer to Jesus.*

• *Build into your job description days alone with God.* The ideal would be one day a week, one week every six months. Paid time where you leave your cell phone, pager, and schedule at the office and go to a retreat center or quiet place just to be alone with God.

• *Because most youth workers are constantly moving, rest.* Yeah, that's right—chill out, sleep, take naps. Don't feel guilty about resting; that's part of your relationship with God. (Remember that Elijah took a nap before he was ready to listen to God! And in my book, what's good for Elijah…)

—*Mike Yaconelli*

priority, your youth ministry will *never* be genuinely healthy. The next section contains ideas to help you out of the spiritual rut you're bound to fall into at some point in your ministry to students.

Staying Connected

Honestly, no one enjoys being told what to do. Our rebellious streak wants to emerge and push against the *shoulds* and *ought to's* from others. In light of that, I write with humility and acknowledge the fact that I'm incapable of telling anyone how to connect with God. The principle of abiding in Christ taught in John 15 gives me confidence to challenge you to stay connected to him, but giving specific guidelines about how to do that are uncomfortably legalistic. I have enough trouble staying on track with my own spiritual journey, so what follows are some actions that have been helpful to me as I try to keep my faith fresh and my heart tender to God's presence.

// Pursue consistency.

If you're noticing warning signs, first evaluate your time alone with God.

Do you have a consistent time to seek God's presence? I love this version of Matthew 6:6—

> Here's what I want you to do: Find a quiet, secluded place so you won't be tempted to role-play before God. Just be there as simply and honestly as you can manage. The focus will shift from you to God, and you will begin to sense his grace. (The Message)

When I speak with struggling youth workers, they often admit their time with God is inconsistent. If that describes you, begin with a few minutes of focusing on God and allow him to take over. Even if it's for five minutes, start there and show up ready to be still and learn. Don't set goals to pray for an hour every day, if it's not realistic (and it probably isn't). That's a sure setup for failure and guilt. Begin with minutes and let God take over.

Pick a time when you're at your best. Are you a morning person or a night person? When are you least likely to be distracted? Set aside your best time for the best person in your life: God. Make a commitment to keep your appointment. And if you fail, make the commitment again and again.

Some of my non-Christian neighbors must think I'm so weird when they see my huge piece of black velvet hanging in the corner of my garage.

"No wonder Doug had trouble parking the car in the garage."
—thoughtful reader of Chapter 1

When they ask about it, I explain that it's the location where I spend my time with God. With three children racing through the house, I made my own prayer closet where I could retreat and focus on God. This bizarre location will never be featured in *Discipleship Journal*, but it's a place that works for me. Actually, I love being in my cocoon (as my kids call it), alone with God. While it's not fancy, it's functional, and it's where I go to be with God. I know he understands even if my neighbors don't.

// Go public.

Be courageous enough to invite a friend to lovingly ask you about your consistency, your desire, and the quality of your times with God. You might say something like this: "Would you consider asking me about my spiritual health every now and then? I need someone in my life to care about my spiritual journey with me. On my own, I'm doomed to fail, and I'd love a little accountability."

Don't ask this person into your life if you're not willing to give honest answers—there's no point in wasting another person's time. Obviously, your friend won't be responsible for your spiritual health, but she can become an inspiration and a trustworthy friend.

I'm so thankful I went public and asked my friend Matt to care about my spiritual journey. I've watched him passionately pursue God. Although we're different people, I know he's spending time with God, and I respect his journey as much as anyone I know. Matt is the person in my life who inquires about my times with God. He wants to know what I'm reading, the questions I'm asking, the prayers I'm praying, the doubts I'm journaling. He's not obnoxious about his questioning; he's caring, gentle, and affirming. Some days I find myself wanting to know God more intimately because I know Matt finds joy in my progress. I'm not only more consistent because of accountability with Matt, but I'm a deeper believer too. Not a day that goes by that I'm not grateful for Matt's presence in my personal and spiritual life.

> I've known Doug for many years, and the qualities that impress me the most are his openness and honesty. When honesty is shared within the safe context of a spiritual friendship, accountability is the result. Doug makes me sound so spiritual in this paragraph, but he's as much a part of my spiritual journey as I am of his. I guess that's the point of having an accountable friend—we all need encouragement to finish the race!
> —Matt McGill

// Return to the basics.

Do you recall John's words written in Revelation 2:4-5?

> Yet I hold this against you: You have forsaken your first love. Remember the height from which you have fallen! Repent and do the things you did at first.

This passage was originally written to address spiritual fatigue. John's advice is simple and to the point: do the things you did when you first believed. Can you remember the joy and exhilaration you had when you began walking with God? Remember the expectation you felt right before you went to church or read your Bible—that feeling of, "I can't wait for this!" Go back to the basics of how you first fell in love with God.

Don't be prideful and label those feelings as *immature*, thinking you're too advanced for baby steps. Nothing could be further from the truth! Anticipation and excitement may be the rut-buster you need to jumpstart your faith.

// Pursue variety.

Some Christians whom I respect have custom-tailored spiritual disciplines that are adapted to their own personalities, schedules, and life stages. In the past, I attempted to imitate others in the belief I would be propelled to new depths of spiritual maturity. I didn't end up there because copying something so personal doesn't work.

What others describe as their meaningful times with God may sound boring and legalistic to you. You don't need to do what they do, but maybe you need to try something new to you to shake up your routine and ignite your spiritual passion. God loves variety, so you can stay connected many different ways.

Consider the following options. They aren't original ideas, but they may trigger a fresh connection with God.

- Journal about a meaningful Bible passage. What are the implications for your life?
- Meditate on a single verse or phrase and consider what it means to you now.
- Seek extended solitude. Be still and listen to God. Don't pray. Simply be quiet and write down what comes into your mind.
- Pray through a passage of Scripture, personalizing it for yourself or a loved one.
- Journal about your life. Examine yesterday's actions. Did you miss what God may have been trying to teach you?
- If your Bible reading plan seems stagnant, replace it with a devotional book or commentary.
- Read a large portion of the Bible quickly. Don't stop to think about every verse. Treat it like a story.
- Read a small portion of God's Word and carefully digest each verse.
- Sing.
- Write your prayers to God in a journal.
- Read from a translation or paraphrase you haven't read before.
- Write down life lessons you've learned recently, for example, what you've learned over the last month.
- Listen to a Christian music CD and meditate on the lyrics.

Typically, I'm a creature of habit, but change can inspire me. While I love new experiences with God, my appointments with him almost always start the same way—by reading a chapter of Proverbs. When I was a teenager I was challenged to read a chapter a day. On the 16th of the month, I read Proverbs 16. To this day, reading Proverbs is my primary method of slowing down and focusing my thoughts on God. My God-time typically extends beyond reading Proverbs, but that simple approach to Scripture serves as my entrance into God's presence.

One of the joys of being part of the body of Christ is hearing about how other believers experience God. Everyone is different, so the variety is amazing.

I once taught youth workers, "You can't take students to deep places if you haven't been there first." But the more I see God use spiritual knuckleheads, the more I realize that's not an accurate declaration.

God doesn't need you to be a spiritual giant to lead students toward maturity. God used evil Babylonians, teachers with incorrect motives, and even a jackass (see Numbers 22) to make a spiritual impact. The Holy Spirit isn't limited by our efforts or spiritual maturity. Consequently, we must have a more powerful reason to desire spiritual health than "the students need me." Spiritual health shouldn't be for the sake of students, but for your Creator and for you.

More Than an Activities Director

The great news about the content of this chapter is that I'm describing something you've already experienced—a dynamic, exciting, spiritual life. Everyone experiences spiritual ruts from time to time, but we can access Christ's power to draw closer to God.

Good youth ministry starts with you and God. Without God's active presence in *your life*, you're nothing more than an activities director for teenagers. God is concerned about your heart—it's the single most important gift you can offer him, your church, and students.

My prayer is that you'll pause to diagnosis the condition of your heart frequently. Be sensitive to the subtle warning signs of spiritual disconnection, and be prepared to take ruthless measures to get yourself right with the Lord. God intends for you to love him first—that's the foundation of every good youth ministry, whether it's your first or 21st year.

The Questions at the End of the Chapter

// For group discussion

- Which personal warning sign do you identify with from pages 69-70? Why?
- What adjectives would you use to describe your current spiritual journey?

// For personal reflection

- Do I spend more time thinking about my youth ministry responsibilities or my spiritual life?
- What external, spiritual acts do I value as signs of someone being spiritually mature?
- Am I aware of the warning signs that lead to spiritual disconnect?
- Now that I'm away from my group, how would I really describe my spiritual journey? Is it different from what I shared in the group? If so, why?
- What keeps me from being consistent in my time with God?
- How would I explain to a student what I do to stay spiritually fresh?

// Actions to consider

- Copy Matthew 22:36-39 on an index card and put it by your alarm clock so you can read it when you wake up the next several days.
- Put a check mark by one of the devotional options on page 76 that you'd be willing to try.
- Spend time, right now, begging God to help you see the difference between doing his work and being his person.

Go to www.dougfields.com and enter your comments under Your First 2 Years: Chapter 3

4

what's most important to students?

being with them

Ian was an intern in my ministry for two years prior to his current youth ministry position. Recently I met a man who attends Ian's church. He gushed, "I love Ian! Actually, my entire family loves him. He's a great youth worker."

As I talked with this Ian fan, he never said Ian's youth ministry was growing, that he has started new programs, or that he was breathing fresh life into a tired volunteer team. I got the impression this father didn't care about the trappings of youth ministry. Instead, all he talked about was how Ian cared for his son, wrote him notes, went to his football games, and occasionally called him. Then, in the middle of praising Ian, he looked at his watch and said, "In fact, Ian is meeting with my son right now!" His eyes watered and a thankful tone emphasized his words as he continued to described this effective youth worker.

I happen to know Ian *has* worked hard to change dead programs and inspire weary leaders; however, I'm most proud of him for how he has cared for students. He knows youth ministry programs are needed and can be effective, but he understands that relationships are the key to a healthy youth ministry. His relationship with Jesus is at the center of his ministry. Relationships with students and leaders are central to his focus. Jesus is *center*; people are *central*. That's an equation for a healthy youth ministry.

Ian's story is a terrific testimony to the power and effectiveness of relational ministry. It's also a reminder that, although youth ministry can offer programs, those programs cannot define a ministry. Too often, youth workers are seduced by the lure of designing an attractive program. They admire the creativity it offers, the potential it produces, the challenge it brings, the wows expressed from observing youth workers—and then they forget the reason for the program.

As you begin your youth ministry, please keep in mind that programs only exist to build and strengthen relationships with God and with one another! Relationships are key to a healthy ministry!

Often people write to me, visit our church, or attend one of my seminars with the hope of finding the secret program. "What do you do? How do you do it? What videos do you show? What songs do you sing? What games do you play?" While I'm happy to give details, I always tell youth workers that observing our programs will be underwhelming. It's not that our programs are horrible—they're fine—but they're not flashy. What our programs do, however, is provide opportunities for students to connect with God, with one another, and with our adult volunteer leaders. Our programs help create relationships.

My Relational Journey...Past and Present

One of the reasons I now value relationships so highly is because of failure during my first years of youth ministry.

In 1979, when I started in youth ministry, I focused only on students and cared little about programs or developing other leaders. At my next church, I spent many years trying to figure out the right program formula to create the perfect experience that students would love. After five years of chaos, I learned that helping volunteers develop relationships with students was a major route to youth ministry health. Thankfully, I continued at my second church for several more years, changed priorities, and saw the fruit of this relational strategy.

When I came to Saddleback Church in 1992 (my third church), I began with the priority of adults investing in students' lives. The student ministry had 35 students hungry for significant relationships. Although I was determined to see evangelism take place and for our ministry to grow, I decided to establish relational priorities from the beginning. As the lead youth worker, I made a commitment to pursue four goals:

- Know each student's name
- Show a genuine interest in each student's life
- Find and develop other adults who would do the same
- Cast the vision for a healthy youth ministry

The position at my church was part-time for the first year. This raised two issues:

- How can I accomplish those four goals in 20 hours a week?
- Youth ministry is only one part of my life. I also have to give time to my relationships with God, my family, and friends; other income-producing work; and health and fitness. How will I balance all these demands?

My four goals were not widely accepted by some parents, mainly because they wanted me to disciple their children. They assumed that, since I was the "paid professional," they were getting a better return on my salary if I ministered to everyone myself. Thankfully I didn't cave to this expectation, and this turned out to be best for our church, our youth ministry, and the leaders involved.

It took a while to educate parents on the importance of building a team of caring adults to love and disciple students. As part of the process, I pointed to Jesus as a model. He hung out with 12 disciples, focused on three, and he was perfect.

During my first few months at Saddleback, I gave my attention to the first two priorities (knowing students' names and showing interest in their lives) during our weekly programs on Sunday mornings and Wednesday evenings. Outside the programming time I worked on finding adult leaders and training them to work with students—which enabled me to gradually transfer the priority of showing interest in students' lives to them—and casting the vision for a healthy youth ministry.

That's how I began at my church in 1992, and that's essentially what I continue to do today. Years later, the foundation of our ministry is our volunteer leadership team—godly and dependable adults who each build relationships with a few students and invest in their lives.

I'm thrilled that youth ministry has become more professional as a result of strong programs at colleges and seminaries and emerging academic books, but it isn't rocket science—youth ministry is about adults loving students, building relationships with them, and pointing them to Jesus. While many components of building a strong youth ministry require education and training, its simplicity rests in lives intersecting lives. To fully understand this during your first two years, let me present some big-picture truths that will help you become even more relational with students.

Big Picture: Put People before Programs

I remember getting excited about a program-driven style of ministry another church was doing that produced fruit (that is, an increase in attendance, which was my definition of fruit). My youth team and I visited the model ministry, interviewed its leaders, talked with their students, and decided, "Let's do it!" We spent hours in preparation, training, and promotion to launch an entertaining program. It completely consumed all of my leaders' time.

And the result? It worked!

Actually, it worked well for about six months, and then our students started to feel like we were using them to grow the group. They got to watch our youth ministry enlarge and see their friends come to Christ, but the cost to them was a lack of authentic relationships with leaders and with one another. I had trained my leadership team to focus on attendance, activity, enthusiasm, and competitive games. Although the result wasn't intentional, we grew at the expense of laughter and genuine one-on-one discussions. Some of our students saw their friends drift from God, in part because they weren't making any significant connections in our ministry and attendance wasn't helping them grow spiritually.

I think I finally got the message when Jamal, a sophomore who stopped attending, wrote me, "Doug, if you ever stop playing games and start caring about people again, let me know. When I became a number and not a person, I felt like it was time to find another church family."

> "I bet this note didn't make it in the ol' affirmation file!"
> —wise guy

Ouch! We had become high glamour but low touch. I soon learned that students cared more about the friendships than the flash. To value people more than programs is a lesson I'll never forget. Working on program details takes time, and if you let it, it will consume the time you set aside for personal relationships. Giving in to this temptation will hinder your ministry and limit your view of what God wants to do in your life and ministry.

Big Picture: You Can't Minister to Everyone

Simply choosing to be relational isn't enough because you'll quickly realize that students need more time than you alone can give. You've got to decide who you're going to spend time with. You can't possibly spend time with everyone, can you? Well, yes, you can...sort of.

I learned a major truth after 10 years of youth ministry, one I wish I had learned in one of my first years. You may want to highlight this statement: *"You can't minister to everyone on your own. You must help others become ministers. Encourage your leaders to develop relationships with students."*

Don't attempt to be the super-hero youth worker who's constantly busy trying to meet everyone's needs. Instead, be the super-connector. If your goal is for students to be known and loved, it doesn't have to be with you. This may require some new thinking. As a limited, imperfect person, you have a finite capacity for meaningful relationships. If you're the only one connecting with students, you'll be a bottleneck to any potential growth and genuine care.

Consider this next question carefully: *do most relationships with students point back to you?*

If so, your ministry will soon plateau.

Here's an idea on how you might use your time ministering to students:

// If you're the lead youth worker...

I'd encourage you to spend 50 percent of your relational time with your adult volunteer leaders and 50 percent of your time with students. Why? Spending time with students keeps you sharp, student savvy, and in tune with the audience God has called you to care for. But spending time with leaders allows you to provide them care and model what you want them to do with students. In essence, you're developing a relational ministry with your leaders.

It works like this: I spend time with a leader making sure he's doing okay (spiritually, emotionally, with his family) and that he's developing as a youth worker. The leader then spends time with his small group of boys. I still love those boys, just *through* him. This relational plan is one of multiplication rather than addition.

My preference is that volunteer leaders spend time with kids of their own gender. I'm not suggesting this is *the* way, but I would advise you think through some male-female guidelines if you need to mix volunteers with opposite-sex kids.

Ideally, you'll communicate this relational ministry strategy as an expectation before you accept a youth ministry position. A way to explain this during an interview is to say something like this: "My goal is that every student is known, loved, cared for, and discipled—but I know it can't happen by me alone. My priority will be to love leaders and model to them what I want them to do with students."

If, at this point, you find yourself looking at an interviewer with an open mouth and a confused look, you may be in trouble—they don't get it.

If you're already at a church, serving in your first two years, share this approach in the context of a review. Explain the benefits of a ministry that multiplies itself. Consider these numbers:

- If I set aside one hour a day to spend with two students Wednesday through Friday, I can meet with six students each week—24 per month.

- But if, during those same days, I spend 30 minutes a day training a leader to spend time with students and 30 minutes a day with a student, at the end of the week I've connected with three students and three leaders. If each of those three leaders spend time with three students during the week, together we'll have ministered to 48 students a month, which is 100 percent more than I could have met with by myself.

These equations are examples to illustrate the exponential growth of multiplication. It's awesome! (But don't misconstrue the illustration by thinking you need to meet with this many people or on this schedule.)

// If you're a volunteer...

Spend the majority of your available time with students. Identify a few students and love them. As this group begins to grow numerically, be on the lookout for another leader who can come alongside and love these students with you.

My friend Terrell, a 50-year-old accountant, is a volunteer youth worker in our church. Terrell views himself as the youth pastor to the five students in his small group. He calls them on the first day of school; he occasionally attends their sporting events; he writes them letters. This is relational ministry, and, in reality, he *is* their youth pastor. From the church's perspective, I get paid to be the youth pastor, but the truth is Terrell is the youth pastor to these students. When I know other leaders like Terrell are caring for students, this frees me up to minister to more leaders who will, in turn, care for other students.

Don't allow the lead youth worker to succumb to the pressure to meet with everyone. By spending time with students, volunteers can relieve the pressure youth workers feel to be all things to all people. Step up alongside her and help her carry the relational load.

// 5-3-1 relationships

I ask my volunteers to think in terms of having 5-3-1 relationships. This means that every volunteer has five students who they know well and care for (a term we use is 'shepherd'). From those five students there will probably be three students who they spend the most time with outside of programs. Typically, not all five students will be interested or available to take the relationship to deeper levels. And, of the three, one student usually becomes the go-to student. "This is the one who you're most likely to develop a life-long relationship with." This takes away the guilt of trying to have a relationship with everyone in the ministry. Now, leaders can *know* five, *develop* three and *focus* on one. That's not too much to ask.

Big Picture: Everyone Doesn't Want You to Minister to Them

Just as some people in your group you don't want to spend time with (you know who I'm referring to), chances are high that your personality doesn't connect with certain students either. Don't take it personally. Instead, view it as a blessing from God that you don't have to personally hang out with _____. (C'mon...I know you can fill in the blank!)

Terrell's five boys are in drama and band, and that fits Terrell's musical and acting personality. I don't understand those students. I don't know what a thespian is, let alone want to hang around one. Likewise, the computer geeks in my youth ministry would rather hang around Brian than me. Brian knows the binary language, and they can amuse themselves about megabytes, RAM, and Microsoft all day long. They understand each other. Personally, I'd rather take a kick in the head than be the small group leader of this bunch. They're nice kids; they're just a little weird, which is okay because so is Brian. He works with them well, and he loves them. Like Terrell, Brian is the youth pastor to his students. Terrell and Brian are great parts of the body of Christ working together to meet the variety of needs and personalities within a youth ministry.

> Thespian: *adj.* Of or relating to drama; *n.* actor or actress.
> —*the editors*

Big Picture: You Are a Model

Whether you're a volunteer or the lead youth worker, students are watching you. While that truth may feel like a burden, it's actually a calling from God—at least that's how the apostle Paul saw it when he said, "Follow my example, as I follow the example of Christ" (1 Corinthians 11:1).

Students are like a sponge, and you're the water. They soak up everything you say and do. They watch, listen, observe, and take notes on—

• Your language when you miss the nail and hit your thumb on the mission trip.

• Your driving when you ignore the speed limit on a barren highway during the mission trip you've considered never going on again because your finger hurts so bad.

• Your attitude when you get pulled over by a police officer on the not-so-barren highway during the mission trip that you've just decided you will never take again.

• Your marriage and how you talk to your spouse when you're asked why you're late arriving home from the mission trip from hell.

Even if you can't personally interact with every student, you're being watched by every student, every parent, all the leaders, the senior pastor...and the janitor! Welcome to the fishbowl called youth ministry!

> "I'll be watching you!"
> —*everyone*

Developing a Relational Style of Youth Ministry

To have a relational style of youth ministry, you and the other leaders must work together to purposefully develop it. You'll find that most of the recommended action steps listed below require attitude adjustments rather than extra time from your week. I encourage you to make sure everyone on your team reads through the steps and uses them as a checklist to evaluate his relational time with students. Some of these steps seem difficult at first, but, given some time, they'll begin to feel more natural.

// Understand the power of presence.

Many new youth workers feel like they have to force conversation to get to know students. Relax. Just be there for a while. Don't expect students to come rushing up to you and say, "Hi. Welcome. Are you a new leader? I'm so glad you're here. Why don't you come sit by me?" This won't happen on Planet Earth. But over time, your presence communicates that you care for students. When you show up at church, at their campus, at their games, at important community events involving teenagers, they'll soon learn that you're not an obnoxious stalker, but that you're a caring adult.

Trust isn't built by pushing your way into a teenager's world. Be there. Be loving. Be patient. Be encouraging. Be approachable. And your presence will communicate concern.

// Take someone with you.

Would you like to do effective relational ministry without adding hours to your work-load? Whenever possible, take students with you as you live your life.

What's on your agenda next Saturday that you might be able to do with a student? Washing your car? Shopping? Painting your house? Eating dinner? Lifting weights? Watching a video? Watching someone else lift weights?

Consider calling a student or two to join you. You won't get anything done as efficiently as you could by yourself, but you'll create great opportunities to talk, and you'll establish memories that impact students forever. Your students will come away with a message: "She thought enough of me to ask me to join her."

// Ask strategic questions.

Asking good questions is one of the greatest attributes you can have as a youth worker. A strategic question draws the focus away from you and allows a student to share as much as he's comfortable sharing, while not simply responding with a one-word answer. For example, you might ask a student, "How are you doing?" A quick, safe response is, "Good." End of conversation.

Instead, try something like, "Tell me one thing you did today." This opens up the possibilities a bit more. Even if a student replies, "Nothin'," a natural nonthreatening response could be, "Well, if you could have done something fun, what would you have done?"

I'll admit, a student with a don't-bug-me attitude can find a way to avoid any question, but most are willing to talk if an authentic listener addresses them with a good question. Asking good questions requires some practice. (Try asking at least six questions before you give up!)

// Learn to listen.

During my early years, I had no idea how important listening was to the health of youth ministry and to the power of relationships. Now, every year I'm more aware of hearing these words from students, "No one ever listens to me." Let's be the exception to that cry for help. Listening (and good eye contact) communicates love and powerful messages like these:

- I recognize you.
- You matter to me.
- I have time for you.
- You're my friend.
- I'm excited to see you.
- I care about you.
- You're valuable and worthwhile.

Don't lose sight of the great ministry opportunities you have with students even when it's just for a few minutes. In my early years, I missed wonderful chances to communicate care because I didn't have good listening skills and I thought students loved hearing my bits of wisdom.

Listen

■ *Listen with your ears. Do your students know you hear them?*

Stop talking and start listening. Ask questions that show you're listening intensely. Don't finish other people's sentences or give them quick-fix answers.

■ *Listen with your eyes. Can your students see you care?*

When talking with students, are you guilty of looking around the room to find another person? Of looking at your watch, at your notes, at your birthmarks, at their birthmarks? Have you ever had a conversation with another person who focuses on the hot dog cart behind you instead of focusing on what you're saying? It clearly communicates his hunger is more important than your heart. Don't let your eyes betray you. Focus on the person you're with.

■ *Listen with your face. Do your students believe you're listening?*

When students share their hearts, your facial expressions should match the impact of the words. It's not good enough to have your face directed at a student but expressionless. Be real. When your students are excited, reflect their excitement back to them. When they're hurting, show concern.

■ *Listen with your hands—Can your students sense you care?*
Appropriate touch is similar to good eye contact in its ability to communicate care and concern. When it's appropriate to give a hug, a high five, a pat on the shoulder, do it! Relational youth ministry requires that you connect with students at a level many of them don't experience from the world. You may be the only one who shows them genuine interest and care that day. A simple hug and a few words are a powerful way to communicate care: "Wow! Thanks for taking the time to share that with me. I can tell it was big, and I'm thankful."

// Be real.

Transparency is risky.

Some people in your church may want you to be perfect in the eyes of your students. They want your life to be so different that you're unaffected by temptation. They'd like you to be above their problems. Well, the only people who aren't affected by temptation are dead, so why pretend that life's struggles don't affect you? If you pretend to be something you're not, it's dishonest, hypocritical, and damaging to students because they'll eventually find out the truth.

On the other hand, I'm not suggesting that you be totally transparent and reveal your worst sins; your students should not serve as therapists. But be real with students and help them see how you're learning to walk through the challenges of life.

One way to do this is to share your fears of being new in ministry. Let students know *some* of the concerns you have and how they can pray for you. Instead of giving a false portrayal of your skills, present an honest picture of who you are as you journey with them in Christ. Exposing your weaknesses won't hurt your ministry; instead weaknesses endear you to students. The result of honest leaders is honest students. Your vulnerability helps students shed their masks and increases your credibility among other leaders.

You'll be in the company of Paul, who says, "We were delighted to share with you not only the gospel of God but our lives as well" (1 Thessalonians 2:8). Paul didn't pretend to be someone he wasn't or keep his distance; he opened up.

// Know when to nudge.

One complaint I hear from youth workers when I emphasize the value of relational ministry is that, if they focus so much on being friends, they'll never get an opportunity to challenge students to align their lives with God's Word.

First of all, our goal for youth ministry is not to acquire more teenage friends (although it's certainly appropriate to be friendly and caring). Secondly, someone who is friendly and approachable is more likely to have an opportunity to share God's truth with a student, at least to a listening student who cares about what you have to say. It's easier to accept confrontation and learn from someone who has earned the right to be heard. A stranger rarely motivates me, but I'll typically listen to any challenge from someone who genuinely cares about me.

When opportunities arise or when you need to challenge students, don't be afraid to nudge them. That's a necessary part of the disciple-making process—to lovingly point them toward Christ or to challenge them to develop new habits. Students expect you to ask about their spiritual lives, their prayer requests, their home life, what they did on their dates, and so on. If they're expecting it, you might as well follow through! But timing is everything. So part of your relational journey is learning when to talk about God and when to talk about other topics.

I have a lot of my meetings at Taco Bell restaurants, where I can afford the food and they refill my drinks. One day I saw one of my small group students come into Taco Bell, pull a cup out of his backpack, and get a drink without paying. A sign is posted that reads, "Free refills during same visit only," but he didn't pay for his drink—he stole it.

I knew that if I said something to him I risked the chance of him thinking I'm a prude Christian. He probably would say, "It's no big deal. Everyone does it." He would be right on the latter comment, but his action *was* a big deal. Integrity is worth talking about, so it was time to nudge him. We had an intense 10-minute conversation. I didn't persuade him to my point of view, but I affirmed my love for him, and we ended our conversation.

> As a teenager, I spent a lot of time with Doug. He was more than my youth pastor then, he was a friend—an old one. When I read this chapter, it forced me to process my relationship with Doug. His greatest impact on me came from opening up his life and mentoring me "accidentally" (or so I thought until I read this chapter). Our time together wasn't organized and planned; he came to my games, and I would occasionally hang out at his house. He showed me how to love my family by inviting me into his own. His imperfect yet transparent life modeled a genuine faith that I wanted to emulate.
> —Andy Brazelton

A week later I got an e-mail from him, in which he told me that the Holy Spirit had convicted him throughout the week about his behavior. He thanked me for taking time to care about "something so insignificant" (his words). It would have been easier on me to let it slide, but I had a wonderful opportunity to challenge a student. God used it to help him mature.

If you challenge students about everything they say, think, and do, you'll find yourself a lonely youth worker. But when the time is right, don't be afraid to capitalize on your relationships and love students toward a deeper faith. Students not only need this type of nudge, but also many are looking for someone to care enough about them to take action. I'm always amazed at the results when I have the courage to speak the truth in love.

// Be available.

Obviously, you can't be available to students 24 hours a day, but relational ministry requires your presence when a tension arises or a crisis hits. It would be wonderful to choose the timing of crises in the lives of adolescents. Since that's not realistic, I ask my leaders to communicate "perceived availability."

For example, I might tell a student, "If you need to talk, I'd love to be there for you!" We might not have an immediate meeting, but the student knows he has access to me.

Or I might say something like, "I know your parents are in the middle of a messy divorce, and I'm so sorry for that. I know it's painful for you. I also know that you're hanging out with all your buddies right now, but please know that you can call me if you ever want to talk about what's going on." By saying that, I'm communicating concern and availability.

Sometimes I'm trying to connect with students. I'll uncover personal interests and then express availability: "I heard you're on the basketball team. Can you get me a schedule? I'd love to watch one of your games."

Being available doesn't mean being on call, but it does mean expressing interest and concern.

// Establish boundaries.

In youth ministry, you'll need to establish some boundaries. Whether you're married or single, you cannot and should not try to meet every need at every hour on every day. If married, your family will love you for learning the art of saying no. If you're single, your future spouse and children will thank you for learning to say this important word and developing good relational habits.

When I first began in youth ministry, I went to a seminar in which a veteran youth worker told about being interrupted during his anniversary dinner by a student who wanted to talk. This particular speaker said that, in the name of good youth ministry, he left his wife at a romantic dinner to be with a student in need. As a 20-year-old rookie, I thought that was admirable.

Today, as a veteran of more than 20 years, I think it was stupid. If it were me, I would answer the door and say, "Are you planning on killing yourself tonight? No? Good for you! Let's talk tomorrow, because if I leave to meet with you now, my wife will *kill me*! I love you, but I've got another commitment right now. It's just not a good time."

> "I wish I read this 20 years ago."
> —a divorced youth worker

If you're relational but you don't establish some boundaries, ministry will keep you from having a personal life.

// Use technology to your advantage.

Don't take every phone call; don't reply to every instant message; don't answer every knock at your door! Instead check voice mail and e-mail when it fits your schedule. As long as you respond in a somewhat timely manner, you can still communicate care to students while also protecting your sanity and your family's emotional health. You need to guard your personal time if you're going to survive long term in youth ministry.

// Learn to refer.

When you do meet with students or parents about significant issues, sometimes the best plan is to listen, pray, and refer to a professional counselor—or at least to an individual with more experience with the subject.

I'm a listener and a lover of people. I'm not a counselor. I've often felt guilty that I couldn't solve every problem. When I tried, there were times when I did more damage than good.

Don't feel guilty about referring. Make it clear that you're not a counselor but you'll be happy to listen and offer the name of counselors to contact for additional help.

Two of the most effective tools of relational youth workers are prayer and referral.

I called Marvin the first week of my youth ministry job. Marvin was in the 7th grade. I met him briefly at a youth gathering where I was officially introduced as the new youth pastor.

My goal that first week was to contact each student either by phone or by way of a personal note. My phone conversation with Marvin went something like this:

Me: "Hi, Marvin! This is Helen."

Marvin: (in a monotone voice) "Who?"

Me: "Helen. The new youth pastor. (Silence. My insecurity increasing.) I was calling to say hi. (More silence. More insecurity.) So...what are you doing?"

Marvin: "Nothin'."

Me: "Wow. Yeah. Well, what are you gonna do this weekend?"

Marvin: "Nothin'."

Me: "Wow. Yeah. Well, what's goin' on at school?"

Marvin: "Nothin'."

Me: "Wow. Yeah. Great. Sounds fun. Well...I guess I better let you go. It's been really great talking to you. Hope to see you at youth group Sunday night."

I hung up the phone, feeling sure the letters "LL" (double loser!) were plastered on my forehead! "Man, this relationship building thing is really tough!" I thought. "And this is what I went to graduate school for?!"

That Sunday I ran into Marvin's mother in the hallway out side the adult Sunday school room. I tried to make a quick about-face when she spotted me and called me. Oh boy...here we go...

"Helen, thanks for calling Marvin," she said. "What did the two of you talk about?"

I was about to say "Nothin'," but before I could she broke into a smile of interest and appreciation.

"Marvin got off the phone and said, 'Mom, that was Helen, the new youth pastor! We talked, she understands me, how I feel, my struggles...'"

Teenagers are often unpredictable, inconsistent, and not easily decoded. I learned that early on as I undertook relationship building. And the old saying, "If at first you don't succeed, try, try again!" bears repeating when you're trying to establish regular communication with students. For some of us, conversation and interaction comes easily. But for many of us, the lurking voices of insecurity drive us from reaching out the way we really want to. It's during these moments that we must remember, "In our weakness, his strength is made perfect." And then our insecurity becomes our greatest gift...because it pushes us toward deeper dependence on Jesus.

Marvin and I became good friends, regular "phone buddies." I'm so glad that my first impressions and assumptions about our first phone call were wrong. And so, 25 years later, I'm still making phone calls to kids. And I'm still surprised at what God does in the midst of my weaknesses.

—Helen Musick

// Understand the power of little things.

I've taught the Bible to students for years, yet I can count on one finger the number of times students have come up to me after graduating from our ministry to tell me how one of my messages impacted their lives.

On the other hand, I've long lost count of the number of times students have reminded me of the little things I did that are forever etched on their minds and continue to encourage them years later.

What's a little thing?

- Calling students on the first day of school and praying for them.
- Sending students photos taken of them at youth group events. (Always get double prints.)
- Dropping by their workplaces just to say hi.
- Attending the last quarter, inning, or set of their games. (Although you can drop by earlier, coming at the end affords the opportunity to interact with your students afterward.)
- Mailing favorite snacks to arrive on their birthdays.
- Calling students' parents just to brag on them. (e.g., "Mrs. Gates, your son Billy is doing some amazing things with computer graphics for our small groups!")
- Taping notes of encouragement to the front door during exams or other stressful periods. (Ring the doorbell and disappear.)
- Actually taping notes of encouragement directly on students.
- Inviting students over for dinner.
- Letting a group of (same-sex) students spend the night.
- Following up a few days after a student shares a prayer request.
- Using your students as positive illustrations in your message or Bible study. (It's always a good idea to get permission first.)
- Mailing goofy postcards for no reason.
- Dropping off brain food (a double cheeseburger) the night before a big test.
- Asking students—on a one-to-one basis—to pray for you.
- Remembering students' names and using their names when you talk with them.

Not all youth workers get the opportunity to deliver a message or lead a Bible study, but everyone can pull off the little things. When you hear of other leaders doing little things for students, share the idea and affirm them during your next leadership meeting. Not only will other leaders hear great ideas, but also positive youth ministry is reinforced and valued. Other leaders are likely to try the same ideas with their students.

So What Do I Do First?

Being relational doesn't depend so much on what you do, but on who you are. Healthy youth ministries have relational leaders who love students and want to get to know them. They have shepherds, not chaperones.

Jesus was the master of relational ministry! Not only did he come to our world to walk among us, but he looked people in the eyes and loved them in the moment. Whoever he had contact with—the hemorrhaging woman, the paralytic being lowered through the roof, Zacchaeus hiding in the tree—Jesus stopped his task and put people first. That's the essence of relational ministry: putting people first.

Don't get overwhelmed. Focus on a few students. All the ideas I've listed flesh out the one important goal that you read about in Chapter 3: the fulfillment of God's great commandment.

Love the Lord your God with all your heart, all your soul, and all your mind. This is the first and most important command. And the second command is like the first: Love your neighbor as you love yourself. (Matthew 22:37-39)

The Questions at the End of the Chapter

// For group discussion

- Do you have the freedom in our youth ministry to invest your life in students?
- What scares you the most about being a relational youth worker?

// For personal reflection

- How can I do a better job remembering names?
- What do I need to do to establish boundaries for when I'm available and when I'm not?
- How do I feel about other leaders "taking" students who I want to invest in?
- What students do I think would refer to me as their "youth pastor"?
- What parts of my life could I reveal to students so they might know more of the real me?

// Actions to consider

- Make a list of the names you would identify as having 5-3-1 relationships with. If you can't list these names, make this one of your goals.
- Make a list of five little things you can do on a regular basis (see page 99). This list can become your go-to list.
- Write an encouraging note to a different student each week.

Go to www.dougfields.com and enter your comments under Your First 2 Years: Chapter 4

how do i work with parents?
becoming family friendly

Of all the chapters in this book, this one emerges from the trenches of trial and multiple failures rather than trial and occasional error. I've made more mistakes in this area than I care to admit and moved so slow in learning how to minister to parents that I'm honestly embarrassed at my educational pace. This is an important chapter conceived through struggle and pain. I'd love to save you from some of the hurt I've caused and experienced.

My Journey…From Viewing Parents as the Enemy to Parents as Partners

Early in my ministry I held an immature perspective that parents were the enemy to good youth ministry. Because I held this view, I battled feelings of intimidation and insecurity when I spoke to parents.

Parents were saying no to my creative ideas. I couldn't believe that Mrs. Moore didn't want us to sponsor a boxing match between student government leaders at the local schools when I thought it would be a good outreach event.

Parents were verbal about my efforts: I wasn't teaching enough Bible; I was too serious and teaching too much Bible. I was playing too much; I wasn't playing enough. The kids were too loud during the service; not enough kids attended the service. I could fill a book with their complaints—complete with the names and faces I easily remember.

Because of my inexperience, I took the comments as direct attacks. I developed a defensive posture—parents versus me—which was evident in my attitudes, actions, and communication. Parents became the enemy of all my ideas to build a strong youth ministry. I felt angry.

Today I parent a teenager who's in my youth ministry. The change in my family's dynamics has also changed how I think about youth ministry. Ironically, I often view our youth ministry as the enemy of family time, since she's more interested in youth ministry events than family events.

During your first two years of youth ministry you won't be able to focus much time or energy on families. You'll be busy learning names, evaluating programs, developing a strategy, getting established. But you can develop family-friendly attitudes during your early years that will influence your future actions. Whether your position within your youth ministry is paid or volunteer, you can't go wrong when you put families first and commit to being a cheerleader to the families in your church—minus the pom-pons and handsprings.

Let me present some caring attitudes and ideas to help you with family ministry during your first two years.

Big Picture: Foundational Truths about Youth Ministry and Parents

It's important that all youth workers gain a big picture perspective regarding the vital connection between youth ministry and family. A family-friendly youth ministry team strengthens your entire church, helps families and students, and makes your youth ministry look good in the eyes of your congregation.

// You're *an* influence, not *the* influence.

I've come to realize that I can have little long-lasting influence on a student's life if the parents aren't connected to the same spiritual transformation process that we're teaching at church. While students may think you're nice and feel safe talking to you, parents are the primary influencers in students' lives.

// Family-friendly youth ministry is important, but it's not easy.

Dealing with families in a real-life environment is different from families presented in the ideal, academic setting. When I was in seminary, the lectures seemed so clear, the ideas so easy, the families so accepting. When the classroom emptied and I walked into the trenches, I found it to be completely different—a mix between "wow!" and "oh, no!" The trenches are messy. But the glimmers of "wow!" are worth the effort we give.

"And maybe even an occasional 'uh oh!'"
—*one who's been there*

I'm writing in the most honest way I can to make you fully aware that, while dealing with families is important, it's not easy. In your first two years, don't worry about setting up a lot of programs for parents and families; instead, focus on understanding families and how you might assist them on their difficult journeys. Lower your program expectations and increase your attitude changes, and some common sense actions will naturally follow.

Six Parent Prayer Ideas

1. Make it a habit to ask parents how you can pray for them.
2. Find a parent volunteer to gather parent prayer requests. Perhaps set up a prayer line by which parents can call in their prayer requests. Pass the ones that aren't confidential to other leaders to keep the volunteers aware of family ministry.
3. Pray for parents if you say, "I'll be praying for you." (This point may only apply to myself.)
4. Ask parents to pray for your leadership team and your ministry.
5. When you gather to meet for a special event or camp, ask the parents to stay for a time of prayer. Recognize and acknowledge that families struggle with strong emotions and anxieties when their kids leave on trips. Consider asking a parent to lead in prayer. (Be sure to ask the parent first.)
6. Ask some of your ministry-active students to pray for specific families in your church.

// Don't teach parents how to parent unless you've parented teenagers.

In my early youth ministry years, I actually thought I could teach parents how to parent. Big mistake! I remember teaching a so-called parenting seminar where the parents looked at me with expressions of, "Yeah, right," "I can tell you don't have a teenager, pal," and "That idea might work on a toddler, but it'll never work on a teenager." Through their facial expressions and body language, they communicated I wasn't a credible source of parenting experience. They were right. I *didn't* know what I was talking about.

Unless you've already finished parenting a teenager, don't try to teach other parents how to do it. As a youth worker, you *know* about teenagers, but, unless you've already raised children, you don't know how to parent them. You may know more about adoles-

I'm grateful for the honesty, insights, and tips this chapter offers youth workers. But sadly, one of the reasons it was written is because for years we've actually been hurting families. Many of us are infected with a disease that can do great damage to the church: We see our ministries to kids as *our* ministries.

Doug notes that we must acknowledge parents as the primary influencers in students' lives. If this is true (which I believe it is), then everything we think, say, and do in the name of youth ministry must reflect this.

Take the issue of time, for instance. We are greatly limited in our abilities to influence—or even forge consistent connection with—kids because we have so little time with them. With the exception of occasional one-on-one, direct conversations, over the course of a week there may be up to three hours of large-group contact with students who show up—and perhaps some of those kids will also benefit from another hour of small group interaction. So, for the *most consistent* kids in your group (who'll still miss some meetings), over the course of a school year they will have been involved in youth group for about 100 hours, plus a weekend or two and another week at camp. This is *far less* time than they'll spend with most of the other caring adults in their lives—parents of close friends, bosses, teachers and coaches. To varying degrees, they *all* care and influence your students. But this is most true for their parents. As influential on kids as Christian youth workers are, we're merely among a large cast of characters whose best work is done in conjunction with and *under the tutelage of* those adults charged by God to nurture our students— their parents.

This often is not the case, however. And it's a major weakness in youth ministry. We think we know, love, and serve kids better than anyone else. But as the father of three children who are rapidly growing up, I've seen youth workers come and go. Some are solid and sacrificial, but many are superficial and inconsistent. Still, all three of my kids can point to one or two youth workers who were *great* for them. The common denominator? These youth workers not only loved our kids for who they were (or are), but they also recognized their number-one job was to *support the family*. From Chuck to Joey to Heather to Scott, they knew Dee and I needed and cherished teachable and committed *partners* to help our kids understand God's intentions for their lives and for his kingdom. It's my hope and prayer that every youth worker will define their role in this way.

—Chap Clark

cent development, more about current popular culture, a few more slang words, what kind of underwear is currently in fashion than the average parent, but when it comes to parenting, save your ideas for your own kids—and you'll quickly learn humility like I did, which was when I moved from the role of self-imposed educator to the role of committed family ally.

Develop Family-Friendly Habits

Parents need to know you're not trying to take their place. You're trying to help them.

// Understand basic family needs.

When you look at youth ministry and parenting concerns, the common denominator is busyness. (See sidebar below.) Yet I often believe I'm the only one with a packed life, so then I'm left wondering why I don't always agree with parents. To develop a family-friendly attitude, embrace the fact that busyness is epidemic and universal in our culture. It's not limited to those doing youth ministry. Universally, families need time...together. When you understand this need, you'll be more sensitive in your programming, your teaching, and your expectations of students and parents.

> "Don't make my teenager choose between our family and church!"
> —a concerned parent

Youth Worker Concerns

- How can I keep the attention of my students?
- How can I grow my youth ministry?
- How can I help my students to grow spiritually?
- What activities will appeal to my students?
- What service projects can I provide for my students?
- What topic should I speak on next Wednesday...next Sunday...tonight?
- What curriculum should I use?
- How can I keep the parents of my students happy?
- How can I stay alive working in a ministry that never ends?
- Why am I so busy?

Parental Concerns

- How will we pay the bills this month?
- How can we have peace in our home?
- How can we get our kids to do their homework?

- How will we be able to afford to send our kids to college?
- How can we get ahead in life?
- Who are our child's friends?
- Is our child having sex? Doing drugs?
- How can we get our children to go to church...willingly?
- Why does it seem like we can never catch up?
- Why am I so busy?

// Always consider your impact on the family.

One practical way to be sure you're sensitive to family needs is to ask—and answer—this question: "How will this activity impact the families in the church?"

When you set the price of camp, what impact will the cost have on each family? How about a family with two teens? To the best of your ability, minimize costs. When you build a casual buffer into your price, the extra cost hurts some families. Do whatever you can to lower the cost of events. If your setting allows, charge less for the winter retreat and have your students eat before they arrive and leave the camp before the last meal to save on food costs—even buying food on the road may be less expensive than eating at the camp. Think through the situation carefully to come up with any and all cost-savers.

> "Okay, Bobby. You can go to camp, but we'll have no money for electricity this month."
> —a financially strapped parent

// Consider the impact on families when you schedule programs.

Minimize the nights you have students out for your events. You can't be a family-friendly youth ministry and constantly ask students to be separated from their parents. If you have students out more than two nights a week, your ministry may not be family friendly.

// Lighten up on the programs.

Since you know that a healthy youth ministry focuses on relationships, emphasize the importance of kids having positive relationships with their families. Consider having a few weeks throughout the year when you cancel everything related to youth ministry and challenge your students to spend time at home with their families. Don't worry. God will still be God, and your students will survive for a week without youth ministry events.

Typically our youth ministry team tries not to schedule events during December. Families with any social life have limited free time during December, and we don't want to further burden their calendars. We also schedule two free weeks right before school starts to encourage families to get ready for school, go out for a last summer family outing, or whatever activities allow them to enjoy time together. Of course if you want families to benefit from the activity blackout, communicate the purpose of the gift to families.

Since Jesus didn't say, "Follow me to programs," constantly pray for discernment and God's wisdom regarding how often you request students to be out of the house. Be careful not to fall into the trap of equating attendance at youth programs with spiritual maturity. Possibly the most spiritual action some of your students will make is to not show up at an activity so they can spend time with their families.

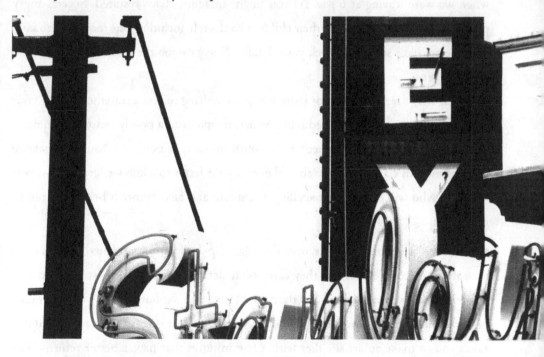

// Master communication as a simple, but powerful, tool.

The simplest secret to winning with parents is to learn how to communicate clearly. I can't count the number of times parents have asked me questions that could have been easily answered through basic communication channels. The parents of my students are smart, but none of them are mind readers. Parents want to be informed about what's going. Over the years I've learned communication to parents should be—

■ *Consistent:* Every month parents should receive a brief list of announcements, your top 5 or 10. Parents will rely on this information if you send it regularly. It relieves some stress for them when they're informed about the youth ministry.

■ *Concise:* Most parents can't keep up with their reading: mail, school reports, newspapers, magazines. They need dates and key details to update their family calendars. Parents don't want all the funny, cute, and inspirational anecdotes; they want details. They need the menu, not the recipe.

■ *Clean:* If you're not a good writer, find someone to proofread your parent correspondence. I once sent out a parent letter designating the departure time for camp as 6 *a.m.* when we were leaving at 6 *p.m.* As you might imagine, chaos resulted. Several angry parents got out of bed to bring their children to church, including one mother who said, "You better have someone check your details." She gave me the idea—with a tone I'll never forget.

This may seem like a minor issue, but poor writing makes a statement about your youth ministry—one about credibility. When people read a poorly written document, they can't help but wonder whether the youth ministry is poor too. You don't have to take journalism classes, but you should e-mail your letter to a knowledgeable coworker or friend who will correct your spelling, grammar, and facts before it becomes a public document.

■ *Clutter-free:* Save the silly, gross, over-the-edge clip-art for your students. Parents don't care about cartoon characters; they care about detailed information. I've never looked at a letter from my kids' school and thought, "This pizza announcement would be much better if there was a picture of a guy holding a pizza while surfing." Replace the hour it takes you to make an artistic flier with a few minutes that have a better return—like personal letters or phone calls to a few parents.

■ *In Advance:* Early communication helps prevent family scheduling issues. Parents should know your big summer events early in the year, so they can accommodate them as much as possible when planning their summer trips and vacations. Save the minutiae for your monthly parent letter when the event gets closer. The bigger the event (not only in terms of effort, but also in terms of spiritual impact), the earlier you should be announcing the date.

- *Cheap:* Communication doesn't need to be expensive. Use e-mail when possible. If you have families who aren't online, leave a few copies on the church information table and encourage parents to pick them up. For the parents of students who don't attend your church, send the information home with students and pray that it arrives—which may be expecting a miracle (but those are good to pray for). When you think postal mail is called for, postcards are less expensive than first-class mail.

- *Honest:* Communicate to parents what time your mid-week evening event is *actually* finished so parents know the "real" pick up time. If your students are like some of mine, they tell their parents, "Pick me up at 9:30," even though the event ends at 8:30. When parents know the real ending time, they can choose how late to allow their children to stay; the decision is in their hands.

- *Helpful:* On the back of your monthly parent letter, give a brief synopsis of your teaching lessons for the upcoming month, which offers parents information to draw from for

---

⟨A VOICE FROM THE TRENCHES⟩

At one time, I wanted to teach a series on sexuality for our students. When word got out about my plan, several parents contacted our senior pastor expressing their concerns. My senior pastor asked me to meet with the parents and hear their concerns.

I had two choices—listen to their concerns with an open mind and heart or listen to them with my mind already made up. Unfortunately, I chose the latter.

Our meeting was a dismal failure. There was lots of shouting and anger. I did end up teaching the series (I won the battle), but it took a long time to regain the trust of those parents (I came close to losing the war).

Looking back, I realize where I failed.

First, I failed to *really* listen to their concerns and suggestions. I only listened so I could make good rebuttals—not to hear their pain and ultimate concern for the children.

Second, I failed to acknowledge that when it came to my students, their parents were indeed the experts. As the youth pastor, I thought I knew what was best for their kids. I knew youth culture, I knew adolescent development, and I established good relationships. I decided, therefore, that a series of lessons on sex was necessary. It never occurred to me that someone else, especially parents, might have other ideas.

Third, and perhaps most importantly, I failed to involve the parents in the decision-making process until it was too late. If I had just taken the opportunity to seek their input, I could have developed allies rather than enemies.

—*James K. Hampton, (formerly) Westside Nazarene Church, Olathe, Kansas*

"And finish when you say you will!"
—*a busy parent*

mealtime discussions. Of course you need to plan your lessons further ahead (I know—another miracle to pray for).

The usual after-church conversation goes like this:

Parent: How was Bible study tonight?

Student: Fine.

(*End of conversation.*)

By letting parents know in advance what the topic is, they might have this conversation:

Parent: Did you agree with Doug's teaching on forgiveness tonight?

Student: Yes.

Parent: How was the teaching?

Student: Fine.

(*End of conversation…but at least it was twice as long!*)

Informed parents are happier, grateful parents. Your youth ministry can't be considered family-friendly if parents are uninformed.

// Don't underestimate little expressions of thoughtfulness.

Often parents value small courtesies the most:

- Returning from an event on time, not 30 minutes late.
- A simple, handwritten letter to a family stating your appreciation for them.
- A daily update left on an answering machine that parents can call during summer camp.
- A smile and the honest words, "I'm praying for your family."

Parent love gestures like these.

I learned the importance of small courtesies when I told parents they were welcome to borrow any of our youth ministry resources for their summer vacations. We had some tents, coolers, walkie-talkies, recreation equipment, and other gear. Although only two families took the offer, I was highly praised for even presenting the idea. I didn't think I had made a special offer since I had been calling church families and borrowing stuff for years. I was simply trying to return the favor. (In fact, half the stuff parents borrowed was theirs to begin with!)

Even a little idea can make a big statement.

// Take the trauma out of transitions.

Transitions such as joining your youth ministry or leaving for college are opportunities to minister to families.

When new students begin attending, call parents to answer questions and address concerns. You don't have to make the call yourself; develop a team of leaders who share the responsibility. Most families will have at least a few questions. By calling, you give parents a forum to ask them, and you have the opportunity to express your enthusiasm for their family's involvement.

Sending kids to college can be tough. Many parents grieve when their kids leave. Send an encouraging note along with a youth group photo of their child to communicate your support.

// Encourage parents on their journeys.

Parents crave affirmation and long for positive reinforcement about their parenting skills; they love to hear optimistic comments about their children. Building up a family with your words is one simple practice every youth worker can pursue regardless of age or parenting experience.

When you return from the winter retreat, don't rush off to clean the van. Instead meet parents in the parking lot, look them in the eyes, and tell them a story emphasizing some positive interaction or characteristic you noticed about their child. When your mid-week meeting is finished, make one phone call to a parent to highlight some positive observation about their child from the evening. Go out of your way every week after the Sunday school hour to find at least one parent to encourage with a genuine compliment. When your comments are sincere and specific, they have impact.

> It's amazing how parents can change when they know you're on their team.

10 Ways to Validate Parents

1. Learn parents' names and who their children are.
2. While attending students' events (recitals, games), visit with parents.
3. Compliment parents on their parenting. Recognize the strengths in their children and give parents the credit. ("You've sure done something right, Mrs. Jones. Your son's a servant. That sure is rare among teenagers.")

4. Send parents a note following a conversation with them ("It was great talking to you at John's game yesterday. I sure appreciate your family.")

5. Listen to parents. Consider their input regarding the youth ministry. You don't have to respond to every suggestion, but assure them that you care about their ideas.

6. Express your feelings about the importance of the family. Let parents know you value their family and respect them. Make your youth calendar family-friendly. Don't ask kids to be out more than two nights a week.

7. Acknowledge that parents love, care for, and do more for their children than you will ever do. Your role in their lives may be significant, but you'll never take the place of a parent.

8. Organize a parent appreciation dinner once a year.

9. Encourage kids to sit with their parents during the church service.

10. Respect parents' time. Return from your events by the time you promised. (We expect parents to be on time to pick up their kids, right?)

Develop Family Friendships

One of the most difficult tasks of youth ministry is developing priorities. Many youth workers don't make time for parents because it doesn't seem like a productive priority. The same can be said about prayer—it doesn't *seem* productive, but prayer is an essential act of living out faith.

Taking the time to develop a few strong relationships with parents is a priority; it may make the difference between having a short, good ministry and having a long, vibrant, family-friendly ministry.

Advantages of good parent-youth worker relationships are—

• You may find a parent to mentor you.

• Parents can become allies who influence other parents positively about you and the youth ministry.

• You learn to see from the parental viewpoint (if you aren't one).

• You have relationships with adults, not just students.

• You hear the other side of the parent-child stories. (There are always two sides.)

• Parents have unique resources and influences to offer the teenagers in your ministry.

• Your ministry extends beyond students.

• You can minister to students through their parents.

- You send a message to students that parents are important and valuable.
- You can get a free meal once in a while.

// Be relational.

Just as you intentionally develop relationships with students, intentionally develop relationships with parents. Obviously you can't have significant relationships with every parent, just like you can't with every student (unless you're overseeing a very small group), but you can pursue relationships with a few.

I tell parents, "I'd just like to get to know you. I eat lunch every day, so I'd love to have you join me to talk about life, your family, your job, and God. I won't break out a Bible study and force you to answer questions. I want to know more about your family."

What might you ask about when you're with a parent for the first time?

- What kind of work do you do?
- What's your favorite family activity?
- How is our youth ministry helping your child grow spiritually? What can we do to help more?
- Tell me about your relationship with God.
- Can I borrow your Mercedes for my next date night?

The process is nearly the same for parents as for students. Get to know them, care for them, listen to them, help them, encourage them…then watch your youth ministry deepen.

My favorite approach is to meet a dad for lunch in his world. After a lunch meeting with Garrett, he invited me to join him for a day in his family medical practice. When I arrived, he gave me a white lab coat, a stethoscope, and a clipboard, and I followed him around for the day. I left with some great laughs (a few rubber-glove stories you'll have to ask me about), fun memories, fresh illustrations, and a new friendship. Relationships like this form the foundation of family-friendly youth ministry.

How to Reach Out to Disconnected Parents

One of the biggest frustrations I experience in my ministry to parents is that the parents who need to be more involved in our programs are the parents who aren't! What can we do to connect with parents—unchurched or attending another local church—who don't seem to want to connect with us?

1. Communicate clearly your desire to get to know them.

2. Express encouragement about their students whenever you speak with them.

3. Enlist their help. Some parents are waiting to be asked.

4. Know their needs before they tell you. Think through issues that affect them and offer assistance when possible (transportation, price breaks for the family with two teenagers, et cetera).

5. Design events they'll want to attend.

- Mission trip reunions

- Parent meetings in which they can observe a program for students.

- Banquets for incoming junior high or high school students. Ask parents for pictures to use in multimedia presentations to be shown at the banquets.

6. Be available during times of crisis.

7. Send parents letters to thank them for the opportunity to spend time with their children. Include a phone number or e-mail address by which they can contact you.

8. Always have a leader who greets parents when they drop their kids off at activities. Go out of your way to be friendly even if parents aren't.

9. Make an appointment to visit or call on the phone to explain what the youth ministry is about. Tell parents you want them to know about the place and activities their student is attending. This gives you an opportunity to go to parents if they won't come to you.

10. Realize you won't be able to reach every parent and family. You do your best (the possible) with faith that God will do the impossible.

Allow Parents to Minister to Parents

While a healthy youth ministry includes a ministry to families, the truth is, parents can—and should—minister to other parents.

Over the years, I've learned that parents can minister to parents effectively, more effectively than my younger volunteers (or me when I was younger). During your first two years, you can realistically find at least one parent of a teenager to organize some of your family-friendly efforts. Start by taking two careful steps: create a ministry description for this parents' ministry leader and find a person for the responsibility.

// Create a point-person ministry description.

Have a clear vision of what you want your parent ministry volunteer to do, so you can find an individual with gifts that fit the ministry. Look at this description:

1. Oversee communication to parents.
   - Create and send a monthly e-mail letter.

2. Plan and oversee parenting events (two to four times a year).
   - Develop a leadership team of helpful parents.
   - Plan parent training (Understanding Your Teenager, Taking the Trauma Out of Transitions, et cetera).
   - Organize and finalize details for each program.

3. Find and organize *been-there, done-that* referrals.
   - Develop a list of *been-there, done-that* parents, people who have offered to share about their painful experiences.
   - Organize the list into like-situation groupings.
   - Make contacts with the referrals to explain their role when hurting parents call.

4. Place interested parents into small groups.
   - After each parent-training event, place interested parents into small groups.
   - Find appropriate material for parents in small groups.
   - Work with and care for parent small group leaders.

5. Respond to entry-level parent problems.
   - When parents call with parenting issues, be their first contact.
   - Refer callers to been-there-done-that parents.

As you read over the list, please realize that I've given you an extensive description to give you ideas about what your volunteer might do. They don't have to all be incorporated into your youth ministry setting within a month or even a year. A healthy parent ministry takes time to develop. Initially you may want your volunteer to only produce and send the monthly parent letter. Whatever the description, write it down and change it when you're ready.

// Find a point-person parent.

Our current volunteer—Kathleen, 45 years old, four children, two high school graduates—manages our family-friendly efforts in about 10 hours a month. This great woman serves God by caring for and loving parents. I wish I could clone her for your church, but it's

> When Doug asked me to coordinate ministry to parents, I didn't think I could handle one more task—I was too busy! But as we talked and prayed about it, I realized that parents would minister to me as much as I ministered to them. So I gave up other activities and made parents my priority. Now I'm blessed to partner with them as we navigate the rocky terrain of adolescence together. In fact, they were amazed that our youth ministry wanted to help and was so concerned for their families. So I'm glad Doug saw the need—and asked me to fill it. I'm a better parent because of this shared journey, and hopefully the other parents are, too.
> —*Kathleen Hamer*

my guess you've got someone like Kathleen waiting to be found and empowered to support your families.

Once you've got a realistic job description, you can begin looking for God's person. When it's time to find the person in your church who can own the ministry to families, consider these ideas:

■ *Ask the children's ministry leaders:* Request the names of three parents who are passionate about parenting well. You may find an individual who is gifted appropriately for this ministry position.

■ *Identify "model" parents:* When you're looking for a minister to families, you'll want someone who practices what he preaches. As I interact with families, I think to myself, "I like how she treats her son," or "I'm impressed with how he communicates with his daughter." Parents like these are good candidates to ask.

■ *Find involved parents:* You've heard the expression, "If you want something done, give it to the busiest people." Active people are doers. Kathleen was participating in PTA, sports, church, and other activities. She was *too* busy for the position, but when I told her more about it, she reduced her other responsibilities so she could focus on our ministry to parents.

> "I may rethink my position on cloning."
> –*a desperate youth worker*

■ *Invite your favorite families to dinner:* This is a hand-selected parent appreciation dinner. Once you have these fine families at your house (about three to five families at a time) tell them how much you appreciate what you see in their lives and within their children.

Then present your dream for finding a point person for this ministry. Share more than needs; let them hear your heart and your vision. Ask them to prayerfully consider the position. Even if no one responds, you have more people aware of the type of person you're looking for.

The most powerful principle I've learned over the years is to ask people eye to eye about getting involved in ministry opportunities. People want to be believed in and empowered to serve God in unique ways—and to make a difference. With little effort you can present the needs and incredible opportunities that exist within your church's families. Look and ask, and you'll be surprised at who God might have waiting as your minister to parents.

> Start dreaming now about how volunteers can oversee your family-friendly efforts.

Caring for Angry Parents

Within every youth ministry, you will find angry parents—angry for good reasons and bad. How you respond to them determines whether you gain credibility or lose respect. Don't try to avoid conflicts or pray that issues will be resolved in silence; they won't. I'm not expecting you to enjoy conflict. I am offering four ideas to help you resolve conflict in your parent and youth worker relationships.

// Don't avoid angry parents.

Angry parents typically call at the peak of their frustration, when they're likely to express themselves with more emotion than reason. Many times I've been glad I was gone when the call came. If I'm in the office, I'll take the call, but invariably the message to call back buys some time. If possible, instead of calling, make a personal visit. In face-to-face communication, you can read nonverbal communication that isn't recognizable over the phone.

// Listen until they finish.

Good communication requires you to allow parents to fully share their feelings without interrupting. It's natural to want to interrupt and clarify their statements; however, once parents have voiced their opinions, you'll have your turn. If the conversation is taking place by phone, take notes and wait until the parent is finished.

// Think rationally, not personally.

When parents are angry, they might express themselves inappropriately. You might hear a comment like, "You're not qualified to be a youth leader," when what's driving the comment is, "I don't know how to reach my son, and I'm afraid for his future. I go to this church, tithe, and I need your help, but I'm too insecure to admit this." Or, "Your trips always cost too much." This may mean, "Money is tight right now, and I could really use some help." Your job is to discern the real issue if it's hidden. Ask God for his wisdom and discernment, before you make contact if possible.

// End on a positive note.

Ending with positive comments does not mean you give into the whining parent. Concluding in a positive way communicates that you want to pursue peace. I try to allow parents to leave our conversations feeling as though—

- They were heard and understood.
- We've taken steps to resolve the conflict.
- Their input is appreciated. (This is essential to leave the door open for future communication.)
- I've said. "I'm sorry. Please forgive me," when necessary. If you've messed up, apologize and ask for forgiveness. Reconcile. You're modeling humility, and humility diffuses anger.

Some conflict creates such turmoil within your soul that you'll feel it in your body. It's difficult to not take criticism personally when you care deeply about what you're doing. You can't avoid conflict. Parents will express their anger in some way. Be prepared, pray, and digest the material in the next chapter on conflict. Learn to face conflict directly because, over time, you'll hone the skills needed for dealing with people. As your skills improve, the situations become easier.

When You're Angry with Parents

As sure as you'll get complaints from some parents, you can also

count on feeling frustrated with and disappointed in parents. Basically, you'll have many opportunities to develop methods of dealing with anger. Consider a few ideas specific to dealing with parents:

// Be slow to respond.

While this idea is important for all conflict, it's especially important when dealing with parents. Believe me, I am not the master of this principle. (As my wife was first reading this chapter, she jokingly said, "Why don't you write about something that you actually have some real-life experience doing?")

I used to be better at this before the days of e-mail. E-mail is so instant. When I receive an attack by e-mail, I can reply before I even think. I've sent some nasty, vicious, and sarcastic e-mail before I even have the time to evaluate whether there might be some truth to the message. I regret it every time. I've got to pause, pray, think, ask questions, share my thoughts and feelings with a neutral person, run a marathon, and then wait until I'm rational and less defensive. A good rule is to wait at least 24 hours and allow someone else to read the response before you send it (if you choose to write back at all) to make sure you respond in an appropriate and godly way. You won't lose when you take your time responding.

// Don't undermine parents.

When you're angry with a parent or group of parents, don't try to get their kids on your side. Do *not* put students in the middle! If students aren't part of the solution, keep them out of the situation.

Take the godly route and steer clear of comments that undermine parents. Parents struggle to keep their children's respect, and you don't help their cause when you demean parents. We already have too many sitcoms making parents look foolish. We don't need youth workers promoting the stereotype—even when it might be true.

// Go to the source.

I've always lost the battle and damaged my reputation when I've tried to resolve conflicts with parents through third parties (their kids, their spouses, the prayer team, other pastors, the local newspaper). Most conflicts are misunderstandings blown out of proportion by overactive imaginations. When you experience a conflict with parents, go to the parents! Even if the parents don't take this approach, you need to take the higher road and deal with the parent face to face.

// Walk in their shoes.

Many problems happen behind closed doors. You'll never see them. It took several years, but I finally learned this simple principle: there are two sides to every story. When I think like a parent, I understand why parents react the way they do to family conflict.

Especially if you're not a parent, put yourself in their shoes and imagine the situation from their perspective.

What to Do with Families in Crisis

One of the most challenging tasks you will face in youth ministry is reaching out to families with teenagers in crisis. You won't be able to foresee every crisis situation the kids in your group may face, but you'll be ahead if you have a response plan in place. Here are some thoughts to get you ready.

1. Minister to families before the crisis hits.

Relationships make dealing with trauma easier—a little bit easier. Being real and honest allows them to be that way, too.

2. Be prepared to listen.

Your presence and actions are more appreciated than your words. Silence is better than meaningless chatter and platitudes. Be available to listen.

3. Don't be afraid to bring up the trauma in conversation.

People want to talk, but they may feel guilty about focusing too much on their hurts. They appreciate it when they're asked to share.

4. Know your resources.

- Who are good Christian counselors in your area?
- What is the number to Child Protective Services? Who is a good contact there?
- What does the law in your state say about abuse? What are you required to report? Who do you tell?
- What books, videos, CDs, and Web sites are available on the different types of trauma and recovery?
- What are the phone numbers of trauma hotlines

5. Offer to meet needs.

- Offer to handle arrangements in the case of death.
- Offer books and other resources for those recovering from trauma.
- Pursue referrals from your list of contacts.

6. Make yourself available; say, "I want to do whatever I can to help."

Parents are more open to help during a crisis than at any other time. They may not have anything specific for you to do, but you send a powerful message when you make yourself available. An even more powerful message is sent when you actually do something to help since so many people typically say, "Call me if you need anything."

7. Don't be afraid of the phone.

When you hear of a crisis, call the family immediately. Don't wait and think others will be calling or the family is too busy to talk. You don't have to stay on the phone a long time. Call. Express your concern and your willingness to help. Then get off the phone.

8. Connect hurting parents with parents who have experienced similar hurts.

This allows parents to connect with others who understand. The bonds created through common experiences builds community among families in your church body.

While writing this book, I've had to face major regrets from my early years of ministry. I've wondered what my life would have been like if I had taken the proper actions in the beginning.

You have the opportunity to begin ministry with correct thinking about parents and families. They're not the enemies of a healthy youth ministry, they're your greatest allies.

The Questions at the End of the Chapter

// For group discussion

- Based on this chapter, how do you feel our youth ministry can better partner with families?

- Why do you think it's difficult for parents to accept authority from youth workers who aren't parents of teenagers? Can this be changed? If so, how?

// For personal reflection

- Do I understand that I represent the youth ministry to parents even when I'm not at a scheduled event? How do I feel about this?

- What do I think about families that drop off their kids at church but never attend themselves?

- How do I impact the family-friendly nature of our youth ministry?

- How can I better communicate with the parents of the students I disciple?

- Dream about how volunteers can eventually oversee your family-friendly efforts.

// Actions to consider

- Make a list of five little things you can do on a regular basis to encourage parents and families. This list can become your go-to list.

- Go out of your way this week to greet parents as they pick up/drop off their kids at your next event.

- Who is one parent you might be able to meet over lunch during the next three months? Call this parent and schedule a meeting.

Go to www.dougfields.com and enter your comments under Your First 2 Years: Chapter 5

why all the conflict?
dealing with difficult people

Francisca was a great youth worker! I've spoken at some of her camps, watched her with students, and always left impressed. She has served at three churches—terminated from two and leaving the last time before she got fired again. It's not her youth ministry skills getting her into trouble; it's her conflict resolution skills and inability to deal with tough times and difficult people.

As I talk with her, I see the tenderness in her eyes and hear the pain in her heart as she grieves her mistakes as well as some missed opportunities to reconcile. I've talked with hundreds of Franciscas who say, "If it weren't for the people, I'd love youth ministry."

I wish I could claim, due to lack of experience with conflict, that I'm not an expert, but I can't! During my years of leadership, I've experienced enough tension to fill an entire book. I've shed tears, caused tears, avoided conflict, started conflict, confronted gently, confronted loudly, made enemies, gained supporters. Some times I've been right, but often I've been wrong.

While this hasn't been my favorite chapter to write, the topic is still important. I'll spare you all my horror stories by extracting principles I've learned that may help you deal with the conflict you're sure to face in your leadership position. You will experience students, parents, and church leaders who—

- Don't like your personality
- Don't like your decisions
- Love to find fault
- Have anger issues
- Act like immature fools
- May be related to Satan

I'm sad to write this, but a few people may actually hate you. You'll find yourself questioning your leadership and even your calling. At times you may want to hide from people; at other times you may consider becoming a missionary...to a people-group that doesn't speak your language. Conflict is inevitable because when imperfect people work in imperfect situations, problems arise. Regardless of whether you're paid or volunteer, as soon as you say yes to a leadership position, you're saying yes to conflict.

But I have good news: some people will like you, listen to you, follow your lead, pray for you, and help you bandage yourself after collisions. You can learn how to soften some blows, increase your chances of restoring peace, and avoid some difficult situations before they start. Plus, tough times can lead to personal growth and enhanced character...for which I thank God.

In my years of training youth workers, I've noticed something startling: the majority of questions asked of me, both public and private, have to do with conflict or how to deal with a difficult person. You aren't stumped by the program ideas, but the interpersonal tension that becomes a roadblock. Conflict is a huge issue in youth ministry! Early on and years later, you'll be forced to make choices regarding conflicts. The main options are—

- Staying in the situation, doing nothing, hoping the conflict goes away, and feeling frustrated.
- Pretending conflict doesn't exist.

- Trying to please everyone with the hope of avoiding conflict.
- Dealing with tough issues as they arise.
- (I tried to figure out a fifth option, but I think it's a felony.)

As frustrating, emotionally exhausting, or hurtful as a person may be to you, *you* choose how you react. While the first three options may seem more attractive than the last one, it's the fourth option that brings results and leads to peace in your life and encouragement in your ministry.

> There's one other unattractive option that some of us seem to slip into far too often. It involves blindly fighting for our own way whether we're right or not. We ram through our agendas, refusing to listen to the voices of others, and in the process we alienate people around us. Youth workers who always have to have it their way almost always kill team spirit and usually don't last long in their positions. And sadly, the damage often affects others for a long time.
> —*Marv Penner*

My prayer is that you learn healthy techniques for dealing with people during tough times. As you model conflict resolution, your youth ministry will become a place where conflict isn't avoided. You'll learn that conflict isn't bad and can lead to growth.

God understands pain, conflict, and frustration, and he accompanies you on your journey. Jesus had plenty of conflict—he started it, avoided it, and sometimes resolved it. Some of the great lessons I've learned have come from conflicts. While I have scars, I'm a richer, deeper, stronger, and more empathetic youth worker because of my experiences.

During Conflict...Be a Leader

The overarching principle I've learned while dealing with many conflicts is that I must be the leader God has called me to be. Most of the time, my response is the same to youth workers who seek counsel for their conflict problems: "Be a leader."

They often protest, "But Doug, you don't understand. This guy created these same problems with other volunteers, and now he's creating them with me."

I smile and say, "I understand. My answer remains the same: be a leader. Talk with him. Go with a grace-filled heart and speak truth rather than waiting for the problem to go away. He'll be creating this tension with the next youth worker, too, if you don't deal with it. Be a leader, even when it's tough and not fun."

// I don't want to hurt their feelings.

Most of the time, my challenge to be a leader is countered with this heartfelt appeal: "I don't want to hurt this person."

I often shock people when I respond by saying, "Why not?" I can see it in their eyes. "Doug, you seemed so nice before...what happened?" Well, I'm not saying you have to be mean-spirited to be a leader. But the most healing balm for conflict is truth, and truth often hurts. The sting can be minimal in comparison to the joy of growing and learning because a brother in Christ made you aware of a truth you didn't see before. The body of Christ has been guilty of shooting its wounded and being silent toward those who need to hear truth.

I needed a loving friend to say to me, "Doug, you come across as arrogant when you try to do everything yourself. I don't sense that you are, but that's how people read you when you don't let them get involved." Do you think that hurt me? A little, yes. But, if I continued to do everything myself, I would have hurt myself eventually anyway, and I would have hurt a lot of other people, too. Truth helped me change!

> Dealing with conflict is never fun—Doug and I don't like it, either. Over the years we've vacillated between dodging bullets and facing the tough stuff. But because we've been committed to building a healthy, growing youth ministry, we know that dealing with conflict is part of the leadership package. A great part of our ministry together—and a part for which I'm very thankful—has been that we've always acted as sounding boards for each other during difficult situations. After working with Doug for more than a decade, I've seen how God has used those very situations to make us better leaders, deeper people, and more dependent on his grace.
> —Lynne Ellis

Your motive when you deal with conflict shouldn't be to humiliate or devastate others, but to lovingly help them.

// I'm too young.

Here's another excuse I hear often: "Doug, you make it seem so easy. But you're in your 40s, and I'm young." Well...Mr. Selective Hearing (I never said conflict is easy), the issue isn't age, it's leadership. The Bible reveals God uses young leaders. Paul told

Timothy, "Don't let anyone look down on you because you are young" (1 Timothy 4:12).

Be a leader and watch God use you. I have some of the same kinds of conflicts in my church today as I did 20 years ago. The difference isn't my age; it's my experience and my ability to lead.

// Not everyone will like the leader.

One of the toughest realities for new leaders to understand is that once you're a leader, you won't always be liked. Leaders must make decisions that will cause some feelings to be hurt. A casualty of leadership is that someone will be disappointed, hurt, or bent out of shape because of your decisions. To finish the marathon, you have to face difficult people and situations.

Why Becca Hates Me

I wish I could brag that all my conflicts have ended well. They haven't.

At our church, we interview potential volunteers and go through a screening process that includes a reference check, among other things. Last year, I found myself needing more leaders for small groups starting a few weeks later. I felt desperate for leaders. When I interviewed Becca, a potential leader, something about her didn't seem right, but I didn't have any tangible evidence to confirm my suspicion.

Instead of taking more time, I moved her through the process quickly and made her the leader of a small group. Within a month, I had multiple complaints about her from the parents of her girls. Because of all I was hearing (and confirming), I knew I had to ask her to step away from her volunteer leadership position for a season.

I was concerned because she was fairly new to our church and not well connected with other believers there. As a pastor, I wanted to see her grow spiritually, but I knew this confrontation would probably result in her leaving our church. I tried getting together with her face to face, but in the end I had to resort to a phone conversation. As much as I tried to be kind, to Becca my words were a hurtful attack that brought judgment and rejection. When she abruptly ended the call, I was crushed—for her, for my actions, and for the mess I needed to solve within her small group.

Within a week, I received a copy of a letter she sent to my pastor about the experience. Her perception of the entire situation was distinctly different from mine. Fortunately, my pastor supported my decision (which enhances my courage to make tough decisions). He told me I made the right choice. I prayed that Becca would end up in a community where she could heal and grow and where others would help her develop her gifts and find a better-fitting ministry.

I'm sure Becca dislikes me, doesn't respect me, and would graciously classify me as a pig. That's not the way I wanted things to end. Conflict cannot always be tied up with pretty, pain-free bows—no matter how systematic I try to make conflict resolution appear. Being an effective leader during conflict requires prayer, dependence on God's power, and confidence in your decisions.

Conflicts during Your First Two Years

It's not *if* you'll have a blow out with Becca-types, it's *when*. Since conflict is inevitable, I want to make you aware of where you're likely to experience it.

// Potential areas of conflict as the lead youth worker

■ *Issues of support:* You're young and the volunteers you're leading have been Christians longer than you've been alive. They're not eager to jump on the go-get-'em train and follow a youngster's enthusiasm. Who knows whether your idea will work? If you're not young, but you are new, the same issue can apply.

■ *Issues of trust:* If your church has gone through three youth ministers over the past two years, what makes students think you're going to stick around or be kept around?

■ *Competition:* Say volunteers have been integral in running the ministry for several years. You arrive with new ideas and enthusiasm. Students like you. Insecure volunteers feel devalued.

■ *Structure and support:* What you thought was new-found freedom in your profession of passion has become a position micromanaged by your supervisor.

■ *Student woes:* The students are enthusiastic about your arrival as the new youth leader. Everyone except for the two who act up in the back of the room. One is the senior pastor's son, and the other is the chairman's daughter.

■ *Inflexibility:* A volunteer wants to keep pursuing his own agenda rather than embracing your new direction.

You'll face more issues. I've just listed a few because I want to inform you, not depress you. What? Don't tell me it's too late.

// Potential areas of conflict as a volunteer

Conflict volunteers experience may revolve around issues like these:

■ *Issues of overload:* The youth committee expects you to meet all the needs of all the students, even though you have limited time and resources.

■ *Babysitting syndrome:* Some parents don't know what you're trying to do with students, nor do they care. They drop off their teenagers expecting you to teach, entertain, and baby-sit them.

■ *Issues of respect:* Since the pastor and some parents don't view you as the youth minister ("real staff"), your ideas are discounted or undermined.

Doug spends much of this chapter talking about ways to bring interpersonal conflict to a peaceful conclusion, and rightly so. The psalmist encourages us to "seek peace and pursue it" (Psalm 34:14), and Jesus blesses peacemakers in the beatitudes (Matthew 5:9). Unfortunately it's not always that easy. There are times when our leadership roles require us to take a position on an issue and stand fast—even when it's unpopular or uncomfortable to do so. Some people won't understand. They may get angry, threaten us, and perhaps even leave the church. It comes down to deciding which hill is worth dying on—and you *will* find some that are.

The challenge is not only knowing how to make that judgment but also knowing how to communicate your position. Our convictions must always be communicated in principle-based rather than personality- or preference-based terms. Our resolve must always be tempered by gentle humility. And it's always wise to filter your tenaciously held position through the wisdom of someone who will tell us if we're wrong. We must find ways to be firm without being obnoxious, to be steadfast without being stubborn, and to be committed without being arrogant. None of this comes naturally.

There are several kinds of conflict issues that could fall into the category we're talking about. You'll notice the absence of programming and scheduling issues—don't rush into battle over less significant matters. Save your big guns for some of these more important issues:

Lifestyle choices that model compromise. We all know how carefully students watch the lives of adults in leadership. The most important lessons are caught, not taught. When volunteers or highly visible adults are living in ways that could cause kids to choose destructive lifestyle choices, that's a hill worth dying on.

Theological heresy that dilutes the power of the gospel. Small-group leaders or Sunday school teachers who communicate theology contrary to the convictions of the church must be challenged. (Just be careful to distinguish between nuances of interpretation and outright heresy.)

Abuse of power that destroys kids and families. As leaders we're obliged to protect those who are vulnerable to abuse. There are times that we simply must step into difficult, often volatile, situations. Usually the abusers are in positions of power and won't be used to being confronted.

Safety issues for which parents hold you responsible. When your adrenaline-driven volunteer leader decides it'd be "way cool for everyone in youth group to leap from the 80-foot high train trestle," be prepared to step in and say no, even though you may be branded a party pooper. There's always a fine line between legitimate adventure and sheer stupidity. As leaders it's our job to define that line.

Moral choices that violate the teaching of Scripture. Sin demands confrontation. One of the responsibilities of spiritual leadership is to discern and deal with issues of moral disobedience in the lives of those we lead. Sexual compromise, dishonesty, stealing, gossip, and other forms of blatant defiance of Scripture must be addressed immediately, aggressively, and consistently.

Non-negotiable legal issues. Good leaders are aware of all legal matters related to their positions and are unwavering in dealing with violations. A pastor friend of mine decided to "help" a sexual abuser with a discipleship program rather than a call to the police, and he was subsequently charged with obstructing justice.

There are times in the life of every youth worker when the burden of taking an uncompromising stand seems almost unbearable. But remember this: Letting these issues slide usually makes them worse. The temptation to overlook the obvious or sidestep the difficult can seem like an attractive, short-term solution, but in the long run it's always best to face the responsibility squarely, firmly, humbly, and quickly.

It won't be pretty, but that's what leadership demands.

Get used to it.

—*Marv Penner*

■ *Hyperactive students:* Your ministry is growing, including the number of students who are climbing the walls with energy. You try to get them to quiet down and listen to the teaching, but they look at you like you're an idiot.

■ *Misunderstandings:* You can count on someone misunderstanding your motives, your message, your actions, your requests, and your presence. It won't take long. Somewhere you'll be misunderstood; it's frustrating!

■ *You versus you:* You begin to question whether youth ministry is worth the effort. Wouldn't it be less painful to volunteer as a crash test dummy?

During the Tough Times

Regardless of your role, people may use all types of tactics—consciously and unconsciously—to test your leadership. You may encounter ridicule, rumors, resistance, or exaggerations. Don't take it personally, even when your character is attacked. Granted, this is easier said than done, but taking shots from people is part of ministry. You've heard it before: leadership isn't easy, and not everyone will like you.

Some difficulties and struggles will be of your own making. Are you having conflict with the janitor because you filled the baptismal with ice and sodas during the lock-in? Sounded good! Perceived badly. Trouble comes. Deserved? Yes.

I can't count the number of times I've made dumb mistakes and poor judgment calls. I've been known to promote my own agenda and vision without considering the consequences. I've bought my own pain, and so will you. That's part of growing and learning.

But some conflict will catch you off guard, and you won't know what to do. Here are a few actions I consciously have to pursue during conflict.

// Give people time to change.

Nobody likes change, and people have a tendency to criticize what they don't like. Be careful about being quick to label people simply because they don't agree with you:

- He has a critical heart.
- She's unwilling to follow my leadership.
- He doesn't support our youth ministry.
- She's threatened by me.
- He's an idiot!

Often the person who's the loudest is either the most insecure or the most passionate. Combat insecurity by affirming and valuing people while creating a sense of belonging. The passionate can become vocal for the change when you win them over.

Clarify from the beginning that change is difficult. If you're the lead youth worker, give one-on-one opportunities for people to share their fears, frustrations, and questions with you (and don't react defensively). By meeting individually, vocal people aren't able to influence the entire group, and they learn that you aren't fearful of change. The time you take to listen shows that you're open to conflicting ideas. People have the potential to change—some just take more time than others.

// Watch for people's strengths.

Often people will be negative because they don't know any other way to get attention. You'll typically find an agenda behind criticism.

When Steve, a structural engineer, made comments about the disorganization of our summer camp, I was hurt and offended. Then I realized Steve had strong organizational skills, but weak people skills. He didn't know how to approach me to say, "Doug, you need my organizational help."

When I finally realized that Steve was awkwardly trying to help, I said, "Steve, I get the impression that you could have done a better job with the details than I did, and I agree, so I would love for you to run the trip next summer. Would that allow you to use your strengths and fulfill your desires?" By taking me up on my offer, Steve used his skills and abilities to design systems that increased our effectiveness and professionalism (though he went overboard by handing out camp blueprints). He freed me to focus on activities that used my strengths during the trip.

Most people don't bother expressing their opinions if they don't have a passion for or desire to be part of the solution. Use their energy, honor their wisdom (sometimes hidden in criticism), and put them to work. Some sage pronounced, "When you get people to row the boat, they don't have time to rock it."

// Turn the mirror on yourself.

Don't be afraid to ask the question, "What can I learn from this conflict?" Be willing to search for the truth in criticisms, complaints, confusions, or even caustic attitudes. You may not like how people communicate their frustrations, but you may learn something from the words or tone. Ask yourself, "What's true in his comments?" When you learn something, be humble and admit it.

> You can't lose with humility.

Occasionally you may need to confront the method or the tone used to share a concern but still admit you learned a lesson: "Linda, I didn't like the way you criticized the Sunday school lesson with others, but I heard your point, and I agree with it. Thank you for your insight. Next time, I'd love for you to come straight to me rather than speaking to others who aren't part of the problem or solution."

If you're willing to learn and grow, you'll find that you can gain some personal insight from almost every situation. You'll be a better youth worker and a stronger Christian when you look in the mirror and see the truths that apply to you.

Consider it pure joy, my brothers [and sisters] whenever you face trials of many kinds, because you know that the testing of your faith develops perseverance. Perseverance must finish its work so that you may be mature and complete, not lacking anything. (James 1:2-3)

One Model of Conflict Resolution

Individual conflicts never look the same because in each situation the characters are different: students, parents, other youth workers, pastors, family members, neighbors, farm animals, aliens, and left-handed pancake flippers.

> What about pastors who act like farm animals?

But the conflict *process* contains common elements that everyone experiences, depending on how we choose to respond. The resolution process can be either positive or negative. This is how I would chart it out for you if I were drawing on a restaurant napkin:

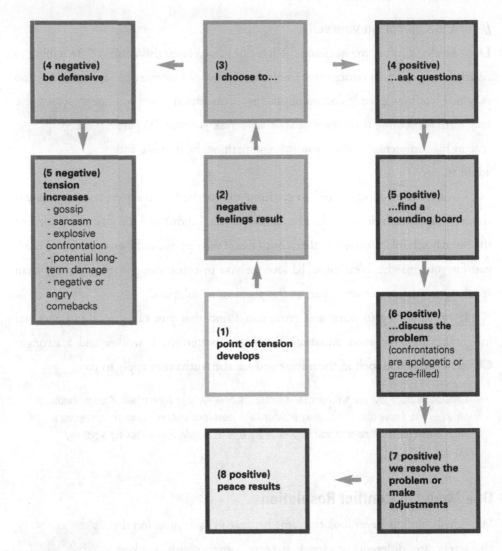

(4 negative)
be defensive

(3)
I choose to...

(4 positive)
...ask questions

(5 negative)
tension
increases
- gossip
- sarcasm
- explosive
confrontation
- potential long-
term damage
- negative or
angry
comebacks

(2)
negative
feelings result

(5 positive)
...find a
sounding board

(1)
point of tension
develops

(6 positive)
...discuss the
problem
(confrontations
are apologetic or
grace-filled)

(8 positive)
peace results

(7 positive)
we resolve the
problem or
make
adjustments

Conflict isn't only negative. When you give thoughtful attention to each of the stops in the conflict process, you and others may experience personal growth. How you deal with the inevitable conflicts will either paralyze you or increase your effectiveness. Look at the chart again (but this time with dice. If you roll a six...move two spaces to the left. Where are Steve's blueprints?)

▪ **(1)** *Point of tension develops:* Tension can arise for any number of reasons. Causes may be as simple as a misunderstanding over words or as complex as personality differences. Another leader may ridicule you or undermine a decision you've made in front of students. Maybe the church secretary makes derogatory remarks about your time management skills. An overzealous parent may constantly communicate his agenda for your life and ministry through the words, "Have you thought about…?" Or the church janitor gets angry because the youth room is a mess. However it happens, tension gives birth to negative feelings.

■ **(2)** *Negative feelings result:* The range of emotional responses that can occur when tension develops are amazing. Can you relate to any of these feelings?

Frustrated: "I don't like this!"

Confused: "What's going on?"

Threatened: "I'll show them."

Insecure: "No one likes me."

Arrogant: "What idiots! They just don't get it."

Defeated: "I can't do anything right."

Oblivious: "Huh?"

Whiny: "This isn't fun."

Unmotivated: "I should have stayed with Amway."

Negative feelings aren't inherently wrong. How you choose to act on your feelings will either solve problems or create more relational chaos.

■ **(3)** *I choose to…:* This is the critical point in the conflict. As your feelings emerge, you must decide whether you move in a positive or negative direction. The easiest, natural route is to take a negative direction even though the route toward peace flows through the positive route. Let's look at both.

■ **(4 negative)** *…Be defensive:* As soon as you become defensive, you've veered toward the negative route. This is a natural, self-preserving move in which you gather ammunition to use in a counterattack. This is usually when the people-bashing appears: "What a fool! He just doesn't get it! He may even be demon-possessed or, worse, a Dodgers fan!"

The most pain I've experienced in my ministry is when I spend too much time being defensive. When I'm defensive, my thoughts and feelings oppose peace, which leads to stronger negative feelings.

■ **(5 negative)** *Tension increases:* When you don't take proper action, tension increases, fueling negative feelings. The more tension increases, the more likely you are to say words and do things you're likely to regret.

If you find yourself caught in this negative cycle, correct your course. Acknowledge your pride and admit your role in the problem. Humility always forces me to the positive side. Even if the difficult person refuses to leave the negative path, take the high road by seeking resolution. You can live in peace having pursued it, whether the issue is resolved or not.

When you're ready to seek peace, the next step is to ask questions.

■ (4 positive) … *Ask questions:* Sincerely gather insight about yourself, the situation, and your response to the situation. Seek to understand the other person before seeking to be understood. Ask yourself some of these questions:

- Have I prayed about this conflict?
- What is this conflict *really* about?
- What do my feelings mean?
- What is the other person thinking?
- Why am I feeling so negative?
- What did I contribute to this conflict?
- Is some outside factor in the other person's life affecting his response to this conflict?
- Who stole the cookies from the cookie jar?
- Has the other person been confronted on this issue before?
- When will the rapture happen?
- What are the other person's strengths and passions? Do these play a role in this conflict?
- What's God's wisdom about this situation?
- What's God teaching me through this conflict?
- Where did I file my résumé?

When you focus on the issues and not on the person's character, personality, or reputation, you'll experience a calm place where you can consider—rationally consider—how to respond.

■ (5 positive) … *Find a sounding board:* Bounce the facts off a wise, mature advisor whom you respect. You can speak in generalities to avoid gossiping and still get the needed wisdom. Using a sounding board doesn't mean recruiting troops to your side. It does mean finding an objective friend who can echo your questions, help with rational thinking, offer godly advice, and pray for you. Finding a safe person is important. A safe person—

- Isn't part of the problem or solution.
- Can add perspective, wisdom, and rationale.
- Won't take sides.
- Listens to you, prays for you, supports you, challenges you, believes in you, and loves you.

■ (6 positive) ...*Discuss the problem:* This is the face-to-face confrontation. It doesn't have to be a battle, and it won't be if you avoid spending time in the defensive stage. Once you've determined that you need to have this conversation, your palms will sweat, your stomach will knot, and you'll find yourself wanting a slow water-torture death rather than face this individual (unless you're one of the rare psychos who loves confrontation). These conversations are tough but open the door to peace. If you're wrong, apologize and ask for forgiveness. If you need to speak truth, offer it with grace.

Before the conversation, you may need to ask yourself these questions:

- Am I confronting the person because of how I feel or because the behavior is a problem?
- What might God want to teach me or the other person in the midst of this tension?

God may have a plan to strengthen you through this, or it may be that he has chosen to use you as divine sandpaper to help work out Christlikeness in the life of the other person. Are you willing to be changed? Are you willing to be used?

I've weaseled my way out of countless confrontations, because I didn't want to say the difficult thing ("I'm sorry" or "I've been hurt by you"). People deserve to hear truth. If you speak the truth in love, people will be given an opportunity to grow. Don't protect emotions of the moment over personal growth that may impact eternity.

- Do I need to begin this conversation by saying, "I'm sorry?"

God can use your humility to heal anger. As you speak calmly and listen carefully (rather than validate your opinions), you dissipate tension.

Confrontation Techniques

You may want to rehearse the conversation before the meeting. It's important that you clarify your intended outcome: resolution, restoration, and peace.

During the conversation—

*Start with an **observation** statement.* Use "I" statements. Describe the situation or behavior without labeling or defensiveness. This focuses the discussion on behavior, not character. If the conflict is about a character issue, stating the behavior gives support for your interpretation statement.

*Offer an **interpretation** statement.* Offer your own interpretation of the behavior. Then ask, "What do you think is the basis of that behavior?" Let the individual respond to your interpretation. She may offer insight into what is going on in her life.

*Tell how you **feel** and how the conflict affects you or the ministry.* This is important. He needs to hear how his behavior is harming you and the ministry. You might share why you have reacted so strongly to this situation. Realize that opening your heart with humility may lead to quick healing, but be wise and appropriate with what you share.

*Share a statement of **desired outcome** for mutual resolution and healing.* What is your goal? Perhaps new understanding or a change in behavior. Describe a specific action plan if the outcome requires a consequence. Also provide a time frame in which you will meet and discuss the outcome again.

The Conflict Process in a Case Study

Lani, a coworker in the ministry, is critical of every idea that involves change. His opposition has increased to the point that he has made negative statements to students about you and other volunteer leaders. Rehearse your approach:

Observation *(apparent behavior)*
"Lani, I'm hearing about negative statements you're making to students about our ministry. You made statements like, 'That won't work' and 'How can we do that?' at our last two midweek programs."

Interpretation *(what you think)*
"I know you care about details, Lani. I'm wondering if you feel like we're not thinking through all of the potential problems. Is that a fair assessment of your thoughts?"

Feeling *(how it affects you)*
"I feel uncomfortable when you make negative comments to students. I feel like it communicates division and a lack of respect for the others on this team."

Desired outcome *(mutual resolution)*
"I'm coming to you because I want to hear your input face to face. You have valuable ideas, Lani. I'm wondering if you'd be willing to outline the details that you think we're overlooking. Maybe we could meet to discuss them privately so our students don't hear about them first. What do you think?"

■ **(7 positive)** *We resolve the problem or make adjustments:* After you've had the difficult conversation, offer a healing gesture within a week. Send a card or e-mail or leave a phone message that says, "Thanks for being willing to discuss this." Even if the conversation didn't go exactly the way you wanted it to, the message communicates your desire to bridge the conflict.

Schedule follow-up conversations and meetings to further evaluate the conflict and resolution.

If the tension is based on personality issues or value differences, it may be necessary to make adjustments in the relationship. These may require you to—

- Redefine your boundaries for relating to and with the individual.
- Limit the amount of conversation about the subject of tension.
- Include a third party in future conversations.
- Appreciate the contribution of that individual and love her without expectations.
- Pray.
- Expect the best outcome versus the worst.
- Build trust over time. (Forgiveness may be immediate, but trust grows.)
- Send five junior high boys over to wrap the person's house in toilet paper.

If the person does not respond to the conversation appropriately in the following weeks, take another person with you for another confrontation. (See Matthew 18 for biblical guidance). If, after you've gone through all the steps in Matthew 18, the behavior hasn't changed, you have the freedom to release the conflict, and accept the reality that you won't "win" them all.

As you approach the situation with pure motives and using biblical guidelines, you're freed to focus on what God has called you to do—impact students. At this point you can gain peace in the situation or with the person.

■ **(8 positive)** *Peace results:* Our biblical goal—

> *If it is possible, as far as it depends on you, live at peace with everyone.*
> (Romans 12:18)

> *Let the peace of Christ rule in your hearts, since as members of one body you were called to peace.* (Colossians 3:15)

Peace occurs as you forgive, release the offender, and recognize that the steps you took are peacemaking actions. You may need to revisit the resolution and adjustment phases until you have a workable and healthy situation, but God will grant you his peace as you surrender to his wisdom when difficult situations arise.

The Conflict Process in Real Life

I sat across from Porter over breakfast at Denny's poised for confrontation. Porter seemed passionate about our youth ministry, but his critical spirit (*point of tension*) was killing me (*negative feelings*). After months of letting the tension ride and building a case for why he didn't belong in our ministry (*defensive ammunition gathering*), I finally decided I couldn't deny this problem anymore (*my choice*).

I began to evaluate the tension (*ask questions*), so I could get a better understanding of the situation. I met with a mentor who offered insight and encouragement (*a sounding board*), and I prayed for the courage to call Porter for a meeting (*discussing the problem*).

Over breakfast, I confronted him with specific statements he had made. I explained how this was hurting the ministry and me. Though my tone was gentle, he felt threatened, frustrated, and defensive. He angrily stormed out of the restaurant.

When he left, I felt emotionally drained but free since I had finally addressed the issue (and quite full since I ate the rest of his omelette). I remember saying a short, silent prayer, "Thank you, God, for giving me the courage to speak the truth." Within minutes after leaving the restaurant, I felt incredible relief (*peace*)...even though he stuck me with the bill. Though Porter and I hadn't identified any resolutions or adjustments, I knew my heart was right and that I had spoken with grace and truth. When Porter left in anger, I was unclear about whether we'd have future, divisive issues (*increased tension*). I felt confident, however, that I had done the right thing and opened up the issue for future discussion. Now I had to leave this conflict in God's hands for his Spirit to work the "impossible."

To my surprise, Porter called me the next day, apologized for his behavior, and thanked me for being honest with him. He then revealed how his dysfunctional family history had influenced his angry retreat. We discussed specific steps we would both take in the future if we had another conflict. He made personal commitments regarding his criti-

(A VOICE FROM THE TRENCHES)

One of my many mistakes in my early youth ministry years—and one I continued to make until just recently (after 14 years of youth ministry, I'm embarrassed to say)—was "dealing" with potentially difficult parents by nicely avoiding them.

My thinking was that I didn't have the time or energy to become distracted by their critical spirits. Besides, if their students didn't have a problem, then I didn't have a problem. Recently I found myself with a parent who seemed determined to make my work harder through what I perceived as a critical spirit. I casually visited with her a few times, and then I just hoped that whatever "her problem was" would go away.

My senior pastor heard about this conflict and gave me some of the best advice I've heard regarding conflict resolution with parents.

He used the analogy of a soccer goalie. When an opponent is coming at the goalie, ready to kick the ball into the net, the goalie is supposed to leave the mouth of the net and *run toward the opponent*. Soccer goalies know the opponent has less room to take a shot when they cut down their angle of attack.

So my senior pastor set up a weekly meeting with my upset parent. We began to meet at Starbucks (buying her mocha didn't hurt) and have continued to do so for the last two months. I've discovered that running toward this parent (and the conflict) has reaped tremendous rewards! Not only has the conflict been resolved, but also I've found in this parent (and I know this won't always be the outcome) a volunteer staff member who's giving incredible time and energy to the youth ministry. I've also found a friend and someone who's become invaluable in resolving conflicts with other parents. Her support and defense of me has been incredible.

I'm still tempted to avoid conflict with parents—I'm beginning this day with a voice mail from an angry parent—because it takes time and energy to resolve conflict. But avoiding conflict only makes the conflict grow larger, which will take more time and energy later to resolve it—not to mention that if we're going to have a youth ministry that honors God, we need to honor our parents.

—Dan Snyder, youth pastor, Mountain Park Church, Lake Oswego, Oregon

cal spirit, and I made a commitment to come to him immediately when I sensed tension. We both felt heard, valued, and restored to one another.

Within the year, Porter became one of the most supportive volunteers in our ministry. To this day I praise God for Porter.

(If you think all of my conflicts end tidily, turn back a few pages and reacquaint yourself with Becca.)

You Can Manage Conflict!

You'll probably want to revisit this chapter, maybe even memorize a few sections. The ideas I've presented in this chapter will help you handle conflict, but they won't eliminate it.

But your ministry doesn't have to be one endless tension after another. As you learn to speak the truth and offer grace to others, you'll build their character, integrity, and godliness. And by dealing with tension in positive ways, you'll reap a harvest of support, trust, and growth. Negative situations will diminish because of your skills, though you won't please everyone. (Don't waste your time trying.) God will honor your humble and obedient efforts.

I know you can deal effectively with difficult people! It's tough, messy, and hard work, but God has called you to love and lead people into a more intimate relationship with him. What a privilege to be used by God—even when it's tough!

The Questions at the End of the Chapter

// For group discussion

- Do you consider our youth ministry environment one where we can speak honestly about hurts, feelings and tension? Why? Why not?
- When was the last time you had the urge to explode at someone in our youth ministry? What was it about? How was it resolved?
- What part of the conflict resolution phase is most difficult for you? Why?

// For personal reflection

- How might my own family history and/or patterns directly affect my conflict resolution skills?
- What do I do when I've tried everything and nothing seems to help?
- Is there anything I'm doing that's leading to recurring conflict?
- Is there anything in my life that's making me hypersensitive and easily angered? If so, what is it?
- What is keeping me from being a leader?

// Actions to consider

- Create a plan of your own to deal with conflict.
- Find another person on the ministry team (or in your church) who will hold you accountable to deal with conflict when it arises.

Go to www.dougfields.com and enter your comments under Your First 2 Years: Chapter 6

who's the leader?

understanding submission and supervision

"Doug, you've got to help me keep my job. Can you talk to my senior pastor for me? He's out of control!"

This desperate cry came during a phone conversation I had with a youth pastor acquaintance. As I listened to Clark's story, I was convinced that he worked for an insecure, arrogant, power-hungry senior pastor who had no concern for youth ministry, no vision for his community, and no respect for his staff's families. The pastor seemed like a man who would argue with umpires at Little League games. I immediately disliked him and wondered why God would allow such an individual to lead a church.

Can you say, "Jump to conclusions"?

As I continued listening, I silently prayed that God would give me something positive to say to Clark. How could I encourage him in the midst of such an oppressive situation? When he finished his story, I asked a few general, open-ended questions. Clark's replies caught me off guard. In fact, they confused me. As I continued to probe with more specific questions, I realized that Clark was the problem. He was defiant, egotistical, and disrespectful toward his senior pastor. I struggled with the emotion that arose in me; I wanted to care for him, but I also needed to confront him. (It's a good thing I had the conflict diagram from Chapter 6 in my pocket).

So I did both. I caught my breath, collected my thoughts, and spoke gently. "Clark, the more I hear you, the more it seems that you might just be the real problem. I feel that you're the one making life miserable for your church, for your ministry, for your pastor, and for yourself. From what you've told me, the problems with your senior pastor can be traced back to your self-ishness and arrogance. What makes you think you can force your view of ministry onto a

church and a senior pastor in your first few months? Attitudes that are selfish and demeaning are what give youth workers a bad reputation."

There was an awkward pause on the other end of the phone line. I didn't know if I should congratulate myself (because I was on a roll) or cry (because I was sad for him and for his church). I decided to wait for a response.

We continued to dialogue, that day, the next day, and several times the following week. Eventually, I met with Clark and his senior pastor to discuss ways they could *slowly* rebuild their strained relationship.

While most staff relationships aren't this unhealthy, all ministry teams have some degree of dysfunction. Simply learning more ministry skills or gaining extra biblical knowledge rarely remedies relational problems. Clark was a talented youth worker who loved God and students, but he lacked skills and understanding about how to work with people in authority.

We all answer to authority. If you're a youth worker employed by your church, you're most likely accountable to the senior pastor, elder board, and janitor. If you serve as a volunteer youth worker, you're probably accountable to the lead youth worker, elder board, and janitor. I've never met a youth worker who ran the entire church and was the boss of everyone else, although I know some who think they're in charge. A youth worker will always have some authority figure to submit to.

When I struggle in my relationships with those in authority over me, it's often because I'm criticizing others when I should be critical of myself. I need to consider the log in my own eye before I point out the speck in another person's eye. (Have you read that somewhere?)

During this chapter, let's take a look at submission as it relates to the two audiences reading this book: volunteer youth workers and lead youth workers. You'll find some practical ways of dealing with those who provide oversight to your ministry position.

For Volunteers: Work Successfully with the Lead Youth Worker

Volunteer youth workers are the backbone of an effective youth ministry and when they commit their hearts to their role and support the church's lead youth worker (usually the youth minister), lives are changed and the youth ministry becomes a model of effectiveness for the rest of the church.

When volunteers struggle with supporting the lead youth worker and publicly question the leadership, the youth ministry team suffers. Why? Because divisiveness has no place in the church! Your battle is with the enemy of this world, not with the saints in your church. If you're a divisive person (look back at the ministries and relationships you've left behind), I challenge you to leave your leadership position and spend serious time dealing with this issue. Most divisiveness is rooted in some sin in a person's life. The Apostle Paul felt strongly about divisiveness and made a deeply emotional plea for unity:

> Now, dear brothers and sisters, I appeal to you by the authority of the Lord Jesus Christ to stop arguing among yourselves. Let there be real harmony so there won't be divisions in the church. I plead with you to be of one mind, united in thought and purpose. (1 Corinthians 1:10, NLT)

I write to you with the same emotional intensity and ask you to prayerfully evaluate your actions and attitudes based on the following questions: [2]

☐ Do I confront or run from divisiveness?

Your leader typically hears complaints from 101 different groups, so be quick to confront any gossip you hear with a simple question: "Have you talked to Taneisha (the lead youth worker) yet?" If the answer is no, walk the person over to the lead youth worker so the issue can be dealt with. Chances are that the critical person won't make it more than two steps.

If you overhear gossip or negative conversation, confront or walk away from it; don't feed it. When you know someone is critical of the lead youth worker, share some examples of how that person is making a great impact in your church. Counteract negativity with positive anecdotes.

☐ Am I supportive of new ideas?

Typically, no one is burdened for the youth ministry more than the lead youth worker. As the lead youth worker presents ideas, it's vital that volunteers support trying them. Programs can and should be negotiable and changeable. Our biblical purposes (evangelism, worship, fellowship, discipleship, and ministry) last forever, not the programs.

Even if your church has "never done it that way before," be open to new ideas. Your sacred cow may need to get slaughtered for spiritual health to emerge. When you

---

[2] If you're the lead youth worker, pray for these questions to arise from your volunteers. Then affirm your volunteers as you see these questions arise.

support a suggested change, you send an I-believe-in-you message that energizes the lead youth worker. You can help your ministry become healthy by embracing change. Go public with your support, and reserve your criticism for one-on-one discussions with the leader of the ministry.

> Obviously there are exceptions to total support. Sacrificing house pets to illustrate Old Testament passages is little bit too much.

☐ Do I support my lead youth worker in spite of his/her weaknesses?

Everyone has weaknesses. Great volunteers recognize this truth and support their leaders in spite of their weaknesses. A common weakness for lead youth workers is taking on too much. Share the burden of responsibility by assisting in the tasks you know are a struggle. By doing this, you communicate your desire to help in a way that demonstrates you care.

Confront weaknesses with solutions. Instead of saying, "You're a lousy administrator!" you might bring up the problem by saying, "Sherrie, I know you struggle with administrative details, but you're so great with students. We want to help with administration so you can focus on the students. Vince and I want to assist you. Would you like us to make phone calls for you next week?"

☐ Do I show love when my youth worker messes up?

Leaders of leaders make mistakes—lots of them! Many youth workers are young and have limited experience. Don't expect them to be perfect. Be their advocate. Encourage them. Affirm their efforts.

Even experienced youth workers make mistakes because they tend to be risk takers, willing to attempt and explore innovative ideas. Encourage their faith and creativity, no matter how long they've been doing youth ministry.

A lot of what I know about youth ministry has been learned by my failures. Failure is a great teacher.

☐ Do I affirm the lead youth worker publicly?

Public affirmation helps your leader thrive and remain in ministry. Verbal praise massages the heart, particularly when the enemy—or a feisty parent—communicates opposing messages. When your church has a setting for public sharing, give specific examples of how God is changing lives in the student ministry, and then affirm the leader's efforts in the life-change process.

Don't worry about your youth worker getting a big head. Remember this is youth ministry, where few affirmations come from students.

☐ Am I the last to leave an event (or do I at least make sure someone else is there)?

Immediately following an event, no matter how successful, the lead youth worker is prone to struggle with low feelings after an adrenaline rush. This time can be particularly difficult, as the enemy often challenges the leader with destructive thoughts and feelings of loneliness and isolation. A leader needs to know she can rely on her volunteer staff during these times. Help by spending an additional 30 minutes cleaning up so your leader isn't left alone.

☐ Am I a positive person?

Being around positive people is always better than being around negative, bitter, nasty people. Positive attitudes make ministry more fun.

Andrew is one of my champion volunteers. He's heard me deliver countless messages to students, so he knows when I'm on as a speaker and when I'm in big trouble. When I am struggling, I can always count on Andrew's nonverbal communication. His smiles and body language help me through. I can see his eyes communicating hope: "I'm on your team. Your message stinks right now, but I know you'll have 51 more this year. You'll be okay."

Be quick to respond to instructions. Replace, "Oh, I can't believe he wants us to do that," with "Let's go. That's a great idea! Come on, you guys! Jump in with me."

☐ Do I actively look for other volunteers to join the team?

Asking others to join the team shouldn't be limited to the lead youth worker; it's everyone's job. You know the people who could become great teammates, so invite them to apply for a position! Be vocal about what God is doing in your life through your involvement in youth ministry. Highlight your spiritual growth and the joy you've experienced. When you share the responsibility of bringing in additional leaders, you're gold.

Jim and Jamie, a couple in our ministry, recruited their entire adult small group to join our youth ministry team. It took a couple of years, but Jim and Jamie are directly responsible for eight great youth workers, all sitting in their adult small group every week. Their friends came because Jim and Jamie spoke so highly about the youth ministry and because they were asked to join.

☐ Do I solve problems on my own?

As a volunteer, when a problem appears, you have the authority to be a problem solver. It's frustrating to have a volunteer come running to me saying something like, "Doug, there aren't enough chairs set out. What do you want me to do?" I want to snap back, "Brilliant deduction, Sherlock. I'm glad the obvious has leapt at you… now set out some chairs." Instead I say, "Thank you. Please go ahead and set out some chairs. Next time, feel free to solve problems like that on your own. I trust your judgment."

Don't rely on the leader to solve all the problems. If you can make decisions, handle them. Save the leader some effort. Bottom line: if you can solve a problem, do so. That's a sign of a valuable volunteer.

☐ Do I have a heart for long-term youth ministry?

The greatest gift you can give your church is to have a long-term view of serving in youth ministry. Working with experienced team members leads to a stronger, healthier, more enjoyable, and more fruitful ministry. The way to build camaraderie and trust is to stick around.

My favorite part of ministry is working with the incredible volunteer leaders at my church. I love them and receive incredible joy by watching them experience God's blessings because they're loving teenagers and pointing them toward Jesus.

Thank you for being a volunteer and supporting the leader of your youth ministry!

Lead Youth Worker: How to Work Successfully with Your Senior Pastor or Supervisor (If you're a volunteer who doesn't work directly with the senior pastor, you can skip to Chapter 8.)

A wise youth leader develops a positive relationship with the church's senior pastor. You want your pastor on your team! Your senior pastor can help you in too many ways to not seriously consider the importance of this relationship. Most of what you'll learn about having a good rapport with your pastor won't be discovered in your first two years. It may take several years to feel comfortable with your pastor, but it's worth the effort to start learning right now. Let's consider a few ideas on how to develop and strengthen this unique relationship.

// Before you begin, ask about management style.

If you're not on a church staff yet, during your interview process, ask the senior pastor to describe his style of managing his staff. Solicit examples. Then inquire of current staff members, elders, and other church leaders about the pastor's management style to ensure that they confirm his self-assessment.

> Out of respect, ask the pastor's permission first. Recognize that a "no" response should trouble you.

Feedback about his management style will give you a better understanding about what your future will be like if you decide to join this ministry team. For example, as a new youth worker, you'll benefit by working for someone who holds you accountable for your goals, provides insight into people problems, helps you craft vision, expects you to establish boundaries, and is available when you're in need of advice or experience.

If you find the senior pastor to be a terrific person but not a good manager, you'll find yourself struggling during your beginning years. (An exception is the senior pastor surrounded by good managers who provide supervision.)

After my first interview with my current pastor, I had concerns. He seemed to know everything about youth ministry. I mean *everything*! Its history, current trends, future thinking, students' name, parents' issues, the details of the programs. In my opinion, he knew way too much. I immediately assumed he was a high-control leader. Yet when discussing his leadership style with staff members, I learned he was just the opposite—a hands-off leader. In the absence of a youth ministry leader, he had done his

Sadly, I have heard many war stories about strained relationships between senior pastors and youth workers. Fortunately, there are also many happy stories about senior pastors and youth workers who soar because they bless each other.

Having been a youth pastor and now a senior pastor over the course of 25 years, I see the issue of submission and supervision from both sides. Since I began Saddleback in 1980, I've had positive relationships with my staff members in almost every case. Those relationships have been a source of personal joy for me and a source of health for our church.

But the relationships I've enjoyed with my staff haven't happened accidentally. They've taken time to develop. It's taken time to build trust and confidence in each other. It's taken time to communicate effectively with each other. And above all, I've learned that I must be intentional about nurturing these relationships. I must work for their progress!

Another truth I've learned is that church health is greatly enhanced when the senior pastor and youth worker maintain a strong, trusting relationship.

Trust.

This is what a senior pastor desires in a youth worker. Someone who can be entrusted with an entire area of ministry. Someone who will lead it well. Someone you don't have to worry about.

When Saddleback was smaller, I had to be involved in all areas of its ministries. But as it grew larger and we added staff, it was a blessing to see God bring on trustworthy men and women to lead our ministries. This allowed me to give my time to other areas that needed development.

Trust.

How is it built? Quite simply, by being *trustworthy*. By the senior pastor and youth worker spending time on their relationship. There are no short cuts. Getting to know each other, praying for each other, serving side by side, laughing together, and learning from each other all create a climate where trust can grow. And where trust grows, unity grows. And where unity grows, both the senior pastor and the youth worker will be richly blessed, and the church will be healthier.

Here are three things youth workers can do in their first two years of ministry that will continue to bear fruit for many years after:

Keep your communication clear and consistent. Your senior pastor doesn't have to know everything about everything that's happening in your ministry, but you do want to communicate the most important things.

Never stop learning. All good leaders are good learners, and the moment you stop learning you stop leading. Some people believe that to develop trust you must never make a mistake in the planning or execution of your ministry. Nothing could be further from the truth! I tell my staff that I expect them to make at least one mistake a week—that it's one of the ways we learn. (Of course, I don't want them making the same mistake every week!)

Stay close to Christ. The issues of submission and service ultimately come down to your relationship with Jesus. The pressures of ministry can easily keep you from your major source of strength. Don't ignore your time with God.

—Rick Warren

homework, learned about the youth group, and adopted concern for its direction. This was good! It communicated that he was interested in the youth ministry and wanted to see it strengthened. His described management style was attractive to me since I was entering my second decade of youth ministry and didn't need a high-control manager. I needed a pastor who would support my leadership and allow me the freedom to soar. That's what my pastor did and continues to do today.

While some personalities are controlling, most senior pastors I've met or heard about don't want to manage you. They don't have time. They want to trust you, believing that you'll do the job you were hired to do and that you'll support and practice the church's philosophy of ministry. If you get a clear picture of expectations, you should be fine. (See Chapter 12 for help with expectations.)

Here's an extra nugget of knowledge you won't learn in school: senior pastors who are superb in the pulpit aren't necessarily gifted in management or administration. Grant your pastor the freedom to grow and develop. Lower your expectations of him to something less than being everything you want and need. Many youth workers are disappointed when they discover their pastors don't have gifts in management and mercy. Senior pastors are a combination of strengths and weaknesses just like everyone else.

// Actions to avoid with your senior pastor.

Add your own ideas to this list each time you learn from a mistake. *Live and learn* makes sense in this area.

- *Don't drain your pastor.* Be a breath of fresh air when your pastor sees you. During meetings, protect your pastor's time by arriving with an agenda and being out of his office in

10 minutes or less. Respect your pastor's time and you'll be amazed at how much more you'll receive from him. When you're viewed as a drain, he may avoid you. Your pastor may be highly relational and love to talk with you; consider that a gift—but he still has other responsibilities, so be conscious of his time.

I know my pastor is extremely busy. I want to respect his time. I don't ask to schedule many meetings with him, so he knows when I do ask for his time, it's to discuss an important issue. I'll start the meeting by saying something like, "I've got three items on my agenda to run by you, two questions and an idea. I know you're swamped, so I'll make it brief." On some occasions I don't even sit down. When I respect and value my pastor's time, he respects my agenda and is more open to giving me time in the future.

> For the curious, if my pastor invites me to stay longer, I do.

■ *Keep your problems your problems.* Your pastor has enough problems that he doesn't need to take on the problems of your ministry as well. If you can't find a van for the upcoming youth event, don't make it his problem. Realize what senior pastors have to deal with. They've got—

- Too much to do.
- Too many expectations.
- Too much to hear (everyone brings complaints to them).
- Too many personal attacks: what they wear, how their children behave, what their spouses overhear about their neighbor's third cousin once removed who lives overseas.

If you have a *major* problem, talk to your pastor. If it's not critical, but you'd like some advice, talk to a trusted mentor or someone else on staff. If you're busy, chances are your pastor is busier.

■ *Don't expect a lot of your pastor's time.* Don't expect your pastor to treat you like everyone else in the congregation. You'll need to be mentored during your first two years, but not necessarily by your senior pastor. He can't be everything to everyone. Free him up from that expectation. Connect with others who can focus on caring for you, nurturing your growth, and coaching your ministry. As much as you'd like your boss to be your pastor, you may need to find someone else to meet that need in your life. Read that last sentence again…let it sink in.

- *Think big-picture—youth ministry relative to whole church ministry.* Steer clear of this belief: youth ministry is the most important ministry in the church. Yes, youth ministry is critical in the life of a church, and, unfortunately, senior pastors often ignore it. This does not give you the right to whine about being neglected or complain about needing more money in the budget—or even getting a budget. Spend time proving the importance of youth ministry by changing lives. Pastors tire of hearing complaints and grow weary of youth workers leveraging for more position. Every task that honors God is important. When you live by that truth, you'll be a valued staff member, not a competitor.

- *Knock over the perfection pedestal.* Allow your pastor to be human. Every senior pastor has issues to struggle with (insecurity, lack of faith, family problems, workaholism, pride, anger). Don't expect your senior pastor to be perfect so that you won't be disappointed when she isn't. The closer you get to a leader—every human leader—the bigger the flaws appear. As a fellow struggler, give your pastor the grace to not be perfect.

(A VOICE FROM THE TRENCHES)

Well, it was that time of year to look for a summer intern to help me through the crucial months of June, July, and August. At the time, I was in a committee-led church, so all of the résumés for the position had to go through our personnel committee. There were three applicants for one position, and although I knew all three fairly well, one person stood miles ahead of the other two. I went to both the pastor and our personnel committee and said that even though they were all good friends, I could only give my recommendation to one particular person.

The problem was one of the other applicants was a recent convert—drinking heavily and leading a very "worldly" life, only weeks before applying. Even though that fact was made very clear to the powers that be, this person had deep family roots throughout the church and even on the committee that was choosing my intern.

I'll never forget when my pastor called me in to tell me that the decision was for the new convert over my choice (who, by the way, is now the youth pastor of one of the largest youth groups in the country). I said I strongly disagreed with the decision, but would support the decision outside of his office. Later he made some phone calls and convinced the committee to change its decision to include both people as interns. (As it turns out, the new convert intern spent time gambling with students during a youth function and almost getting into a fight with another student on church property.)

My point? There will be many times when you feel you're right, and those in authority over you are wrong. And the best way to handle the conflict is by being real about your feelings, but also by supporting their decisions. I believe that disunity within a church staff is one of Satan's biggest tools to disrupt the Body. So guard the unity of your staff and never talk behind their backs—even when you know you're right. Practice encouragement and building them up. That's the one thing that you can and should do behind their backs!

—*Tim Nussbaumer, minister of students, Piedmont Baptist Church, Marietta, Georgia*

// Actions to take with your senior pastor.

My philosophy about working with a senior pastor is to do whatever I can to make his life easier. I want him to succeed and to know that he can trust me in every situation. If you concur, consider these ideas:

- *Care for his family.* Love his children. They don't need to be discipled by you personally, but you should make sure they're properly cared for. Give them extra hugs at camp, watch out for them at programs, and help them get dates with teenagers who are not serving jail sentences. Value and protect his family time. Affirm him when he puts his family first.

- *Support his dreams.* Listen to his dreams and look past his unique idiosyncrasies. Sometimes his dreams may become your nightmares, but your encouragement is crucial. Be a listener who gets excited about what's on your pastor's heart, without providing critical analysis unless it's requested.

- *Encourage.* Senior pastors need affirmation, too! Let her know when she's helped you. Be specific with your praise. If you note something worthy of commendation, point it out.

During a recent staff meeting, my pastor taught a Bible study that inspired me to action. Not only did I take the time to thank him for his spiritual leadership, but I also "stole" his teaching and taught it to my students. (Youth workers often refer to this as "research.") I told him about that, too, so he received a double affirmation.

■ *Take the heat.* If you can protect your pastor and take the heat or listen to a complaint directed toward your pastor, do it. Senior pastors need to know others on the team will absorb some of the pain and provide temporary relief.

■ *Invite, then uninvite.* Invite your pastor to all the youth events but don't expect him to attend anything. Let him know you'd love his presence, but give him a guilt-free opportunity to decline. If your pastor showed up at every event in the entire church, he'd always be exhausted. If your pastor does show up at every event, you're probably at a small

(A VOICE FROM THE TRENCHES)

I'll never forget my first church board meeting at my first church as a new youth pastor. I came all dressed up (even wearing a tie) looking as professional as I could. Looking at the agenda I saw a line item that read, "Youth Concern." To make a long story short, the "concern" was that during my first (and very successful) youth event at the church, someone had taken a bunch of the sugar packages for the adults' coffee the next morning.

Yup. My leadership was seriously questioned over some missing sugar. I reacted by writing off the board as completely out of touch with reality. And that was a big mistake—because it caused me constant frustration over the next year.

Here are some ways I've dealt with church board conflict:

• I've made sure that at every board meeting I've had on paper what I've been doing with the students, what I'm planning to do, and how all my plans will accomplish my mission for the ministry.

• I realize that some adults are always going to be suspicious of me and of teenagers, because teenagers can be intimidating to adults.

• When something happens that causes conflict (like the time I sponsored a rock concert in my youth room, forgetting there was a conservative, adult Bible study happening below us), I try to handle the issue head on. So after I realized we'd really bugged this Bible study group, I visited the class next week with some donuts, apologizing for our noise and thanking them for their patience and telling them we'd be more sensitive next time.

• I make sure my senior pastor is informed about any conflict, and I seek his advice and try to acquire his support. There are few things worse in youth ministry than having your senior pastor upset because you didn't keep him or her informed. The same applies for the board chairman.

• Depending upon the seriousness of the conflict, I don't always go alone. Often my adult/parent leaders stand with and support me.

• I come to every board meeting prayed up—for patience, understanding, and a non-defensive spirit.

The average lifespan of a youth worker at a church isn't very long. I believe that this sad statistic is due in part to the mistakes youth pastors make in resolving conflict with their church boards. My first 3 churches supported this statistic. However, after applying the above strategy, I've averaged over 3-4 years and hope to stay in my present church for more than 10 years.

—*Dan Snyder, youth pastor, Mountain Park Church, Lake Oswego, Oregon*

church, and one of the reasons it may be small is because your pastor shows up at every event.

Before our annual summer kick-off family picnic, I invited my pastor by saying, "We'd love to see you there, but I know it's a busy day for you (Sunday), so stay home after church and get some rest. I'm not expecting you." That particular day, he didn't show up. When he does come to an event, I'm thrilled, and when he doesn't, he's thrilled. Either way, our church wins. If my attitude is to serve my pastor, I want him to be thrilled.

Warning: Don't go overboard (e.g., "Gee, Pastor, why don't you take the year off? I don't think people will notice.")

▪ *Speak highly of your pastor.* Particularly do this behind her back. Your pastor needs to know that, when she overhears you talking about her in the hallway, you're saying positive, encouraging words.

▪ *Inform, but don't overwhelm.* When you're briefing your pastor on a situation, focus on the facts without all the time-consuming, negotiable details. Wait for him to ask for more before sharing all your interesting stories.

▪ *Save your senior pastor for your "biggies."* Be strategic about when you ask your senior pastor to persuade others concerning youth ministry issues or needs. Tactically leverage his leadership since he probably has more all-church influence than you do.

One spring some parents

> Having been a senior pastor for nearly 20 years, I know both the thrill and the pain of working with staff. When it's all rockin' and rollin', there's nothing better—but when there's tension, conflict, or dysfunction, there's nothing worse. Doug has successfully navigated the waters of a good senior pastor-student pastor relationship, and I get to see it firsthand as a peer in ministry. Because of that, Doug's ministry is fruitful, the student ministry is highly honored at our church, the Kingdom is advanced, and as an added bonus, Doug has modeled his supervision/submission approach for his own team of leaders to learn from and duplicate.
> —*Brad Johnson*

were angry because our traditional summer camp dates had to be changed. I understood the parents' frustration, but nothing could be done about it. On a Sunday night many of our parents were attending a mission trip reunion. As part of our reunion program, my pastor was to give a short, we're-proud-of-you message to the students and families. I also asked him to address the camp situation in a positive way. He not only addressed the tension about camp, but he also affirmed my leadership and communicated his belief in all we were doing.

He said what I couldn't say. He was able to influence the parents to accept the change because of the weight his words carry. If your congregation respects your pastor, be wise and strategic about when to use his platform.

■ *Pray.* Pray for your pastor's leadership (and for your willingness to follow it). Pray for your pastor's relationship with God and for his marriage and family. Ask God to encourage his heart. Pray for your pastor to continue growing and learning and for spiritual protection from our enemy. One practical way to affirm him is to periodically remind him you're praying for him.

When it comes to the lead youth worker's relationship to the senior pastor, I've heard these adjectives: great, good, average, bad, awful and near-death. As much as one might think that this partnering relationship would be filled with joy and godliness and free from conflict, that's not reality.

Pray for the wisdom to apply these ideas, for the sensitivity to care for your pastor as a person (not as a boss), and for the courage to talk face to face with him when you sense tension or have a hurt in your own life. Don't underestimate the ability you have to change this relationship for the better.

I wish the story about Clark and his pastor at the beginning of this chapter was unusual. Unfortunately, too many youth workers are losing battles with authority figures in the church. Too many lead youth workers don't know how to interact and respond to their senior pastor. Volunteers secretly write to me asking how they can change their lead youth workers, never considering changes for themselves. All of this saddens me. The stories are the same. Only the names are different.

Working relationships aren't easy because many conflicts arise when we're dealing with people in authority. Your response to the authority figures in your church will be reflected in your ministry's effectiveness.

The Church Board and Youth Ministry Team Working Together

At the mention of the church board, most minds rush to images of bureaucracy, meetings, arguments, donuts, and politics. Sometimes, the boardroom is a messy, mean, and sinful place. Do you have people on your church board? If so, you'll find sin, mixed motives, political alliances, and ministry favoritism. Your entire youth ministry team should be aware of how to work with board members.

Realize that perception can be stronger than fact.

When board members hear rumors of messy youth rooms, see typos in parent letters, call private investigators to find missing youth ministry receipts, and rarely see students in the church service, they form an impression of your ministry—mostly negative. Whether fairly or unfairly, they may judge your ministry on hearsay: what they think they saw rather than by the truth. Many of the decision-makers who approve your programs and decide your budget may never observe one of your youth meetings. That's unfortunate. Because perception is presumed to be fact, your youth ministry team should investigate how your ministry is perceived. Then decide what you can do to change negative perceptions and reinforce positive perceptions.

Respect the board, but don't be intimidated by its members.

Pray for and honor the board members, but realize that they're just men and women who aren't always the most spiritually mature individuals in the church.

At my previous church, the elder assigned to oversee youth ministry was a spiritual infant. He was a generous giver, and he was popular among people in the church who voted him into eldership. As I spent time with him, I realized that many of his decisions were based on his secular experience, not on Scripture. I found myself mentoring this man who was twice my age. I respected his position but struggled to respect him as a mature believer.

The men and women who make the significant decisions do not walk on water. They're fallible human beings trying to serve the infallible God—just like you and me.

Invite them to be involved.

Ask board members to attend some of your youth events to see first-hand what's happening. Invite them to open your meetings in prayer. Expose them to the students in the ministry. Involve them in your ministry. When they're involved, their perception will be more accurate and, as a result, they're more likely to be supportive.

Minister to the board members.

Get to know the board members personally. Don't have an agenda, except to care for them. When you care for people, they're more likely to champion your ministry.

Ask direct questions.

Many who occupy board positions are business people. They're comfortable with spreadsheets and bottom lines. Don't be afraid to ask direct, probing questions. "Here's what I'd like to do with our midweek program. What roadblocks do you see? What's the best way to get this idea backed by the decision makers of our church? Can you sell your home and donate the profits to the youth budget?" Your directness won't offend them, especially if you've ministered to them and they know your intention is to gather support for youth ministry resources.

Keep them informed.

Since board members don't visit youth ministries frequently, provide facts—brief brag sheets—on what's happening within your area of responsibility. Be your own marketing director. If board members have an in-box at the church, fill it. If not, provide this material prior to their regular meetings. The key, however, is to inform on an ongoing basis, not just before the budget meeting.

Realize that servanthood goes a long way.

Make every effort to communicate that you and the student ministry team care about the church's success, not just the youth ministry. Demonstrate that by offering statements like—

- Let our youth ministry team handle that responsibility. We want to be part of the big picture.
- We'd love to stuff the bulletins this week. We want the students to serve their church.
- I'll make sure someone on our team makes those phone calls. We're all in this together as a church.

Obviously, you don't want the student ministry to be viewed as a doormat for every little project, so you'll need to learn to balance your enthusiasm to serve with occasional firm rejections. I once had to decline an opportunity: "We'd love to do that project, but it's right before our summer camp. Our leaders are going to be swamped."

Your church board members will respond more positively to a serving attitude than a territorial attitude. It's hard to lose when you serve.

Train the board about your youth ministry.

Many board members may not know the real reason for youth ministry. When they refer to students as children or as the "church of the future," use that opportunity to respectfully educate them. You might say, "I appreciate your concern regarding the future of the church, but I prefer to think of our students as part of today's church." Many times, people make statements out of ignorance, not spitefulness.

An influential board member called me to ask if I would cancel our midweek evening program. He wanted me to bring the students over to his house to help baby-sit and clean up after one of his business parties. Frankly, I was shocked at this request. I took a deep breath and assertively replied, "I'm sorry, but I don't think that's a good idea." (It's so much easier to write years later than it was to say that day!) I then asked this man what he perceived as the purpose of youth ministry in our church. As he was articulating his response, he realized what an irrational appeal he was making. I followed up by saying, "I'm so thankful that you understand and support our student ministry."

At my going-away party several years later, this same man publicly said, "Doug is the first leader in this church to tell me no to one of my stupid ideas. I have always respected him for that." I'm not sure he always respected me, but I'm positive he understood our student ministry wasn't a bunch of kids doing nothing except waiting to be called to serve the church board's business functions.

> Remember that commitment you made in Chapter 1?

Encourage and pray for the board's efforts.

Ask some parents and student leaders to each pray for and care for a board member or two. Look for parents or volunteers who are willing to send an occasional note to a specific board member saying, "We appreciate your ministry. Thanks for serving the Lord! The youth ministry is praying for you." Over time, those simple, thoughtful cards and comments will go a long way.

Redefine church politics.

Yes, politics exist within the church, but you can give it a positive spin by defining politics as "the ability to gain support for the ministry God has entrusted to you." One of my roles as the youth worker is to help my church board have a clear, positive image of our youth ministry. I want the board to feel confident and excited about what we're trying to do for students and families.

The Questions at the End of the Chapter

// For group discussion

- Of the 10 questions listed in this chapter (pages 152-153), which area is your strongest?
- Which one of the 10 questions is going to require some changes and/or adjustments on your part?

// For personal reflection (change these depending on your role: lead youth worker or volunteer)

- How can I regularly affirm the pastor/lead youth worker?
- What can I do if my relationship with the senior pastor/youth pastor seems awkward?
- What is one forum where I can make my pastor/youth pastor look better?
- If I were the senior pastor/youth pastor of our church and I brought on a youth pastor/volunteer with my strengths and weaknesses, what could be some points of friction?

// Actions to consider

- Make a list of your pastor's/lead youth worker's strengths. Write an encouraging note to him/her and highlight a few.
- Pray for unity within your youth ministry team.
- Choose a leader (board member) in your church and begin to pray for this person.

Go to www.dougfields.com and enter your comments under Your First 2 Years: Chapter 7

where do i get help?

working with a team of leaders

At our imaginary meal, you and I have finished dessert and our waitress is wondering if we're ever going to leave. I say, "Do you want to leave and pick up later, or do you want to talk about volunteers—how to find them and what to do with them?" You order another dessert, lean closer, and say, "I'll stay! I really need help with leaders."

A Note to Youth Ministry Volunteers

Unless you're the lead youth worker, you can bypass this chapter. Consider my invitation to skip or skim it as an early Christmas gift or belated birthday present. If you're interested in understanding a critical role your lead youth worker has, you may want to keep reading. In addition to being reminded how vital you are as a volunteer, you'll also gain insight into the importance of identifying and inviting the right leaders to join your team. Teamwork is an essential element to a healthy youth ministry. Thank you for being a supportive part of the team!

A Note to Lead Youth Workers

If you're the lead youth worker, you may want to memorize this chapter or tattoo the principles on your forearm so you won't forget them! You need to be done with superhero, do-it-yourself, solo youth ministry. Healthy ministries rely on the gifts, talents, passions, and energy of other leaders. As someone once said, "I am more than I am, but less than we are." To make healthy youth ministry a reality, don't just find teammates, but partner with the *right* teammates, regardless of your church size. If you don't have many students, build a team of leaders for when the students arrive. Being part of a team will lengthen your work in youth ministry and strengthen your church.

> Do I hear an "amen!"?

Why a Team?

Learning how to develop and work with a team is the second most important topic (next to Chapter 3 on spiritual health) for a new leader. Developing leaders is essential to building a healthy youth ministry.

My greatest joy and most difficult task is building a team of other adults who will love students and disciple them. I wish it were easier. If you find, develop, and empower leaders, you'll be a valuable asset to your church and set yourself up for success in future youth ministry.

Some uninformed people in your church may believe you're the hired gun. Their attitude is, "You're the youth leader. You must do it all." I'm sorry, but you may be at the wrong church. I hesitate to write this bold statement, but I strongly believe our role is to equip the saints to do ministry (Ephesians 4:12). Your church did not buy a professional to entertain the teenagers.

This attitude may not come from everyone, but if the decision-making leaders within your church have the Lone Ranger mentality (you do it all by yourself), you'll either have to change their thinking (good luck), struggle, or pray for God to lead you in a new direction.

Some churches won't change, so they'll continue to destroy youth workers. You may not be able to escape others' ignorance completely, but you can combat it with success when you develop a team who will provide greater care and discipleship than you can alone. You'll have a more successful, vibrant, and healthy ministry when you minister with and through others.

For more extensive discussion about developing leaders, read through chapters 15 and 16 in my book *Purpose-Driven® Youth Ministry*.

You need a team! Let me give you some reasons why.

// With a team, you don't bottleneck growth.

Your ministry will eventually stop growing if you're ministering alone. Face it. You can only care for a few students personally. Jesus hung out with twelve disciples, but he spent the most time with three, and he had a better grasp on ministry than you and I do.

If all the phone calls, responsibilities, and needs of people are directed toward you, you'll forget or ignore some, your passion will dissipate, and you won't be able to adequately care for the students in your church. Because of this, you must make the mental shift to "I can't be everyone's youth pastor." This may be tough at first—it was for me. (Note: This is a *very* important, difficult mental shift to make—don't skim this section!)

> Doug has convinced me, as a volunteer, that I'm the youth pastor to my group of guys. Doug has REACHED me:
>
> **R**eceived me as part of a team and views my time as a gift to it
> **E**mpowered me to minister, using my gifts and talents
> **A**ffirmed me in my efforts to minister
> **C**ommunicated why our ministry exists, in clear terms
> **H**elped me to help my students by modeling his minister's heart
> **E**xpected my mindset to reflect a pastor's
> **D**edicated time to developing my ministry abilities
>
> That's the theoretical part; here's the practical application. Several years ago I helped lead my first mission trip to Mexico. My wife and I were assigned a group of students, as well as a village where we'd minister for the week. At the end of the week, I led our students in communion. Later that day Doug approached me and said, "The highlight of my trip was watching you minister to your students when you led them in communion." That was incredible to hear. Doug has REACHED me!
> —*Jim McNeff*

We're the leaders, and our natural tendency is to want everyone to know we're in charge. We want students to rely on our ability to minister. But kingdom work is bigger than any of us can handle alone. When we learn to allow others to have some of the credit, take over portions of the ministry, and invest in relationships, the result is a team that soars with enthusiasm.

Recently I spoke with Laurie, one of our new volunteers. I asked her, "Now that your small group is dismissed for the summer, how did you feel about your first year serving as a small group leader?" She said, "I fell in love with my girls." I loved to hear her say *my girls*, a phrase of endearment and ministry ownership reflecting a pastoral heart. I couldn't possibly minister to those girls the way Laurie has. I love it that the girls think of Laurie as their pastor and not me!

When asked, my volunteers would tell you that the most empowering phrase they hear is, "You are the youth pastor." I encourage you to get out of the way and let the students interact and be cared for by others within the body.

> You may grieve this loss at first. It's natural.

// With a team, you'll have more energy and last longer in youth ministry.

God never intended for you to minister alone. He's all about relationships. Everything from Creation to the Trinity points to God's relational design. In Exodus 18, Jethro, Moses' father-in-law, saw how hard Moses worked. Jethro basically asked him, "Why are you the only one to solve disagreements? You are not doing this right. This is too much work for you; you can't do it by yourself." Jethro told Moses that a team approach would help more people. That's a great reason for developing leaders.

Most discouraged and fatigued youth workers are usually ministering all by themselves. Doing everything alone is draining.

// With a team, your church is stronger.

Years ago I heard the story of a comedian who, while entertaining war veterans, watched two men clapping. Each man had only one arm and, as they sat side by side, they each used one hand to clap the other's with joy and laughter. What a great picture of teamwork. These men could accomplish something together that they could not do on their own.

The same is true in youth ministry. No matter how much you love God and students or how gifted you are, you'll never be able to accomplish as much on your own as you can with teammates. When other people in your church experience the joy of serving and pointing students toward Jesus, their faith grows, they're stronger followers of Christ, they'll be better youth workers. Because I believe this so strongly, I view our youth ministry as a place that Christians need for their spiritual journey. I need leaders, but Christians need to serve, and youth ministry is a spot that stretches their faith.

> Believing that Christians will be stronger when they minister isn't arrogant—it's truth.

When You Inherit a Team

I receive phone calls from overwhelmed youth workers during their first few months on the job, as well as frustrated senior pastors. Most of these calls concern lead youth workers interacting (or not) with the existing leadership team.

Some new lead youth workers get rid of every existing volunteer, so they can start new programs without dealing with old issues. Thus the calls from frustrated senior pastors. Others want to work with the existing team members, but they're intimidated or inundated by their expectations. Thus the calls from overwhelmed youth workers.

While a new president of the United States governs for about 90 days before being attacked and criticized, some youth workers get about 90 minutes—if they're lucky. To make the most positive impact at your church (and to buy a little time), here are wise strategies you can adopt:

Honor the previous youth pastor.
It's irrelevant if the last person was terrible. Don't bring it up. Don't criticize. Commit to speaking positively about your predecessor. Be creative, if necessary ("You guys lost money on every fundraiser? Hey, at least you kept trying. That's perseverance!")

Honor the previous youth pastor and your current team by affirming the members of the youth ministry team he assembled. Develop the mentality of honoring others. (Review the fourth commitment on page 28.)

Learn your new ministry's context and resources before you develop your plan.
If others ask what you you're planning, share your heart, not your strategy. Focus on building relationships first. This doesn't mean you're ignorant of strategy or that you have no vision. It does mean that laying a solid relational foundation comes first. If you're planning to work at your church for a while, the strategy and vision will arise in time—and it will be received better through established relationships.

Meet the leadership team members and get to know them before making personnel decisions.

Get to know them. Hear their stories. Listen to their hearts. Pray for wise realignment. Sometimes people just need to be encouraged or offered a new role in the ministry.

When I arrived at Saddleback, half the leadership team wanted to quit because they were tired of ministry without a point-person. Some barely had a pulse. I was tempted to say, "Great! Don't let the door hit you on the way out!" I was concerned that fatigue would translate into negativity. Instead of immediately escorting them out, I spent time with each of them individually. I heard their stories, gauged their spiritual health, and thanked them for their invaluable service. I learned a lot about the ministry, the church, the church's perception of youth ministry, and the climate for change.

Tell the senior pastor your plans.

Sit down with your pastor and agree on goals for your first month, first quarter, and first year. Ask him to write an endorsement letter on your behalf and send it to the existing volunteer team. Your pastor's credibility and stamp of approval enhances your authority.

Evaluate your motives for change.

When youth workers inherit their ministry teams, their egos are easily wounded because they expect every volunteer (and student for that matter) to immediately follow their lead.

I recommend you push to discover the motive behind the expectation. Why do you want immediate buy-in? Is it for your own needs or for the needs of the youth ministry? What's your motive? Some existing volunteers may be slow to accept you because of their continuing loyalty to the previous lead youth worker, or perhaps they're resistant to change. Some may feel a deep sense of ownership in the youth program and perceive you as the new kid on the block. The old program is more meaningful to them than the new person. (This changes over time.)

// With a team, your impact broadens.

Working with a team helps you reach different types of students. Although my wife and kids think I'm pretty hip, that's the last description my students would use to describe me (using the word *hip* proves I'm not).

They would say that Brad, one of our volunteers, is way cool. (Of course they wouldn't say *way cool* either. Okay...I'm a dork.) Personally, I don't see what's so great about Brad. Besides having an earring, multiple tattoos, and the looks of a model, he plays guitar, leads worship, and has a fantastic voice (but I know I'm smarter than him). When Brad speaks, students listen and laugh—and that's good enough for me.

Some students who connect with Brad don't connect with me. Different types of leaders reach different types of students using their own styles, interests, ages, and experiences. The more varied your team members, the more varied the students you'll be able to care for. If you want a wide impact, seek variety in your leaders.

If only they'd laugh at my jokes!

// With a team, your ministry skills will increase.

When you work with other leaders, you'll continually learn—regardless of your age and experience—by watching how each one works with students.

I was convinced that I knew *the* way to lead a small group discussion until I observed Woody's small group. As he began, he broke every written and unwritten rule for small group leadership. I was embarrassed for him as I watched him lead his group. I wanted to interrupt at least a half dozen times to correct him, coach him, and save him from being humiliated. But I waited. After he closed in prayer, I jotted down some notes, planning to gently correct and encourage him after such a horrid display of discussion techniques. I couldn't imagine how bad he must have felt.

I never got a chance to talk with Woody that night because the students continually surrounded him in his group. The boys were talking to him, thanking him for his insight, and sharing their deep concerns. I couldn't remember the last time students in my small group thanked me for anything (maybe the one time we finished early).

I left the house, got into my car, and jotted down more notes, this time for me based on what I learned from Woody. He wasn't a great teacher or facilitator, but he had unbelievable compassion, tenderness, and mercy for his boys. I learned something new watching Woody. He has made me a better small group leader. That's what a team does—it sharpens others.

// With a team, you'll have more fun.

One of my favorite times of year is June because during the last weekend of the month our leaders take a few days to get away and play. We don't talk about ministry, we don't dream about the future, and we don't brainstorm solutions to our challenges.

What do we do? We eat, play tennis, eat, sleep in, eat, go to the movies, goof around in the pool, and, after a long day of playing and laughing, we eat some more. I love the people I do ministry with! They're some of my favorite people on the earth.

Fortunately, I have the freedom to take extended time away with my leaders. If your schedules won't allow that, don't miss the principle: it's more fun to do ministry together when you like each other and have shared experiences. If ministry is worth doing, it's worth doing as a team!

I can imagine telling you my thoughts about why teamwork is so important. You're excited about the possibility of creating a team who is loved and at the same time effective. Then you gesture animatedly and cry, "I get it! It all makes sense, and it sounds wonderful! But how do I build a team if I don't have any other leaders?"

I'm glad you asked. Slow down on your dessert.

What If I Have No Leaders?

If you're starting as a solo youth worker, the good news is you'll get to influence the type of leaders you bring to your team for years to come. What's the bad news? You have to do it alone…at first. God has the leaders in your church; you just need to find them. Remember, God is more interested in the students being cared for than you are, and he'll provide the shepherds for the sheep within your flock.

Here are some principles you may want to consider before you begin to actually build a ministry team.

// Realize that building a youth ministry team gets easier.

The more you work on building a team, the easier it gets. And since looking for quality teammates is something you'll need to do on a regular basis, you might as well enjoy it. As you find and develop leaders, an increasing number of students will be growing in their faith, so you'll need to find more leaders. As students

(A VOICE FROM THE TRENCHES)

Kristi and I spent three years as volunteers under Brian. We were envious at times of the credit he got from the work we all did, as the eight of us together had complete ownership of the youth ministry. Nothing happened that we didn't agree upon. After Brian graduated seminary and left for an appointment in Mississippi, we lost four volunteers to job moves. We hired a new youth minister, and we felt as though we'd made the right choice. But the young seminarian was given little room to make an impact because of our stranglehold on the ministry, and he left within a year.

His leaving happened to coincide with me surrendering my life to Christ—and to the ministry, which insisted all youth volunteers be Christians. I was subsequently hired to fill the youth pastor position, and I proceeded to make some incredible mistakes—the biggest was forgetting how Brian had empowered me just four years before.

I was blessed with several volunteers. My newfound fire was complicated by my pride and my desire to be the youth leader. It wasn't long before my friends began finding other volunteer areas of ministry. Blindly, I accepted their departures, thinking Kristi and I could handle it all ourselves. After all, we were experienced, we felt we had sacrificed much more than even Brian had during his stay, and we loved being with youth.

In less than a year, I lost every single volunteer, my first child was born, and my senior pastor began what turned into a battle that no one won and ended with him leaving wounded.

Through months of prayer, and on the verge of being burned out, God convicted me of my selfishness, and after year three of doing youth ministry practically alone I wrote a letter asking some of those former volunteers and some others for help. Some refused, and others came to my aid. And after I specifically asked people to do and own a specific ministry, the program has blossomed into a far greater wealth of resources than I could've ever imagined.

Sure I had tried asking folks for help in a general sort of way before; I just said, "We really need some help. Is anyone interested?" I can't think of a single time that I received a response.

Help only came after I confessed to God that I was a fallible leader and began pleading for wisdom regarding whom I should ask. Some rejected me, others were overjoyed to help, and still others hesitantly joined me. I can gladly say that since that moment, I've never lost a single volunteer and have only added to their number.

mature in their faith, they'll be inviting their non-Christian friends, so you'll need more leaders to accommodate the growth.

Don't misunderstand me. Finding new leaders isn't easy, but it does get easier. Also quality people attract quality people.

The moral of the story? No matter how small your church or how small your youth group, never think that you can minister alone. Always ask God, "Who else can be of service in the building your kingdom?"

Because if you think you can do it alone, soon you'll find yourself doing it alone.

—*Robert Smith, director of student ministries, Georgetown (Kentucky) First United Methodist Church*

// Pursue clarity before pursuing people.

Talking to potential youth workers is similar to a sales job. This doesn't mean you have to act like a used car salesman, but it does require you to think through your "product" and clarify the answers to questions like these:

- Why should people join our youth ministry team?
- What is the compelling vision our ministry offers?
- How can I convey the positive aspects of adolescents to counter negative stereotypes?
- In what ways might adults participate with our youth ministry team?

If you can answer these questions, you'll inspire others and, at the same time, motivate yourself as you share about the thrill of working with students.

// Be picky…not desperate.

One quality leader exceeds three mediocre ones without question. Share your passion for students and their families with everyone, but only invite a few to work with you. It can be gut-wrenching to fire a volunteer, so save your stomach and the money you'd spend on antacids. Be slow to say yes to potential volunteers. Desperate choices come back to haunt you. (Remember Becca from Chapter 6?)

Once you select a few people who love God, who like students, and who want to play on a team, your group will naturally attract other quality youth workers. So seek out the right people from the start.

How to Remove a Volunteer

Some people may criticize me for including this discussion, but the topic is one that may be most frequently referred to. During every seminar I teach on volunteers, someone sheepishly asks, "Uh…well…I have this one leader…and…well, she's been there a long time…and…uh…well…" Since I've heard the same scenario a thousand times I say, "And you want to get rid of her but you don't know how…right?" The crowd laughs awkwardly and the person who's asking sighs with relief when she finds out she's not alone.

In my many years of youth ministry I have had to ask people to step away from their leadership positions. A few times, the volunteer was relieved to go. Most of the time I faced a sweaty-palms, intense, conflict-filled, difficult conversation. And every time our ministry was healthier once this person was removed.

Consider these principles:

- If God has called you to be the lead youth worker and the church has given you the mantle of leadership, then lead. You don't have to be mean-spirited to lead; you just need to be willing to lead. Leaders have to make decisions and take actions that aren't easy. Letting someone go is one of them. Your youth ministry is too important to lower your standards and overlook someone who is causing problems. Difficult leaders damage morale, hurt students, cause continual grief, and hinder your ministry from growing.
- As the lead youth worker, it's your responsibility to put a team together that's going to pursue health and move in the right direction. Not everyone will go there with you. Remember what Paul and Barnabas fought about in Acts 15? They went their separate ways because Paul didn't think John Mark had what it took to minister with him. You're not the first leader in the history of Christianity to make a tough decision about leaders.
- It's always easier to bring people onto the team than to remove them. Remember that when you're about to say yes to a potential volunteer who gives you an unsettling feeling. Trust your gut and say no.
- Realize the difference between a person who's a chronic problem and a person who needs immediate intervention (moral failure, a nonnegotiable rule broken, et cetera). Volunteers who just aren't cutting it are going to need more tenderness, grace, and chances than those who knew the consequences of their choices and chose poorly.

Removing a leader is your last resort, a step taken only after you've done everything you can to help this person succeed.

Before you remove the volunteer

- Have a conversation with your supervisor. Tell him what you're planning to tell the person. Ask for advice, coaching, and prayer. Don't make important decisions in isolation. Get a second opinion. Supervisor support is crucial since backlash is likely.
- Be in prayer.
- Have strong evidence and anecdotal illustrations to support your decision.
- Confront a problem volunteer about specific issues before removing them. (See Chapter 6 for help on this.) It may be an issue related to attitude, performance, or team fit. Be honest. Tell the volunteer you need to see specific changes (note them!) or else you may ask him to step away from the ministry. Tell the leader you'll give him a month to see changes. During this time, check this person's pulse regarding commitments. I've found that some will confess, "I'm just not into it any more." Then give the leader the opportunity to step aside gracefully.
- Set a date to meet and review again in a month.

When you remove the volunteer

- Be tender but strong. Grace and truth are needed when having this difficult conversation. Grace says, "I care about you." Truth says, "You're not working out in this ministry, and here's why…"
- Don't beat around the bush. Be clear. "Sandy, things haven't changed since our last meeting, and I would like to ask you to step away from the youth ministry for a season." The season can be six months, a year, two years, the rest of the 21st century. It doesn't need to be decided right away.
- Don't ask the volunteer to stay until you find a replacement. Think through that ahead of time. Be ready to accept the responsibilities this person is leaving behind.

After you remove the volunteer

- Immediately following the meeting, spend time alone. Review, reflect, and pray. Do some activity in which you can relax and express the emotions you have. I'm always so stressed before the meeting and so relieved after that my emotions are tender.
- Follow up with a letter. Tell people you're thankful for their service and that you're sorry things didn't work out and that you'll be praying for peace and reconciliation.

- Don't avoid the person.
- If it's appropriate, offer the person's name to another ministry in the church.
- Expect some people to be angry. This is natural, and it can take time to heal.
- Talk about the meeting with a trusted friend, your mentor, or another youth worker who can relate to what you've gone though.
- Don't obsess over it. You made the right decision. Move on. Lead your team. Hopefully it will be a long time before you remove a leader again. Oh yeah…you will have to do it again…some day.

Two lifesavers

■ *A signed commitment.* We establish standards by having leaders sign a commitment each year, myself included. Each leader agrees to attitude, direction, participation, unity, and certain lifestyle standards that go with the commitment. (This is done annually to give leaders an easy out if they don't feel they can commit for another year.)

As we sign these commitments (during our first leader's meeting of the new school year) I say something like, "My prayer is that everyone here will outlast me as a youth worker at this church. I want to be honest, though, and let you know that I will be candid with you if I feel like you're not living up to your commitment, and I'll ask you to make changes." The clearer your expectations are from the beginning, the easier the removal conversation will be. (See appendix a, page 279, for an example you can use or modify for your own group.)

■ *Periodic reviews.* A few times a year, meet with leaders individually to discuss their attitudes, performances, and fit with the team. When reviews are frequent, it's easier to address potential trouble before it gets out of hand. If things are going well, the review is a great opportunity to affirm the leader.

When you form a youth ministry team, you invest in your ministry. Reflect on how each person you invite adds value to your ministry. Before you start building your team, you'll also want to consider the obstacles you may face. At this point I imagine you asking, "How do I go about getting the leaders my students deserve?"

Great question. Let's talk about it.

How to Find the Right Teammates

// Know the type of leader you're looking for.

Don't be deceived by a friendly smile and a few slick responses to your questions. Some of the most faithful, gifted youth workers come in outlandish shapes and sizes. Remember the Lord's instruction to Samuel when he went to anoint Israel's future king:

> But the Lord said to Samuel, "Don't judge by his appearance or height, for I have rejected him. The Lord doesn't make decisions the way you do! People judge by outward appearance, but the Lord looks at a person's thoughts and intentions."
> (1 Samuel 16:7, NLT)

There is no ideal youth worker. Some are tall, others are short; some recite every verse of the Bible, others can quote every baseball team's starting lineup; some are funny, others are funny-looking; some look hip, some like hip-hop music. Over the years, I've learned that the best youth workers are *not* the young, funny extroverts. They're the ordinary men and women who love God and like students.

I've found that one of the greatest ways to attract potential youth workers is to show off the youth worker who breaks all the stereotypes. Older team members who wear dated clothes are good. Tell their stories and the ways they currently contribute to your team. When others see these ordinary people, they may think, "If that guy can do it, I can too."

> In other words, I show myself off quite a bit!

Good youth workers are everywhere; you just have to know what to look for. I look for two characteristics in potential youth workers:

- They love God.
- They like students.

Good youth workers don't have to walk on water (although that would be an asset and make a fun video), but they need to be Christians who have an authentic relationship with God. And don't say yes to adults who are looking for teenage friends. Allow them to get a life first. Leaders shouldn't need to be around students to complete their lives. Expect leaders to love God and like students. If they possess those qualities, they're potential candidates regardless of their age, style, or how high they wear their pants.

17 Ways to Find Volunteer Youth Workers

1. Ask students who they like.

2. Ask parents who they trust.

3. Ask existing youth leaders who they know.

4. Ask the pastor who he sees as an emerging leader.

5. Go to colleges and seminaries at the beginning of the school year to get unconnected students involved in your ministry.

6. Check the church directory and call someone who looks like the type of youth worker you need. (And since there is no specific *look*, anyone could fit. Just say, "I was looking through the directory and you look like you'd be a great youth worker!")

7. Check out local parachurch organizations (Young Life, Youth for Christ, et cetera) to see whether any of their leaders aren't plugged into a church body.

8. Use parents.

9. Look within your own youth ministry. Have mature high school seniors work with junior high students or college students work with high schoolers.

10. Challenge newly married couples to start marriage by ministering together.

11. Make a request at the church membership class.

12. Find the sports coaches who attend your church. Many coaches are good with kids.

13. Write a letter to your congregation requesting assistance.

14. Ask some children's workers whether they might "graduate" with some of the their students to join your junior high team.

15. When you have the opportunity to speak to classes or other church groups (singles, couples, seniors) tell them you're looking for introverts. Many introverts don't think they make good youth workers because they're not wild and crazy. But they make great youth workers because they talk with students and go deep with them. While the extrovert runs around and says hi to everyone, the introvert engages students.

16. With the same group, ask listeners to raise their hands if they grew up in a youth group and had a good experience. Seek them out. One of the reasons they had a good experience was because of caring leaders. Now it's payback time for their good experiences by becoming leaders in your youth ministry. These people are usually warm to the idea of youth ministry.

17. Look for people who are tired of singing in the church choir.

// Identify the excuses people will make.

Before talking to others about serving in your ministry, make a list of possible hurdles that could prevent someone from joining your team. Include reasonable excuses such as—

- I don't have enough time.
- I don't have enough experience.
- I don't have enough talent.
- I don't know the Bible well enough.
- I'm not young enough.
- I don't know what to expect.
- The church doesn't value people in youth ministry.

Of course, since you want to be prepared for anything, be sure to list the unconventional excuses as well:

- I'd rather chew glass.
- I'm afraid to get too close to people who have multiple body piercings
- I'm uncomfortable belching into microphones.
- I don't know enough swear words to understand youth vocabulary.
- I don't know any wrestling moves for junior high boys.
- I'm scared of the pastor's kids because they know more about the Bible than you do.

Take time to list possible solutions for every excuse people might make. Your goal is to have a solid response so their excuses seem irrelevant. Value their concerns, but help them see a solution to every issue.

If you've got some time-conscious potential volunteers, offer options to serve within varied amounts of time. Draft a list of ways volunteers might meaningfully contribute if they served 30 minutes a week, two hours a week, or five hours a week.

If your potential volunteers don't know how or where they'd fit in, simplify your serving opportunities by providing numerous entry points for them. If they can't serve at your weekly programs, add them to a prayer team or to the team for occasional needs (speed boat for camp, their house for a small group, their pool for baptisms, their time-share in Hawaii for your next vacation).

Remember, the more people are involved, regardless of their level of commitment, the more likely they are to stay involved in the future.

// Master "the ask."

Most people serve because you value them enough to look them in the eyes and offer them an opportunity to take part in something bigger than themselves. There is power in asking, but to ask effectively—

- You've got to ask! I'd hate to miss the obvious.
- You've got to ask clearly. Get to the point. (See "Pursue clarity before pursuing people" on page 180.)
- You've got to ask specifically. Don't mislead or manipulate.
- You've got to ask expectantly. Be shocked by a *no*.
- You've got to ask persistently. (*No* might really be *not now*, so ask again in a month or two—especially a strong candidate.)
- You've got to ask creatively. Don't be afraid to use those who can only serve for a season (say, the summer) to help with projects.
- You've got to ask graciously. Leave a positive impression.

- You've got to ask prayerfully. See Matthew 9:37-38.

- You've got to ask confidently. Since you're not desperate, don't whine, beg, or create guilt. Don't be ashamed. (See "With a team, your church is stronger" on pages 174-175.)

When I train youth workers, I ask a dozen people to stand up. Then, one by one, I ask, "How did you get into youth ministry?" The most common responses are—

- I was asked by someone.
- I felt God's call.

It seems obvious: you've got to look for people you can ask. Those who are called by God are going to hunt you down for an opportunity to join your team, but the remaining individuals are waiting for you to ask.

Don't limit your recruiting attempts to ads in the church bulletin. Most people look at requests like that and think, "It's too bad that the students need leaders. I'm sure someone will respond." Bulletins can spark interest in your need, but they won't have the power of asking in person.

// Be visible.

Don't allow your youth ministry to be an underground, private club. Get the word out: your church has a great youth ministry! Set a goal that everyone in your church knows who you are, not to inflate your ego, but to establish a ministry presence. Some easy ways to introduce yourself and your ministry to all visitors, new members, and old members include these:

- Teach your church's membership class (or show up to it).
- Make announcements during church.
- Greet people as they arrive at church.
- Introduce yourself during Sunday school classes. Let the participants know the youth ministry is praying for them. (Don't forget to pray).
- Have informative, attractive promotional materials accessible at key locations.
- Visit the children's ministry, especially the classes that graduate into your youth ministry.
- Update the church's prayer ministry with youth-related requests.
- Host parenting seminars.
- Send out e-mails, and use a Web site to pitch your volunteer team.
- Send Christmas cards from the student ministry to church attenders.

- Schedule a "thank you for supporting student ministries" event that's attractive to adults and families.
- Have your students and volunteers call church attenders to wish them a happy Easter from the student ministry.

The more visible you are, the more likely you are to talk to people about your needs, address excuses, and identify whether they love God and like students.

// Expect other leaders to help.

Finding quality leaders should not be the sole responsibility of the lead youth worker. (See Chapter 7, pages 154-155.) Create the desire within your leadership team for other quality adults in your ministry. Everyone works to find other teammates to help.

Recently, I was talking with an employee at my local grocery store. I commented about how friendly the employees are. He said, "You're a friendly guy, too. Are you interested in a job?"

I asked, "Do you have the authority to hire me?"

He replied, "No, but I've been given the responsibility to find people who would fit in with our team."

He wasn't the store manager, but he had been adequately trained to be on the lookout for potential team members. I love that! While I declined his offer, I did offer to work as a food sampler. I'm waiting to hear if I'm hired.

Everyone should be on the lookout for quality youth workers. You may want to challenge your leaders to talk to at least one other adult each year about joining the ministry team.

And don't forget students are your greatest resource when inviting others to apply for a youth ministry position. It's one thing for an adult to be approached by you, the point person of your ministry, when others may instinctively put up the *uh-oh-here-she-comes* shield to deflect your invitation. It's altogether different when students swoop in, since their requests are often perceived as a compliment. The same request from a different presenter gets results!

// Be professional.

I use a packet of information to describe our programs and inform potential volunteers about the commitments they might make. We ask each one to complete a short application, then schedule a face-to-face interview. This process communicates to potential volunteers that we take youth ministry seriously in our church, and we are making sure we know the people joining our team.

> You don't need to recreate this process. I've spent more than 20 years developing forms and processes you can use. Some are available for free at www.dougfields.com. Click on freebies at the bottom of the home page. Or you can purchase *Saddleback Resource Notebook* (150 pages of forms) from the online store.

In addition to the message it sends to the potential volunteer, the process also sends a message to the parents of our teenagers that we're looking for sharp people in the church who families can trust with their children.

Some Final Thoughts

A friend of mine recently graduated from our two-year intern program and is now the youth pastor at a great church. He's thriving and loves his job. But in the midst of his happiness and feelings of fulfillment, he's been through some painful experiences with existing volunteers. He begged for an early read of this chapter. After he read it, he said, "I outlined your chapter into 10 action steps, and it's really been helpful to me." I asked

I agree with Doug 120 percent. (That's a lot, huh?) Aside from tending to your own spiritual health, working with a team of adult leaders is the most crucial area to which you'll give energy as a youth minister. Doug references Ephesians 4:12, which speaks of equipping the saints for ministry. Later Paul underlines that concept when he asserts that only when each part of the body does its own, special work can the whole body grow.

And "each part" doesn't refer to paid ministers only! We must continually find and mobilize other adults whom we can empower to minister alongside us. When we approach youth ministry this way, everybody wins. Our volunteers get opportunities to exercise their God-given gifts, to be spiritually challenged, and to build up the whole body. In turn, our students get a clearer picture of how the Body of Christ should operate as many different personalities relate to God and serve him.

Concerning how we find other adults to empower, I'm a firm believer that our attitudes and perspectives determine our successes or failures. If we believe, for instance, that resources are scarce and there are "probably not enough volunteers to go around," then we're thinking too small. Does God lack resources? Do you think the one who fed 5,000 with two small fishes and five loaves is wringing his hands in heaven, wondering, "Wow! How am I ever gonna find volunteers for [your name here]'s youth ministry?" God wants to provide for your students' spiritual health! But what's your perspective? Do you have a "scarcity mentality" or an "abundance mentality"?

Several of Doug's suggestions deserve extra confirmation and comment. Do take to heart the importance of being "picky," identifying numerous entry points and levels of time commitments, and addressing potential volunteers' excuses for not wanting to help. (Because excuses usually aren't attempts to get out of being a part of your team as much as they are fears that potential volunteers are hoping you can address!)

And if you believe your adult team is really your most valuable asset, you'll spend a lot of your energies empowering and caring for them. You can assemble a great looking team, but only spiritually alive volunteers will truly minister to your students. Each volunteer brings a different set of skills and experiences to your ministry and, as Doug suggests, it's wise to provide each with more and more opportunities to grow and develop those skills and draw on their experiences to benefit kids.

Furthermore, you should continually look for ways to nourish and challenge your volunteers' spiritual lives. How are you helping them fan the flames? Something I learned while leading a group of volunteer leaders is the importance of connecting them to *each other*. As much as I believed I could relate to all of them and be their sole, primary means of support, they found the most support and solidarity with each other. If this is the case in your group, don't take it personally! It's a good thing—and merely a result of their collective feeling of commonality. So I worked at finding creative ways to keep them connected and spiritually challenging one another.

Working with volunteers is hard work, don't get me wrong. But just imagine the joy of seeing not merely a handful of your students grow in Christ, but hearing story after story after story of many other students who're growing as well—those you would never have been able to reach on your own. Then add to that the joy of serving alongside adults who share your enthusiasm for youth and are growing and discovering new ways that they can serve Jesus. Does it get any better?

—*Jana L. Sundene*

him to share them with me, and I thought they were so good that they should be included here:

- Pray for new leaders and current leaders.

- Identify the type of youth worker I'm looking for.

- Bring new adult leaders on the team in appropriate ways.

- Provide volunteers with specifics regarding how I want them to spend their time.

- Allow them to pastor students. You want to hear your female volunteers referring to "my girls" and your male volunteers saying "my guys."

- Start where they are, and help them take the next growth step.

- Give them ownership and get out of the way.

- Remember they're called to serve God.

- Shepherd your youth workers. Care for them.

- Offer every-other-month reviews. Your leaders need to be encouraged, so you can honor them, as well as adjust their job descriptions. Do this over a meal so it's informal.

I don't fully understand my retirement fund or how it works, but I understand the simple principle *invest today or I'll be hurting in the future*. You don't need to know everything about volunteers during your first two years, but you can understand one simple principle: *invest in your leaders today and they'll pay kingdom dividends in the future*. Invest in your leaders.

The Questions at the End of the Chapter

// For group discussion

- Why do we need to be needed so much that we try to do things ourselves? Where can this insecurity lead?
- What qualities do you think a youth worker should possess?

// For personal reflection

- How will I feel if our team grows and I become a less crucial part of the team because more people are helping the ministry?
- Is our current approach to inviting/recruiting potential volunteers a motivating and attractive one?
- Am I doing anything in our ministry that's bottlenecking growth?
- Am I afraid to ask others to get involved? If so, what are my specific fears? How can I overcome those fears?

// Actions to consider

- Compile a list of potential volunteer youth workers in your sphere of influence.
- Prepare a job description for volunteers in your ministry. Be sure to include some of the values listed by your group. People need to know what they'll do with their time.
- Look at your current group of volunteer leaders and find out why they got involved. When you know their reasons, you can use that to your advantage when talking with others in your church. (For example, if your current leaders came from the church membership class, then you should be at every church membership class.)

Go to www.dougfields.com and enter your comments under Your First 2 Years: Chapter 8

can students handle responsibility?

investing in student leaders

Philip is a friend, but more than that, he's an outstanding student leader in our ministry. He's not outgoing, and he won't impress you with flash or a witty joke. But if I want something significant accomplished, I talk to Philip. Just as likely, Philip sees the need himself and takes the initiative to accomplish the task. While he doesn't stand out in the crowd, he epitomizes effective student leadership. I can't imagine youth ministry without student leaders like Philip.

I also have students trying to convince me that they're leaders. Their rationale for being in leadership is that they are outgoing, they hang out with the popular crowd, they're involved in many school activities, and, my favorite, they need "leadership experience stuff" for their college applications. Would you be eager to have that type of student lead your next mission trip? No? Neither would I.

I love teenagers, and I value leadership. I've learned that developing student leaders is a top priority. In the last several years, publishers have served the cause by making a myriad of resources available: student leadership devotionals, curriculum, videos, Bible studies, discussion guides, interactive CDs, Web sites, seminars, conferences, and rallies. While these products are great, they can be overwhelming, particularly when each resource advertises itself as *the answer* to developing student leaders who will grow your ministry and rule the world. I've reviewed and used many of these resources. Some have been helpful.

In the end, though, adult leadership is what makes the difference in developing student leadership. It's neither published models nor the high profile students. No resource helps, regardless of the guarantee, unless your adult leaders have a healthy understanding of growing student leaders. Small group leaders who care for a few students are the most likely to spot leadership potential. When you find and develop it, you can change students' lives.

Why You Want to Develop Student Leaders

Without question, developing student leaders should be on your radar during your first two years. God often uses leadership opportunities to help teenagers develop spiritually. If you allow students to lead, you'll have the privilege of encouraging, validating, and shaping their faith.

Leadership can positively alter the mind, heart, perspective, and self-esteem of teenagers. Students who experience leadership find significance by serving others, develop unique skills that strengthen their roles in the church, and grow spiritually.

Vanessa was growing in her faith consistently and serving God actively. She had many opportunities to stretch her leadership wings at school, but those options bored her. She was certain God could use her, but she wasn't sure where or how. I invited her to apply to lead a summer missions team, cautioning her that it would require a deep commitment to Christ and a large amount of planning time during the semester, neither of which fazed Vanessa. She accepted the challenge, did a tremendous job with her tasks, and grew in her spiritual, mental, and emotional life.

// Student leadership provides an enticing opportunity for students to consider full-time ministry.

Besides challenging students to live God's way every day, one of my greatest joys is casting the vision for students to serve God vocationally. Aspiring lawyers, doctors, teachers, trash collectors, and parachute jumpers need to see that the skills they're developing can be used in full-time ministry.

While it's essential for committed Christians to fill professional roles in the secular marketplace, most students don't even consider the possibility of being employed in Christian ministry. Student leadership can allow them to use their skills for God's kingdom, interact with full-time ministers, and open their eyes to a unique way of spending their vocational lives.

I'm in youth ministry today because I was given an opportunity to work with junior high students when I was a high school junior.

// Student leaders aid your youth ministry.

Effective student leaders advance the church, reach more people, grow in their own spiritual journeys, and relieve adult leaders of some of their workload. Don't let pride or small thinking dissuade you from believing that you need help, even help from teenagers. We all need support and encouragement, and if you've got students ready to contribute, put them to work in the ministry!

One of our student leaders recently took ownership of a worship program so one of the adult leaders could spend more time with her family. At first it wasn't as strong, but now it's healthier than it ever was, and the adult leader's family is also healthy.

When we were preparing to go to Mexico for spring break, I asked two teenagers who were serving in our children's ministry to help with the Mexico crafts, curriculum, and games. They did a better job than I could have done, even if that were the only task on my plate. They understand children's ministry. I don't.

// When you involve eager students in ministry, your own faith benefits.

Student leaders will challenge you with their readiness to serve, inspire you with their faith, and convict you with their pure motives. They haven't yet experienced the hardships and challenges of ministry (actually you may not have either), but they will soon enough (and you will, too!) Invite them to serve, and be with them when they face trials in the future. You'll grow stronger as they grow spiritually.

// Developing leaders is a biblical command.

The Bible challenges us to live our lives serving others. But God doesn't stop there. He envisions his children as runners in a relay race, passing the baton from one runner to the next. We're to equip others to minister effectively and enable them to reproduce spiritual life in others. Paul speaks to Timothy regarding this issue in 2 Timothy 2:2 when he writes, "Pass on what you heard from me to reliable leaders who are competent to teach others."

The responsibility of passing the baton is not reserved for adults or trained professionals, but for all believers in Christ regardless of age (yes, junior high students can be leaders in the church). When a church decides to develop young leaders it communicates messages students need to hear: "We take you seriously. We believe in you. You're making a difference!"

I frequently pray that our church will graduate genuine Christian leaders. When students exit our ministry, go to college, or enter the workforce, I want them to have developed the understanding that if they can't find a church in their area, they need to start one. That attitude is only realized if the youth workers continually move students toward taking leadership roles and doing ministry.

I'm convinced that if students aren't given leadership opportunities, the chances increase that they'll graduate from their faith when they graduate from our ministry.

> Most teenagers are dying for an adult to believe in them.

Warning! Warning! Warning!

While I've listed some persuasive reasons why you should develop student leaders, please understand this critical point: focus on developing leaders, not on creating a student leadership program or a leadership team. Leaders? Yes! Team? No—at least not now. You have enough to focus on during these two years, so develop leaders today, and build a student leadership ministry tomorrow (actually, in a few years).

At my first church, I read a youth ministry magazine article that communicated that *the* way to build a student ministry was by creating a student leadership team. With less than a year's experience, I created one—that week. I chose the students who seemed respected and asked if they wanted to be part of a youth ministry cabinet. Most of them shrugged and said, "What's a cabinet? Sure. I guess."

I had two problems. The students I chose weren't leaders, and I wasn't ready to direct them. The formula I read included meetings in which I would teach on leadership and assign tasks. Well a young leader teaching nonleaders about leadership is like a kid with a learner's permit teaching infants to drive a car. The audience wasn't interested, the tasks were too complex, and the driving instructor didn't know how to drive.

Within a month we disbanded the cabinet, and I went searching for the next youth ministry article. This time I needed some reading on how to handle failure and depression.

I believe in student leadership teams, which is why our ministry has one, but I didn't have one during my first two years of ministry—or even my first five years. I've always developed leaders, because that's part of fulfilling the Great Commission. But don't buy into a program or video curriculum guaranteed to develop leaders in 30 days. It's not realistic.

How to Identify Student Leaders

Before you begin your search, you need to remember that Jesus' view of leadership is dramatically different from what the world teaches. In the secular leadership model, leaders are in charge of others. Leadership is often a position of power, like a 15-year-old lifeguard with a whistle. The role gives him responsibility, and the whistle is the sound of authority, but an arrogant attitude evaporates all credibility.

Jesus' approach calls leaders to be servants.

> Jesus called all the followers together and said, "You know that the rulers of the non-Jewish people love to show their power over the people. And their important leaders love to use all their authority. But it should not be that way among you. Whoever wants to become great among you must serve the rest of you like a servant. Whoever wants to become first among you must serve the rest of you like a slave. In the same way, the Son of Man did not come to be served. He came to serve others and to give his life as a ransom for many people." (Matthew 20:25-28, NCV)

One of the ways I find potential leaders is to "look up, look toward, and look around."

My act of *looking up* is to see who's doing the jobs that other students believe are beneath them: picking up trash, stacking chairs, and cleaning up. When I *look toward* the corners, I hope to see students reaching out to the unconnected or shy students, the ones in the corners who keep their distance from the crowd. And when everything appears to be done, I *look around* to see who has stayed behind looking for an opportunity to help with anything. It's easy to slip out the door and miss seeing a few students offering to work when everyone is tired. These three groups of students provide relief and give me ideas for potential leaders.

Keep in mind, someone who helps clean up or goes out of his way to welcome a shy person might simply have the gift of serving, not leading. Service doesn't equate to leadership. But, based on Jesus' model, leadership must include service, every time. Servanthood is a nonnegotiable characteristic of leadership. As you look for student leaders, raise the standard to reflect servanthood.

Here are some additional guidelines to identify student leaders:

// Consider a different look to leadership.

Don't be mesmerized by up-front leaders, thinking they're the types to eagerly develop. While those with strong personalities can be wonderful assets, don't miss the potential in the ones who are behind-the-scenes leaders (those who make things happen without being noticed) and the skill leaders (those with abilities in music, the arts, teaching).

I'm especially sensitive to this principle because my wife doesn't fit the stereotypical leader image. She's quiet and prefers being behind the scenes, the exact opposite of me. People tend to dismiss Cathy and look to me because I'm outgoing and give the appearance of making events

> The best parts about being a student leader in Doug's youth ministry are the friendships I've developed with adult leaders. That may sound "unspiritual," but I'm being honest. What I love most is the privilege of getting to truly know some of my "heroes," as they've given me the chance to minister alongside them. They've treated me as a leader long before I ever was one, and they did this by investing in my life—just as if I were one of their friends. I'm a student leader today because caring adults convinced me that I have something to offer.
> —*Ryan Holladay*

or programs happen. After more than 20 years of watching Cathy's leadership, I've seen what an incredible leader she is as she serves in a reserved manner. She'll put together a Christmas party for our adult leaders without ever using the weight of the stage and the motivation of the crowd. Behind the scenes, she calls and e-mails. If I were only taking flashy, charismatic types, I would have missed out on one of my best leaders. Any ministry will break without the behind-the-scenes servants who don't pursue attention or accolades.

// Cancel the cute, fun, and popular clique.

The cute, fun, and popular need not be ignored (if that were even possible), but don't immediately place them in leadership simply because they're influential on their campus or in your youth group. Maintain your standard of servanthood regardless of popularity.

If a girl doesn't have a servant's heart, she isn't a leader. Get her input if you want. Seek her advice, and allow her to contribute by planning events or making calendar decisions. Anyone can help with those activities, because those aren't uniquely leadership actions.

However, don't refer to popular students as leaders if they're not servants. They're key influencers in your group, but that doesn't mean they're leaders. You may want to figure out how to leverage their people skills, but reserve the leadership label for those who consistently offer unsolicited help and reach out to others.

// Battle favoritism with established leadership criteria.

Objective, written leadership criteria protect you from complaints of favoritism. They allow students to discern for themselves whether they're spiritually ready for leadership and give them time to meet the requirements. Gather your adult leadership team to develop criteria by asking, "In addition to servanthood, what other nonnegotiable qualities are important?"

Having established standards won't be new to students. Most of them have to meet expectations to be a part of the school band, sports teams, or other activities.

Consider these "heart" and "action" qualities. The student—

HEART	ACTION
• Is a servant	• Serves in small ways
• Has a positive attitude	• Looks out for loners and visitors
• Is a devoted follower of Christ	• Understands the programs' purposes
• Displays an authentic Christian lifestyle	• Greets at meetings
• Is humble	• Speaks highly about the ministry
• Is friendly	
• Is approachable	

One way to avoid playing favorites is to make student leadership available to everyone once you've established criteria. Begin by teaching a series on leadership, spiritual gifts, making a difference, or other leadership-related topics. Series like these expand students' vision and challenge them to consider taking steps of faith. After teaching on leadership, tell all your students they're welcome to become leaders if their heart reflects the established criteria and they have time to follow through with the expectations. At this point, you're giving them an opportunity to say, "That's me!" or "I'm not there yet" or "How did *you* get hired for *this* job, Doug?"

While it's important to give everyone the chance to apply for student leadership, it's essential to focus on getting a commitment from those who you know are ready to be involved beyond attending a weekly program. Some students need to be nudged, because they don't believe they have what it takes to be a leader. Others simply appreciate your kind, affirming belief in them. Don't be concerned about whether it's appropriate to personally encourage students to apply. Asking is a positive leadership action.

Some truths to remember—

• Developing leaders is not an event or a summer program; it's a mindset.

• Students watch student leaders as much as (if not more than) adult leaders. Student leadership is peer pressure at its best.

• Be prepared. The most unlikely students will surprise you. Don't forget, the early church wasn't built on likely candidates. Look for potential in everyone, even the obnoxious students in the back of the room. If someone hadn't believed in me many years ago, you wouldn't be reading this book. Imagine what students can become if Jesus fully invades their lives.

• Some preconceived "stars" won't shine. Often those with the best "résumés" fall short because they're stretched in too many directions. While it's natural to be disappointed, move on and go with those who have an interest in servant leadership.

> "Using the word *obnoxious* in reference to Doug as a teenager is too mild an association."
> —*Jim Burns, Doug's former youth pastor*

Before entering full-time student ministry, I worked for several years as a high school football coach. Many of the lessons I learned as a coach have served me well and have enabled me to prevail in student ministry. One of those lessons is recognizing and understanding the key role of leadership and leadership styles—in students.

As a coach, I knew that building a championship team would take leadership—not only from the coaching staff, but also from the players. In fact, I learned that in order for our team to succeed, student leadership was needed not only from the best athlete (who was not always the best leader), but also from a variety of players, each of whom exhibited different leadership styles. The same truth applies to student ministries.

Gary Willis, author of *A Certain Trumpet,* describes how some leaders have enormous impact because their leadership styles mesh perfectly with corresponding leadership needs. Years ago I heard my pastor, Bill Hybels, explain how this same principle can work in the church. As he named several different leadership styles, I realized that many of these styles were evident in our student ministry, too. That revelation enabled me to direct student leaders more strategically and give them a clear picture of how God had specifically gifted them to lead their peers.

The following are five leadership styles you can look for and develop in your own students:

1. The visionary student spends hours dreaming about what your ministry could be. You'll often hear this student saying things like, "What if we could…" or "Why couldn't we…". The visionary student has the ability to get other students excited about your ministry's potential and displays endless enthusiasm in pursuit of it.

2. The managing student wants to make sure things get done right. This student gets excited about setting up for your program or helping plan the logistics of your summer camp. The managing student has the ability to organize the ministry for success and finds satisfaction in maintaining the systems it's built.

3. The motivational student has the ability to keep other students inspired and often recognizes those who need encouragement. You'll often see this student helping his or her friends with problems, writing encouraging notes, or making calls to friends who feel down.

4. The shepherding student loves to care for other students. This teenager makes an excellent small-group leader or apprentice. The shepherding student is relationally focused and possesses the ability to make new students feel comfortable and core students feel nourished.

5. The team-building student realizes it takes a group of students to get things done. This student is able to recognize gifts in others and knows where they should be placed for maximum effectiveness. The team-building student also sees the need for group activities that build a sense of community among peers.

Spend a few moments thinking about the students in your ministry. Are they in the best places to realize the full potential of their unique leadership styles? Strategic placement of your student leaders will allow them to build a strong team environment that will more effectively reach (evangelize) and lead (disciple) this generation to Christ.

—*Bo Boshers*

When a Student Leader Isn't Making It

A lot of students can be leaders, but being a leader in a youth ministry requires a different mentality than secular leadership: a right heart, an attitude open to change, and the action-steps of serving. I tell all my students they're welcome to apply for student leadership if they believe they meet the established standards.

You'll probably find your students are tougher critics of themselves than you are. Still, you may end up with some student leaders who don't live up to the established expectations. What do you do then?

▪ *Be specific.* The more articulate you are about your expectations for leaders, the clearer it will be to the students when they don't meet the expectations.

▪ *Don't believe all the rumors.* Before you convict a student about his behavior, give him an opportunity to respond to what you've heard. Instead of saying, "You can't be a leader anymore because you get drunk on weekends," say something like, "I want to ask you about something I've heard." This honors the student and allows him to come clean if it's true.

▪ *Don't be afraid to confront issues.* What you ignore will eventually bite you.

▪ *Be liberal with grace, compassion, and tenderness when confronting a student.* Consider giving her an opportunity to change before removing her.

▪ *Be clear about why you're asking a student to step down.* Provide a time frame. Consider saying something like, "I think it would be good if you took a season off from leadership and perhaps take on a leader role again in the fall."

▪ *Keep the specific details of the conversation between you and the student.* If other student leaders ask why, be vague so you don't assassinate the student's character. Consider saying, "Juan's taking a break and doesn't need the extra responsibility that comes with being a student leader right now." If you're pressed for more, tell the inquiring students you promised Juan you wouldn't talk about it and you're not going to. Let them know you would pay them the same respect, too.

▪ *Don't forget the student.* Follow up with phone calls, meetings, encouragement, and lots of love.

- Students are waiting for an adult to believe in them!

- Expect disappointment. Despite the high hopes you have for student leaders, they'll let you down. Don't place them on a pedestal. It's not fair to them or to the ministry.

- Student leaders require direction and attention from an adult leader. Be patient. The amount of time you and your volunteers invest will pay off.

What to Do with Student Leaders

Each student leader should have one adult pouring into her life. Is this another example of playing favorites? No. It's a strategic use of time. Since you don't want to have a shallow relationship with everyone in your ministry, it's important to focus on a select few. (Remember the 5-3-1 principle? See page 88.) Working with student leaders maximizes your time and energy. Investing in these students will pay the greatest dividends since they facilitate other aspects of ministry and help students get connected.

> If this isn't realistic now, don't worry. Make it a goal for the future.

Investing in student leaders doesn't mean you ignore the other students; however, your primary focus is on the leaders, which gives you the freedom to say no to numerous student opportunities. Saying no to some students allows you to say yes to the student leaders.

When I invest in student leaders, I focus on challenging their hearts and developing their skills.

// How you might challenge their hearts

■ *Bring a few together.* One of the greatest ways to encourage student leaders and foster their passion for the Lord is to allow them to be with others who are like-minded. Iron sharpens iron; sharp students will sharpen their leadership peers. Gathering them together doesn't need to be a monthly structured time, but look for occasional spontaneous opportunities to accomplish this.

Last year I took a car full of junior high and high school leadership students to our local convention center to see a popular charismatic healer. I'd seen this guy on TV, and I thought it would be interesting to take some leaders and expose them to a side of Christianity that they never see at our church. The outing wasn't planned in advance, and I didn't make any fliers. I simply called a few students and we went. When we got to the convention center, we waited in a long line for about an hour. We were intrigued—watching people, asking questions, laughing.

When we clearly weren't going to get into the service because it was full, we walked around and talked to people about their hopes for healing and their opinions about the man drawing the crowd. We left, bought some ice cream, and had a great discussion about God's power, sovereignty, and free will. Even though we never went inside, we had a night those students will remember. This spontaneous, three-hour trip with leadership students deepened their faith and their leader-to-leader friendships.

> If he was really a miracle worker, we would've gotten into the convention center!

■*Provide heart resources.* Whether one-on-one or as a group, make student leaders a priority. Take them with you to leadership-building events and buy them copies of great books you're reading.

When I was in high school, John, a 50-year-old adult volunteer, gave me *Spiritual Leadership.* I wasn't eager to read it because it was…well…a book, and it didn't have any pictures. But John was a respected youth worker in my church. He told me, "Doug, I see leadership potential in you, and I want you to read this book. It's influenced me, and I think it will be helpful for you. I bought it for you as a gift, and you'll give me a gift back if you read it so we can discuss it."

A gift? Wow! I couldn't believe he thought enough about me to buy me something. After I read it, we talked about it. Some of the principles in the book have shaped my life, but the most important influence was that an adult leader invested in me when I was a student leader. I'm a different person today because of people like John who have taken the time (since I was in junior high) to point me toward resources and experiences that have made me a stronger Christian and a better leader.

■ *Lead by example.* You must model what you expect from others. If I walk past empty soda cans or trash at church, so will my student leaders. They'll follow my lead. If I only have superficial conversations about the weather, sports, or school, they'll never learn to ask questions that prick the hearts of others. Leadership students watch everything you do, pay attention to what you read and the music you listen to, and take notes on how you treat your family. They're the sponges and you're the water. Your example of leadership will be a significant part of their personal development.

- *Hold them accountable.* I don't wake up looking for trouble, but when I avoid confrontation in my relationships, trouble finds me. Ignoring students who frustrate you or avoiding the tough conversations hurts everyone. Students need to be lovingly challenged so that they can learn and grow.

When teenagers commit to be student leaders, tell them you're going to go face-to-face with them when the need arises. If you find behavior inconsistent with the established leadership guidelines, talk to the student. You'll model leadership by having the tough conversations.

In addition to a willingness to confront students, you need to unashamedly hold students accountable for significant issues, such as supporting your ministry's strategy, setting and achieving goals in their spiritual lives, and living a lifestyle above reproach. Student leadership isn't a divine right; it's a privilege that needs to be reevaluated every semester.

// How you might develop their skills

- *Start with small responsibilities.* Allow students to have some ownership of their ministry! Giving students responsibilities develops new skills. Allowing student leaders to choose where to buy the pizza and how much they should order is much different than allowing unproven students to lead small groups. Give your students baby-step responsibilities before larger ones. This decreases the potential for them to make huge mistakes, while helping them build confidence.

Each year we take students to Mexico for a seven-day mission experience. I give our leadership candidates and new leaders minor responsibilities like holding the van keys, keeping the water cool, counting the freshmen, or making sure the van mirrors are attached. Everyone has a job, and each task is important. In reality, each person is participating in a series of leadership tests, a subtle but effective way to determine who is ready for leadership. Those who are faithful with the small responsibilities are ready for increasingly larger ones.

■ *Provide multiple service options for proven student leaders.* Every student is unique, so offer unique roles in ministry. Your image of student leaders might include those who can lead small groups, share testimonies, befriend loners, and clean the church van. Those are great, but don't limit students to a few obvious tasks. Student leaders can serve in many ways, if you consider ministry in broad categories:

Working with stuff
- Preparing and cleaning the meeting room
- Working the sound system
- Making videos
- Taking pictures
- Creating bulletin boards or photo albums
- Overseeing the Web site
- Designing promotional materials
- Chasing the rats out of the youth room

Working up front
- Sharing testimonies
- Leading worship
- Giving a message
- Performing dramas
- Giving announcements
- Leading games
- Praying
- Praying that someone will listen to announcements

Working with others
- Counseling peers
- Leading small groups
- Sending cards or e-mails to encourage students
- Following up with visitors
- Overseeing a ministry (greeting, video, music, et cetera)
- Discipling a younger student
- Teaching the youth pastor about Jesus

■ *Get out of the way.* Once you give students jobs, stay out of their way. Coach and encourage, but give students the freedom to accomplish their assigned tasks. Give them enough rope to do the jobs well or hang themselves (figuratively speaking, of course). People don't like others constantly looking over their shoulders. If you're frustrated or displeased with how things turn out, discuss your feelings later. Until then, allow students to succeed or fail on their own.

■ *Get student leaders in front of church leadership.* Invite student leaders to participate in church meetings; introduce them to the pastor and adult leaders. Encourage students to share what they're learning and how they're developing in their ministries. Enable church leaders to share leadership insights with them. Talk highly about them. Build them up. Let the church members see who they are and that teens are not *the future* of the church—they *are* the church.

■ *Prepare students to lead.* A simple process may help prepare students to take the next step in their development. This uncomplicated four-step method serves as an easy reminder when training students to lead:

   Learn—I do it and you watch.

   Help—We do it together.

   Practice—You do it and I watch.

   Lead—You do it on your own, and I train someone else on a new task.

Eternal Investment

I know plenty of students who, over the years, have walked away from the Lord. While I continue to pray that they'll run back into the open arms of God, I'm still disappointed and defeated over the choices they've made. One truth that continues to motivate me, however, is that many former student leaders have served God faithfully beyond the youth ministry and today live for God and love him with all their hearts. They're significantly impacting their homes, their jobs, and their churches for the kingdom of God. Leaders make a difference!

Begin looking for the next set of young leaders and help them develop into servants for God's church. You'll invest in eternity, and they'll continue to motivate and challenge your own leadership and youth ministry.

The Questions at the End of the Chapter

// For group discussion

- Are we effectively using student leaders in our ministry? If so, how? If not, why not?
- What are adults doing in our ministry that students could be doing?

// For personal reflection

- Do I really believe that students can do the work of the ministry? What makes me feel this way?
- Do I know what to look for in discovering student leaders?
- Do I consciously consider how I can reproduce myself in the life of another student?
- What resources have influenced my life that I might be able to pass on to some student leaders?

// Actions to consider

- Make a list of potential student leaders.
- Begin working on a list of qualities that student leaders should strive for. Add to your list the specific actions you want them doing in your ministry and in their schools.

Go to www.dougfields.com and enter your comments under Your First 2 Years: Chapter 9

10

are we doing the right thing?

evaluating youth ministry programs

I have a friend who isn't too excited about going to the dentist. Most of humanity falls into this category, but this particular friend avoids the dentist like I avoid weighing myself in December. He used to skip his check-ups because he couldn't stand the scraping, deep flossing, polishing, and sandblasting. Even the end result—clean teeth and the prevention of tooth decay—didn't motivate him to keep his check-ups.

Recently, something happened that changed his life and his view of dentists. Now, he's all about dental check-ups. He's crazy about them. He talks about them to others constantly; he's practically a dental evangelist.

The cause of his attitude shift was pain. After more than five years of no dental check-ups, he showed up to the dentist's office with 21 (count 'em—21) cavities. He had 16 cavities on one side of his mouth and five on the other. He had so many cavities that the dentist had to take breaks from drilling because his hand was getting cramps. When your mouth wears out the dentist, you've got serious problems.

Youth ministry programs need regular check-ups to stay healthy and prevent youth ministry pain. You may be thinking, "Why evaluate? I've barely started my ministry?" The earlier you get in the habit of performing regular check-ups, the healthier your ministry will be. You don't want to wait for major decay to appear in your ministry before you act.[3]

> This isn't fun, but it's too important to skip.

The Importance of Evaluation

Ministry evaluation can be categorized as a biblical command. Many Scriptures urge believers to examine the condition of their hearts.[4] Since we can't separate our hearts from ministry, it makes sense that we should also examine the heart (or condition) of our ministries.

Consistent and accurate evaluation humbles me, and humility is a great way to be used by God. When I take the time to honestly evaluate our ministry, I find glaring weak spots. If I ever think our ministry is strong, a little evaluation quickly dissipates my pride. It's also humbling and exciting when evaluation points to the work of the Holy Spirit. When I depend on God's power, I inevitably experience things that can't be explained except by acknowledging the Holy Spirit did it. I love these moments since I don't want everything in youth ministry reduced to human explanations.

While some evaluation reveals the spontaneous nature of God's Spirit, most evaluation requires a degree of structure. Structure is a scary word for many youth workers. Skin grows clammy, hearts are locked in terror, and fear descends upon them from the shadows of doubt (okay, possible overstatement). I know these feelings firsthand, but I've overcome the sweaty palms, fear, and doubt. I'll remove some of the mystery with questions to help you evaluate your ministry.

Four Evaluation Questions

I'm not a great chess player, but I love it because it's the ultimate strategy game. Before playing chess, you need to know the basic capabilities and limitations of each piece so

---

[3]*Purpose-Driven. Youth Ministry* is a companion to this book. In it you learn how biblical purposes for ministry are more important than programs. My intent with this chapter is for you to learn how to evaluate programs once you've implemented the biblical principles.

[4]See Psalm 4:4, Lamentations 3:40, 1 Corinthians 11:28, 2 Corinthians 13:5.

you can create a plan of attack. You ask key questions of each piece: "What move can the knight make? Who is more powerful, the knight or the rook?" Your strategy will be incomplete and ineffective if you don't give careful consideration to the role of each piece.

Youth ministry requires, as does chess, a clear image of the essentials of a youth ministry program. When you know the essentials, you can evaluate them by asking directed questions. I use four questions:

1. Have we identified the primary biblical purposes for this program (evangelism, fellowship, discipleship, ministry or worship)?

2. Are we reaching our target audience with this program?

3. Have we met our specific intended outcomes for this program?

4. Are leaders fulfilling their responsibilities for this program?

Let's take a closer look at each.

// 1. Have we identified the primary biblical purposes for this program?

I don't need to convince you of the importance of having a solid biblical foundation for your youth ministry. If your ministry isn't built on God's Word, please stop until it is. God has clearly communicated the purposes for his Church. Several New Testament passages reveal his purposes, but two famous passages summarize all five biblical purposes.

The Great Commandment
*Jesus replied: "**Love the Lord your God with all your heart** and with all your soul and with all your mind.' This is the first and greatest commandment. And the second is like it: '**Love your neighbor as yourself.**'"* (Matthew 22:37-39)

The Great Commission
*Therefore **go** and make disciples of all nations, **baptizing them** in the name of the Father and of the Son and of the Holy Spirit, and **teaching them to obey** everything I have commanded you. And surely I am with you always, to the very end of the age.* (Matthew 28:19-20)

The five biblical purposes are clear and comprehensive:

If you've already read *Purpose-Driven® Youth Ministry*, this is a good review.

Biblical command	Familiar term	Definition
• love the Lord your God	• worship	1. celebrating God's presence in our lives and glorifying his name
• love your neighbor as yourself	• ministry	2. meeting needs through love and servanthood
• go and make disciples	• evangelism	3. sharing the Good News of Christ with the lost
• baptizing them (symbol of fellowship)	• fellowship[5]	4. Christians connecting with one another through powerful and authentic community and relationships
• teaching them to obey	• discipleship	5. teaching Christians God's truth and the necessity of obeying his Word

God's perfect design for his church is captured in these five biblical purposes.[6]

Everything you do for students should be an attempt to fulfill one of these biblical purposes in your youth ministry and in students' hearts. Evaluation begins by determining that you do indeed have at least one, primary biblical purpose for each program.

[5] Of the five purposes, the connection between baptism and fellowship is the toughest to grasp. Rick Warren explains it this way in *The Purpose-Driven® Church*: "In the Greek text of the Great Commission, there are three present participle verbs: going, baptizing, and teaching. Each of these is a part of the command to 'make disciples.' Going, baptizing, and teaching are the essential elements of the disciple-making process. At first glance you might wonder why the Great Commission gives the same prominence to the simple act of baptism as it does to the great tasks of evangelism and edification. Obviously, Jesus did not mention it by accident. Why is baptism so important to warrant an inclusion in Christ's Great Commission? I believe it is because it symbolizes one of the purposes of the church: fellowship—identification with the body of Christ...Baptism is not only a symbol of salvation, it is a symbol of fellowship" (page 105).

[6] For further reading about the five biblical purposes, see *Purpose-Driven® Youth Ministry*, Chapter 2.

// 2. Are we reaching our target audience with this program?

After you have determined whether each of your programs has a primary biblical purpose, decide whether you're targeting—trying to reach—the right group with each particular program.

Consider your personal life for a moment. You treat people in different ways depending on your relationship with them:

- Your next-door neighbor
- Your boss
- A casual friend
- The restaurant server
- A stranger
- Your best friend
- A coworker who isn't a Christian
- Your spiritual mentor
- The telemarketer who calls during dinner

If all of these people came to your home, you'd probably act differently with each one. For example, you wouldn't invite a stranger in to your home to show them your baby photos. You wouldn't be surprised if your best friend walked into the kitchen and opened the refrigerator. Chances are, you wouldn't share deep-rooted doubts about your faith with a nonbeliever. And you'd show a unique respect to your spiritual mentor because of her influence on your life.

Imagine you need to communicate a spiritual truth (such as God's available forgiveness) to the people listed. You'd do that differently as well. With your best friend, you'd need to live forgiveness before you could teach it. With a non-Christian coworker, you'd use simple terminology, avoiding Christian words she wouldn't understand. You would keep your target in mind as you seek to communicate God's truth clearly.

Consider your youth ministry programs as being like personal, one-on-one relationships—only bigger. A single program cannot effectively target all the different spiritual audiences that your ministry contacts. Since your ministry exists to spiritually impact the lives of students, you should consider students' varying spiritual commitments.

This is important to understand because any one program typically frustrates people who aren't part of the target. It's that simple, and it's that complex. You won't please everyone with one program. That's okay.

To best understand this evaluation question, consider the word *discernment*. You want to discern the type of student you're trying to reach with each particular program.

Your ministry may have several different examples of target groups. For example—

2 Targets
- Non-Christians
- Christians

3 Targets
- Nonchurched
- Churched
- Christian leader

4 Targets
- Forced to attend
- Attends for social interaction
- Confesses Christ
- Student leader

5 Targets
- Community
- Crowd
- Congregation
- Committed
- Core[7]

[7]Community students are committed to *not attending church*—they are living apart from Christ; Crowd students are committed to *attending our church*—they are hearing about Christ; Congregation students are committed to a *small group*—they have a relationship with Christ and with other Christians; Committed students are committed to *spiritual habits*—they are growing in Christ; Core students are committed to *doing ministry*—they are serving because of Christ. (See Chapter 5 in *Purpose-Driven® Youth Ministry* for more detailed definitions of the target groups.)

When you aim for a specific target, you can deemphasize other targets during that one specific program. If your Sunday school program targets committed Christian students, you understand when non-Christians attend and don't comprehend everything. Likewise, if your Sunday school targets non-Christians, you'll understand when committed Christians don't feel challenged.

> "So is that why everyone hates coming to my Sunday school class?"
> —a confused youth worker

One of my student leaders recently said, "Everyone in my small group lacks spiritual depth. No one is ever serious." While I dislike hyperbole (*everyone, no one*) I tried to use his comment as a positive teaching moment. I responded, "That particular Bible study isn't intended for you. You've grown up in the church, heard all the Bible stories, and know all the answers. Most of the students who show up aren't like you. They know little about the Bible, and they need the basics. You're not the target for that type of small group. We have a different small group that would be more suitable for your spiritual depth."

Spiritual growth, without exception, involves some level of frustration. When a program targets a specific spiritual commitment, those less spiritually mature are critical and say, "We don't need that." The significantly more mature are frustrated and say, "Why aren't we going deeper?" Comments won't sting when you have taken time to specify the target for your programs. You can respond to criticism with confidence, rather than defensiveness.

In my early years of ministry I was crushed by the comments of students and parents directed at our programs. I tried to make everyone happy, and I was a miserable failure at it. I can remember coming home and angrily saying to Cathy, "People want it their way, on their day, and want it taught with what they'd say." She tried to be empathetic, but we both realized I had just spat out a lame rhyme, and we both began to laugh. Laughter released the tension I felt trying to meet all the needs.

When I learned how to target programs, I became a confident youth worker. I was much happier. Some people were still disappointed that

> You don't need five different programs to fulfill all five biblical principles and reach all your targets.

we were pursing evangelism on Wednesday night when they wanted discipleship. Even when I pointed them to discipleship venues, they wanted it on the night we were focusing on evangelistic programs. Instead of feeling inadequate, I'm able to say, "I'm sorry.

We have what you're looking for. It's just not tonight."

// 3. Have we met our specific intended outcomes for this program?

In addition to evaluating the biblical purposes and target audiences, seek to identify the accuracy and relevance of the specific intended outcomes for each program. There's a big difference between an evangelistic outreach program (targeting the unchurched) and a program that equips mature Christian students to share their faith. Both programs fulfill the biblical purpose of evangelism, but their intended outcomes are different—one presents the gospel and the other trains students how to present the gospel. Evangelism is a broad biblical purpose. You can't hope to fulfill all that's evangelistic with a single program.

Doug!
It so totally worked! Okay, are you ready?
It's time for our monthly board meeting, and the board members start talking about why we do church and how nothing ever seems to change. So I say, "Well, do you mind if I give my report? Because I think what God has revealed to me as a youth pastor could really help our church." The pastor said, "Sure."
I talked about discovering the biblical purposes for youth ministry (I had the Scriptures right there). I explained the different target audiences and took the board through each of our programs, demonstrating what our purpose was for each. I explained how we evaluated the youth ministry after my first year, discovered we were heavy on fellowship and zero on evangelism, and finally how we modified what we were doing so we could continue moving toward a healthy, balanced youth ministry.
And God moved.
The lights came on, man! The board members started asking me questions, and by the end of the meeting my pastor said he would break down all the church programs according to their biblical purpose and defined target audience.
You need to understand that our church was dying. This was a turning point for us. A really big deal! I wanted to write and tell you about and thank you for challenging me to evaluate.
—John-Michael McGinnis

Even with the same target in mind, a single biblical purpose may be fulfilled in different ways. Say your purpose is discipleship and your target is mature believers. One church may offer discussion groups about controversial topics from the Scriptures while another church uses a lecture format without discussion. Both are discipleship programs for the same target audience, yet they look different. That's fine!

This third evaluation question requires you to have a specific list of your intended results. You answer the questions, "What do we want to accomplish with this program? Do we actually accomplish it?"

Let's apply these two questions to our small group example. The primary biblical purpose for our groups is fellowship. We're trying to connect Christian students—our target for this program—with other believers. A secondary biblical purpose that emerges is discipleship. For us, an ideal small group has an intended outcome of 70 percent fellowship and 30 percent discipleship. Percentages communicate to leaders what we want to accomplish. We want our students to grow closer to one another (fellowship) and deepen their walk with Christ (discipleship), using the Bible as our primary focus for discussion.

> There's no single, ideal formula for finding balance with all your programs. But without evaluation, you'll never find it.

The intended outcomes we're looking for in small groups are—

- Group interaction (I call it life-on-life)
- Studying Scripture
- Personal sharing and prayer

When these outcomes are known, small group leaders can evaluate on their own every week.

Do you notice that our small group strategy isn't designed to reach everyone? When a student says, "My non-Christian friend didn't feel comfortable at small group last night," my response is, "I'm glad you care enough about your friend to teach him about Jesus. But these small groups are designed for students who are already followers of Christ. Of course, we won't kick out your friend, but you may want to bring him to our Saturday night program instead. It's specifically designed to introduce non-Christians to the teachings and person of Jesus Christ." This conversation is easy to have when your purpose is clear, your target is identified, and your outcomes are known.

// 4. Are leaders fulfilling their responsibilities for this program?

The final evaluation question involves leaders (adults and students). The success of a program is often directly related to the quality of leadership. To help your leaders succeed, you must clearly communicate the attitudes and actions you're expecting. If you expect them to act as shepherds, make that clear to them or they'll end up as do-nothing chaperones.

> Chaperones don't last. Shepherds do.

Let's return to the example of our small group program. I ask my small group leaders to embody the following roles:

- *Lover of God:* Maintain a healthy personal relationship with God.

- *Pastor/shepherd:* Know the spiritual condition of your small group members.

- *Leader:* Maintain a small group focused on our intended outcomes (group interaction, life-on-life, studying Scripture, and personal sharing and prayer).

- *Servant:* Serve; goes hand-in-hand with being a leader and is reflected in the unseen ways.

- *Communicator:* Know what's happening within our youth ministry and inform your small group.

I also request that leaders follow through on the following:

Once a week:

- Prepare for leading your small group.
- Pray for all leaders and small groups.
- Show up when your small group is scheduled to meet.
- Contact anyone who visits your small group within one week.
- Contact anyone who has missed two weeks or more.

Once a month:

- Make contact with your regular students through a phone call, a letter, or a one-on-one or same-sex activity outside of your small group time.

- Have a conversation with your coach (the person overseeing the small group leaders) and share your victories, struggles, and questions.

Now that you have a general understanding of these four questions, we can be more specific about how to get the answers and what to do with them.

Once You Know the Questions to Ask...

Take these four steps as you attempt to answer your evaluation questions.

// 1. Discern the real.

In spite of the pain it may involve, begin your evaluation by determining "the real"—what is right and wrong in a particular program. You're seeking truth. Your evaluation will only be as effective as it is honest.

■ *Strive for objectivity.* It may be difficult to be objective depending on how much blood, sweat, and tears you've invested into a particular program. We often see only what we want to see.

■ *Observe without responsibility.* If you play a major role in the program (say, teaching the lesson), then find someone else to take over your responsibilities for a week or two so you attend to observe. Other responsibilities can hinder objectivity.

I find it difficult to stand back and only observe. I've tried to fool myself into thinking, "I can teach during this program and evaluate everything else." It doesn't work. I'm busy reading my audience, thinking about my message, wondering who the student is that's flirting with my daughter while I'm speaking and so forth. My best evaluations happen when I show up with no responsibilities.

■ *Talk to others.* Get feedback from others regarding particular elements in your program. You don't need to walk these people through four evaluation questions. Simply ask a few directed questions: "As a leader of this program, what do you feel your responsibility is?" or "What do you think about the music on Wednesday nights?" Seek feedback from a variety of participants.

- *Write down your conclusions.* I've found that when I don't write down evaluation responses, I can't piece the evaluation together completely and don't remember who said what. If you're young, you may think memory is an age thing, but what you may not realize is…well…uh…it's on the tip of my tongue…never mind.

- *Review with a trusted source.* Wisdom is found in the counsel of others. Find a safe individual who will listen to your findings and offer honest, caring feedback.

// 2. Define the ideal.

Once you've assessed what you actually have, consider what it ought to be. The operative word is *dream*. Paint a fantastic mental picture of God working powerfully in the lives of those involved with the program. This stage is fun. Put your head into the clouds to dream about the magnificent what-ifs. Don't abandon reality, but create a picture of what the perfect program would look like. When

{A VOICE FROM THE TRENCHES}

Being new youth pastors (just six months old!), my wife and I are creating and carrying out our events and small groups for the first time. Our "great" ideas don't always go as planned, so we write what we call "post-event reports" (we want to remember what specific things went really well, and what didn't).

We start off the report by stating the goal for the event (this is also good to do at the beginning of the event, in order to stay on track). The goal is specific: for instance, "To provide a place where our students can bring unchurched friends." Then we summarize the event—e.g., when, where, cost, what advertisements we used, concerns, reactions—in two paragraphs. Third, we evaluate the event based on the goal we set, and we state whether or not we thought the event helped us achieve our goal. We try to be brutally honest with ourselves and get feedback from youth, sponsors, and parents—and include those comments in this section. The last suggestion consists of our suggestions for future use. This is very helpful when planning other events, because after a while, we establish patterns and trends regarding what works well in our group.

This Post Report has become a valuable tool for us, because it allows us to study a completed event and figure out what we can do better next time.

Post Game (Post Report, Fall)

Post Game ran from August 31 through October 12 on Friday nights from 9:30 p.m. to 11 p.m.

Goal: To provide students with an alternative to negative after-football activities.

Summary: Basketball was the main activity at the first two Post Games, but since our outdoor activities disturbed the neighbors (lights and noise keep them and their baby awake), further activities were held indoors. On most Fridays, Nintendo was set up in the main sanctuary, students played with instruments on stage, and sometimes they played games in the A building. One time we all played Sardines in the dark in the B building. Between nine and 15 students (mostly guys) attended each Friday night.

October 12 was Broomball Night (10 p.m. at Gateway Ice Center). The cost was $5 per student. The 22nd Street Baptist Church went as well. Thirty-three students from CCF attended the event, making it the most highly attended Post Game activity. We returned to CCF at 12:30 a.m.

evaluating at this stage the four questions are slightly altered:

- What primary biblical purpose or purposes *should* this program fulfill?
- Who *should* this program target?
- What exactly *should* be happening?
- What *should* the leaders do at this program?

In the first evaluation step, you discerned what is; in this second step you define what ought to be.

▪ *Be in prayer.* Seek God's direction by asking him to reveal truth to you and through others. Your ministry is his ministry. It's one thing to poorly execute the first step—discerning "the real"—because the only negative consequence is misperception. Leading God's people down a path that isn't in his plan is another problem entirely.

Evaluation: By far the most successful (as far as attendance and the fun factor) Friday was Broomball Night. Students brought friends, and new, unsponsored students also attended the event.

The rest of the Post Games were pretty boring, unstructured, and not well attended. Because the purpose of this event is to provide an alternative to after-football stuff, it's important that our Post Games are high-energy, fun events that students want to attend with their friends. Our Post Games were unsuccessful in achieving our goal.

Suggestions: Next fall, Post Game must have more energy and must be fun every time. We hope the following suggestions achieve the excellence we're after:

- Post Game will not occur every Friday night. Perhaps only once a month.
- We'll collect ideas for more enjoyable Post Games over the spring and summer. Some we're already considering include broomball, laser tag, visiting Buckaloo Farms (for Pumpkins and the corn maze), and Funtastiks.
- We'll publicize Post Game by highlighting specific events. We'll give students flyers that they can give to their friends.
- Costs will be subsidized by the student budget as much as possible to allow unchurched students to attend for free.

—*Jeremy Veatch, pastor to the next generation, Community Church of the Foothills, Tucson, Arizona*

> Prayer should be part of all the action-steps.

▪ *Learn from others.* One of the most important characteristics of healthy leadership is learning. If you hope to guide your ministry toward change, expose yourself to the ideas, creativity, and wisdom of others. Being an isolated visionary is overrated. Vision often comes as a result of shared thoughts.

// 3. Determine the growth areas.

Now compare the two pictures—the real and the ideal—you've created. Identify the differences. List all the changes you need to make to move to your ideal. No matter how wide the gap is between what you have and what you want, take time to determine what it will take to get there, including interim steps.

You may know what you've got and what you want, but you're baffled about how to move toward your goal. That's fine. Don't get too hung up on the how-to just yet. Commit to write down every action step it will take to move your program closer to the ideal. Don't allow yourself to become emotionally paralyzed when you list more tasks than you can possibly manage. Just because you write them all down doesn't mean they must all be accomplished. This step forces you to identify what needs to be done.

// 4. Make adjustments.

This final step is proactive. Now it's time to make the necessary changes to your ideal. This stage is so important that I've devoted the entire next chapter to this subject. Chances are that the list of steps to move from the real to the ideal is overwhelming—and some factors are impossible to change.

You'll want to begin with the most important and most-likely-to-be-accomplished actions. Discern which changes should happen first; then move forward.

No one is thrilled by missing the mark. One man's performance review is another man's firing squad. Evaluation can be intimidating. But serious youth workers cannot afford to gloss over evaluation. "The wisdom of the prudent is to give thought to their ways" *(Proverbs 14:8)*. Evaluation won't always be a pleasant exercise, but it's an important one.

"But, 'If It Ain't Broke...'"

I know. You agree with all of that. Evaluation is important. But as you thumb through the pages of this chapter, you're likely tempted to say, "I don't go to the doctor unless I feel sick (for, like, a month straight), I don't take my car to the mechanic until the dashboard lights cause me hypnotic episodes, and I don't go to the dentist...umm...*ever.* So why should I consider evaluating my youth ministry when everything's going so well?"

Let's put it this way: From what we can tell, the first few days aboard the Titanic were delightful; it was the latter part of the cruise that needed some serious help. And by then, it was a little late.

A wise helmsman always scans the horizon for potential hazards, even when the sky is blue and the sailing is smooth.

Maybe it's broke, and we just don't know it yet

In C.S. Lewis' *The Pilgrim's Regress,* the Guide warns his fellow travelers, "You all know...that security is mortals' greatest enemy." Sometimes in ministry we're lured from our posts at the helm of the ship by the common mythologies of youth work—mythologies that often breed false senses of security.

Myth #1: God's blessing means God's sanction. It's an unwritten rule in the Christian community that if a ministry is growing and flourishing, then there's nothing wrong. "God is blessing us, right? Therefore, we must be okay...right?"

Well, not exactly. A flourishing youth ministry is no absolute indication that God sanctions either its methods or attitudes. Poor youth ministry doesn't always bear poor fruit right away, either. (Even a bad crop can look good before harvest.) It will take several seasons of ministry before you see the full and true fruit of your work, especially in youth ministry.

In fact, we may even seriously struggle in our ministries precisely *because* we are doing God's will. (Consider Moses, Elijah, Jeremiah, Jesus, and Paul.) God's blessing on our ministries says more about his abounding grace than about whether we've chosen right or wrong courses. We can't excuse ourselves from evaluation just because God is "blessing" our work.

Myth #2: We've been doing this for a while, and we pretty much know what we're doing. With that arrogant assumption, we put off evaluation, smugly assured that no one knows how to do the job better than us. We've peaked. There's no way we can improve on what we're doing. (Remember the Titanic: "Full steam ahead! Nothing can bring this boat down.")

In their classic work on corporate management, *In Search of Excellence,* Thomas Peters and Robert H. Waterman judge that the most discouraging fact of big corporate life is "the loss of what got them big in the first place: Innovation." As the company grows, it typically becomes more careful, less willing to take risks. They note a National Science Foundation study (reported in *Inc.*) in which researchers found that "small firms produced about four times as many innovations per research- and-development dollar as medium-sized firms, and about twenty- four times as many as large firms." Peters and Waterman conclude that excellent companies give employees the freedom to discover better ways to do what they do.

When a youth program is small, the leadership is hungry and desperate, willing to try anything. Sparks fly. Some mistakes are made, but creativity happens, and kids get excited. As the group grows, however, the leadership often becomes more conservative, less willing to try new ideas, more conscious of trying to maintain current standards than trying to reach for new goals.

The corporate claim of Hewlett-Packard is, "We never stop asking, 'What if?'" Unfortunately the claim in many churches (and their youth ministries) is, "We never stop asking, 'Why should we?'" One of the dangers of a "successful" youth ministry is its tendency to assume there's nothing to learn from other ministries. That kind of myopia blinds us to innovations that might strengthen our programs. Sometimes good evaluation can help blind eyes see.

Myth #3: The experts know best. We love the safety of doing what the experts say. That gets us off the hook. "Thus saith Youth Specialties...." "Thus saith Willow Creek...." "Thus saith Group...." That places upon *the experts* the responsibility for *our* ministries. But remember, just because a method has been published in a youth ministry book somewhere doesn't mean it's the best one; it just means it's the best one known to that author. The experts are only experts because they've made almost every mistake at least once!

Myth #4: "But it works....!" She came up to me just prior to the last session of a weeklong camp. It had been a wonderful week, and she thought of the perfect way to finish it out.

"I brought this CD with the song, 'Thank you, Lord.' Why don't we play it for the kids in this last session? Every time I've played it at other camps, *everybody* has cried...."

It was a totally sincere comment from a big-hearted leader who loved her students and wanted to maximize their experience. But the premise troubled me: *If we can find a way to get all the kids crying, it must be a good programming idea.* In other words, one of her ways of evaluating a youth ministry idea was, "Does it make kids cry? Does it move them emotionally? If it does, it must be worthy."

Just because a programming idea "works"—whether it's a coffee house or small group program or innovative media or unique evangelistic approach—doesn't alone make it valid. Your church might host an evangelistic "kegger" and have an unbelievable outreach—why *wouldn't* unchurched kids show up from miles around? But that doesn't make it a good idea. The question is: *What does it work for? What does it work toward? Is there another way we can attract kids?*

That's why this chapter's emphasis on goals and targets is so critical. A good surgeon doesn't perform gall bladder surgery on every patient just because it's been helpful in the past. She diagnoses the problem and then works to heal. Don't pull out your scalpel and clamps until you've taken time to probe.

The basic lesson of this chapter is an important one: If your ministry "ain't broke," nobody's saying to break it; however, it just might be wise to (at least) break it open long enough to look inside—long enough to ask the tough questions, long enough to check the scriptural vital signs. Don't operate until you evaluate.

—*Duffy Robbins*

▪ *Keep the big picture in mind.* As you determine specific areas that require change, don't lose focus of other areas of your ministry. Youth ministry is the sum of many elements. Don't allow one program to consume all of your time and energy.

▪ *Master the good-enough principle.* If you put too much time into a project, you may end up with a creation far above what you need. Not everything needs to be perfect. If you spend 10 hours designing the supreme promotional flier but only 20 people will read it, you've wasted time. You could have called all 20 people and had an in-depth, 30-minute conversation with each one about the program! If something is good enough, then everything above that is a waste of time and energy.

Now that you're acquainted with the evaluation process, solidify and personalize these ideas by putting them into practice. Begin by selecting one program within your ministry and working through all four steps. Understanding this evaluation process is useless unless you apply it.

Evaluation should be ongoing, especially for major areas within your ministry.

When and What to Evaluate

Up to this point in the chapter, I've focused on programs. Now, let's turn to other types of evaluations. Evaluate the nonprogram areas of your ministry (your spiritual well-being, your relationships) throughout the weeks, months and years.

// What you might evaluate weekly (volunteer and lead youth worker)

▪ *Your spiritual health.* (See Chapter 3.) We often wait for a big bomb to drop before we make changes that affect our spiritual journey. At least once a week, briefly consider the condition of your heart. Spend time in silence before God and rest in his grace.

▪ *How you spent your time.* Make the most of every opportunity God sets before you. He's given you just the right amount of time. The question is, "Did you maximize it?"

This doesn't mean you're always busy with a ministry task or responsibility. The best use of your time may be to relax and be rested. Overworking is the most common ministry plague I've seen—for rookies and veterans alike. This is one of the most important areas of your life to evaluate. Your management of time will be important to your future.

// What you might evaluate monthly (volunteer and lead youth worker)

▪ *Personal relationships within the ministry.* Consider the quality of your relational connectedness with people involved in your ministry. What friendships need a little extra work? Which ones are strong? How are relationships with students in your small group? Who needs encouragement or direction? Have you left conflict unresolved? Monthly evaluation guards against the accumulation of relational baggage and hinders ministry.

// What you might evaluate quarterly (lead youth worker)

▪ *Leadership care structure.* As you develop leaders for your ministry, it's important to care for them. You'll spend more time with leaders than students as your ministry grows. Four times a year, review your system for shepherding your leaders.

I can remember going to lunch by myself to evaluate my volunteers. I wrote their names on a napkin so I could throw it away without anyone but me knowing the results. Next to each name, I gave them an A, B, or C grade:

A: Great volunteers. Praise them.

B: Good volunteers. Help them to A; don't let them slip to C.

C: Volunteers in need of coaching or a transition. Help them make a better fit or move to a different ministry.

Obviously, this wasn't scientific, but the process kept my volunteer staff fresh in my mind and helped me act on behalf of my volunteers later on.

■ *Debrief special events.* Evaluate a special event as soon as it's over, so you can capture your best thoughts. Write down what went right, what went wrong, and what you might do differently next time. Consider gathering the opinions and insights of leaders who participated.

■ *Primary programs, general review.* Don't let more than three months pass without doing a general review of your *main* youth ministry programs. Without regular evaluation, you revert to autopilot. Negative patterns go unchecked. You don't need to do spring cleaning every three months, but dusting prevents difficulties from becoming problems. Schedule an hour for this review. Put it on your calendar as an appointment so you keep it.

// What you might evaluate yearly (entire youth ministry leadership team)

■ *Programs, specific review.* Put all your major programs under a microscope once a year. Get radical. Challenge everything you do. Use fresh perspectives from others. Don't be afraid to make hamburger out of the sacred cow. You don't have to examine all of your programs at once; use strategic times throughout the year to thoroughly evaluate. Our small groups break for the summer, so that's when we evaluate them.

When I consult for other churches, I encourage them to cut half of their youth ministry programs if they want to be healthier. Sometimes they already knew to do this; they just needed to hear it from a neutral party. Remember: bigger isn't better; healthier is better.

■ *Leadership effectiveness.* Evaluate the effectiveness of your volunteers. Every year, I give my leaders the opportunity to resign if they need to take a break for a season. This opportunity communicates the value of health. My leaders know that the condition of their hearts is their most important gift to our ministry, and if their hearts aren't right, they should get a break.

Remember: health will take time.

■ *Spiritual health of all students.* Get a grasp on the collective spiritual pulse of the students in your ministry. Since you probably don't need new information about each student, use an anonymous survey to help you get an accurate assessment.

■ *Training materials/job descriptions/leader orientation packets:* Evaluate all the materials you give to your leaders. This allows you to rework or enhance your written information each year.

At this point, we've looked at four questions that need to be asked about a youth ministry program, four steps of evaluation, and a yearly schedule for evaluation. Now take some time to evaluate your programs.

As you evaluate, try to imagine a balanced youth ministry that expresses all five biblical purposes. You may have three awesome programs, but if collectively they only fulfill discipleship and fellowship, you're out of balance.

Balance doesn't mean adding more programs or jamming all the biblical purposes into a single program. If you simply add more programs, you'll burn out your students and leaders and make them dependent on programs for spiritual growth. If you try to implement all the biblical purposes in one program, the result is a diluted program that's usually ineffective.

Balance doesn't happen overnight. That's okay. But it won't ever happen if you don't evaluate.

The Questions at the End of the Chapter

// For group discussion

- What one program do you believe is our strongest? Why? Which one is our weakest? Why?
- What could we do to enhance our evaluation times?

// For personal reflection

- Are the five biblical purposes apparent in my own life?
- Do I know the target audience(s) and biblical purpose(s) for each of our programs?
- Am I normally supportive during times when we evaluate and consider changing one of my favorite programs?
- How would I evaluate myself as a youth worker?
- What do I need to evaluate on an on-going basis?

// Actions to consider

- Establish some specific dates when you can evaluate areas of your ministry described in this chapter.
- To find out answers to the second bulleted question (under "For personal reflection," above), ask the appropriate leader.

Go to www.dougfields.com and enter your comments under Your First 2 Years: Chapter 10

how do i make changes?
navigating the phases of change

After many hours of outlining, writing, editing, and rewriting this chapter, I got the giggles. My laughter was rooted in hysterical memories of countless youth ministry experiences when I anxiously sought guidance to figure out how to make changes without getting killed by the people who would be hurt by the changes. I laughed so I wouldn't cry remembering the painful experiences.

Change has a way of making or breaking youth ministry leaders, especially within their first two years. Some leaders boldly and blindly rearrange their ministry regardless of people's responses. Others are paralyzed by the thought of suggesting change because they fear negative reactions. You have no easy, magic-formula, works-every-time procedure to implement change, but you can take some definitive actions to minimize conflict. Before discussing the phases of change, let me introduce a few basic truths regarding change.

Truths about Change

// There is no change without pain.

I'm sure you've heard the phrase, "No pain, no gain." While this usually applies to weight lifting, it's also true in ministry. You can't experience the benefits of change without experiencing a little pain. Even small changes can create pain.

When we changed from sitting in rows to sitting around tables, people were hurt. I wanted to say, "Come on, folks! Are you seriously angry over how we arrange chairs? This is crazy. People are dying of starvation in our world. Get mad about that instead."

I've caused pain by changes as simple as adjusting a meeting time by a half hour, moving locations, using a different color for our bulletin, teaching with more than one Bible translation, and by removing a couch from our youth room! These seemed trivial in comparison to the biggies: canceling programs, changing camp locations, asking volunteers to make different commitments, replacing a favorite curriculum, or performing a live Old Testament sacrifice.[8]

Why does change bring pain? Because change brings loss, sadness, and disappointment, understandable feelings when the outcome is unknown or untested. Even though I made many changes over the course of my career, I understand why people hate change. It scares them, even when change brings good results.

// People love to repeat the familiar.

Have you heard any of these phrases?

- If it's not broken, why fix it?
- We've never done it that way before!
- We've always done it this way.
- This new idea won't be better than the way we did before.
- Why does it need to be changed?
- You'll be referred to as the antichrist if you change this.

The familiar is comfortable. The past taps into all of our rational senses. Can you imagine a critic saying, "I can know about the present because I've lived in the past, and I saw

---

[8] Okay. Hopefully by now you recognize my humor attempts and at least realize that I would never, *ever* replace a favorite curriculum!

that program work. It's a proven winner. Why mess with it? Let's just do what we've always done. It's too risky to change."

In the Old Testament, Moses dealt with this issue of accepting change. God instructed him to speak to the rock and the water would flow (Numbers 20:8). The Israelites were thirsty and complaining. Instead, Moses did what he had done in the past when he was in a similar situation—he struck the rock with his staff. Even though Moses had direct orders from God, his actions communicated, "We've never done it that way before. I've struck the rock in the past, and I was successful. I don't want to try getting water in a new way." His disobedience had severe consequences. He didn't get to lead the people into the Promised Land.

The people who typically resist change are the ones most deeply rooted in the past, those who believe there's only one way to get water. They'd rather disobey than try a new way. But, if hearts are right, these people can be more easily moved toward accepting change than people with impure or hardened hearts. One's spiritual maturity corresponds with a willingness to accept change; even though one would love to repeat the familiar, a right heart is open to change.

// Programs can and should change.

As our world changes, the church has to change methods without changing or compromising its message. New problems require new solutions, and new situations require attitude shifts. Change isn't a theological issue (God isn't against change) as much as a sociological problem (people don't like change). Since the biblical purposes are eternal, the youth ministry programs should adapt when they don't achieve the biblical purposes they're designed for.

For example, Sunday school began as an evangelistic way to teach people how to read. The original idea was to give illiterate people a Bible and a formal education on the one day of the week when they didn't work—Sunday (hence the name Sunday school). Starting Sunday school was a brilliant idea to get people into the church while meeting a social need.

Today in many churches, Sunday school has become a sacred tradition. Most youth workers couldn't change the format of Sunday school if they brought a written note from Jesus himself. Is Sunday school the problem? No! Please don't misunderstand what I'm trying to communicate. Sunday school is wonderful if it fulfills a biblical purpose and has a target audience. (See Chapter 10.)

Most Sunday school programs are discipleship oriented, which is great…if the audience has Christians. Why do students complain about Sunday school? Because the church is trying to force discipleship on uninterested and non-Christian students.

Instead of evaluating and reinventing Sunday school to reach uninterested students, we fight to maintain status quo and confidently proclaim, "Sunday school is for discipleship and we won't change it until the Rapture." Most of the time, this statement shows ignorance of the fact that Sunday school has already changed over the years since evangelism isn't the focus. If you're unwilling to change a program, you'll soon find it ineffective.[9]

// Change requires flexible leaders.

If you're the one standing in the way of change, I challenge you to evaluate your heart's condition. What are you holding on to? Why are you resistant? What are your motives? Are they pure? Might you be blocking the work of God in your youth ministry because of your pride? Have you evaluated the real reasons for your inflexibility?

If you haven't pursued a self-evaluation, please do so soon. When you find yourself resisting change, defending status quo, or fighting to repeat the past because it worked before, watch out! Like Moses, you may be on the verge of losing your place of leadership.

Healthy youth ministries have leaders who are confident, wise, discerning, humble, and flexible. They watch with anticipation to see what God might be doing. God is creative. He's not limited to your ideas of how he should work.

// Change requires faith-filled leaders.

Remember when you were a child and your friend wanted you to do something risky, like running away after ringing a neighbor's doorbell or calling a classmate of the opposite sex for the first time? Your heart raced. You were scared. But you went through with it, and you didn't die. You may have been caught or tripped and fell. You may have acci-

---

[9]You may want to reread the last paragraph before you run to your elder board and quote me as being anti-Sunday school. I'm not anti-Sunday school; I'm against continuing the same program year after year without any pause and evaluation. Okay, now you can quote me.

dentally burped into the phone. You took the risk and lived to tell the story. That's the risk-taking type of leader I want to see in youth ministry.

Imagine the regret in this statement: "Because you did not have enough faith, you will not lead your youth ministry into the land I (God) promised." Ouch! Even scared and uncomfortable leaders need to be willing to take risks by faith. You'll know if your team is depending on God if the whole team is willing to try what can't be done without his help or what can't be explained in human terms.

Understanding Seven Phases of Change

I grew up a few miles from the stadium where the California Angels play baseball. I was a big fan, working at the stadium during my high school years. I love watching the Angels play. I've seen hundreds of games.

While I can't predict the score of each game, I'm fairly attuned to the phases of each game: pregame warm-ups, the national anthem, walks, strike outs, catches, arguments, hits, the seventh inning stretch, and the final score. Some innings take five minutes; others last more than an hour.

Just as baseball has familiar phases, so does change. I've experienced enough change to describe the basics, regardless of the specific details of individual circumstances. I

I'm an old guy. And by now I know that introducing change in any church program can cause a lot of trouble if not handled properly. In my years working at a local church, I was beaten up emotionally by not doing the sorts of things Doug outlines here. Too often I thought I had a direct line to God and knew what was best for the youth program. I then played manipulative, managerial games to get other people to go along with my ideas.

What I lacked was a theology of the church and an understanding of how God works through the church. I now believe the Holy Spirit mystically moves through the gathered church (Matthew 18:20) and that Christian leaders must patiently listen to what God is saying through the group. In the power plays of contemporary society, leadership comes from the top down—but in the life of the church, the Holy Spirit often leads from the bottom up. The Spirit, according to Scripture, often chooses to reveal the will of God through those who may not be "knowledgeable" or "competent authorities"—i.e., youth. But rather than burdens, teenagers should be treated as people who, interacting with each other, can be vehicles through which God's will is discerned. Therefore youth leaders seeking to affect change should be prayerfully sensitive to what the Holy Spirit wants to reveal through their students about potential change.

It's important to note that the early church often prayed itself into harmony (Acts 5:12, 15:25) before making decisions. The church desired total unanimity when seeking God's will. What's more, the early church was sensitive to those who "held out" in spite of majority opinion—perhaps they were hearing something important from God, too! Good leaders don't impose their ideas on groups; they participate in decision-making processes as equals and create settings in which even the weakest members are empowered to participate. Remember: people are more important than programs. In the end, when changes are made, all members should feel "we decided on this" as opposed to "our leader had some terrific ideas, and we went along with them."

And while leaders shouldn't flat out prescribe the vision for their groups, that doesn't mean leaders can't, through knowledge of Scripture and sound teaching, help their groups develop a vision of what could and should be accomplished for Christ. Good leaders also should question and prod the group into asking what God wants done for those *outside the group*. It's been said that a youth group is the only club in the world that should exist for the benefit of non-members.

Finally, ask yourself if the change you want is absolutely necessary. Doug is quite right about change being upsetting. Often you can achieve the same objectives by other means instead of disrupting current structures. For instance, as churches have moved toward contemporary forms of worship in order to attract youth, many have initiated second services rather than doing away with their traditional worship services. Thus, they initiate something new *and* still preserve older, revered forms of worship—and everybody is happy. Remember that Jesus says "the Kingdom of heaven is like an owner of a house who brings out of his storeroom new treasures as well as old" (Matthew 13:52). Jesus knows it's best to hold on to what's good about the old while initiating great new ideas, too.

The most important thing to consider when initiating change is how it will fit your group's overall ministry vision. "But," you say, "there is no collective vision in my group!" Then you need to resolve that problem—and it is a problem! When there is no vision, the Bible says, the people perish. And from my experience, the leader perishes most of all.

In his Pulitzer Prize-winning book, *Denial of Death*, Ernest Becker contends that youth was made for heroism, not for pleasure. Teenagers want to be caught up in something bigger than themselves—something that gives their lives meaning. That's a tall order. But as a youth worker, you're in a position to encourage your group to attempt great things for God—and to expect great things from God. Bear that in mind when you're looking to navigate change in your group. And bear this in mind as well: when change is implemented, your group must be able to say, "By God's grace, look what *we have done*."

—*Tony Campolo*

can't tell you whether your change will take five minutes, five days, or five years to complete, but I can coach you through the phases so you'll have knowledge to help you navigate the change that's bound to be coming your way. Here are seven phases of change, as I've experienced them:

These phases aren't always neatly divided. Sometimes they will overlap

1. *Personal Preparation Phase.* Being prepared spiritually for God's leading.

2. *Idea Phase.* Gathering ideas about change from God and other leaders.

3. *Testing Phase.* Talking out the idea with a few safe people.

4. *Question-Asking Phase.* Asking and answering questions that critics will ask.

5. *Selling Phase.* Communicating changes to your people.

6. *Opposition Phase.* Dealing with your critics.

7. *Waiting Phase.* Trusting God's timing and moving toward being personally prepared for the next change.

Now, let's take a more detailed look at each phase.

// 1. Personal preparation phase

With every change, leaders need time to prepare themselves spiritually to be sensitive to God's leading. This element of change requires leaders to be ready for the wave of opportunity that will arise in God's timing. My pastor, Rick Warren, has driven this idea into the leaders' hearts at our church by saying, "We don't have to create God's next wave of change. We just need to be prepared to catch it." So how does a leader get ready?

▪ *Prepare yourself spiritually.* As you read the Bible you'll see a common element in the lives of people of change—prayer. During this phase, it's crucial to be before God listening and praying. Too often we go to a seminar or read a book and get ambitious about change without consulting God or wanting to know his agenda for our ministry. Without significant prayer and an attitude of dependence on God, don't even consider change. You're not ready.

"Are you going to weave pieces of Chapter 3 into every chapter?"
—an astute reader

■ *Be forward thinking.* During this phase, leaders need to be thinking about what's next for their ministries. Some people are naturally gifted visionaries; but vision also comes from considering what's ahead and evaluating what has happened in the past. You don't need to be a visionary to do this; you need a right heart and a clear mind.

■ *Challenge the status quo.* Ask challenging questions about what you're currently doing. This type of thinking is in opposition to the we've-never-done-it-that-way attitude. It forces you to evaluate: "Is this still an effective program? Are we being the best stewards of our time? Are we reasonable about what we're asking of students?" When you desire to simply be a faithful servant of Christ and be open to his leading, ask questions that analyze your current use of time and energy.

I'd much rather have one of my volunteers ask me, "Are small groups still the best way to connect students with one another?" than blindly attending her group each week and perhaps resisting God's lead.

// 2. Idea phase

Being connected to God, the source of ideas, generates not only several ideas, but also the right ideas. When leaders are connected to God, ideas flow supernaturally in God's timing. Here are a few tips to help you:

▪ *Be open to ideas from everyone.* When others' thoughts are valued, ideas pour in from many avenues. If the lead youth worker is the source of all ideas, teamwork will be diminished, spiritual gifts will be devalued, and ideas will be quieted that the Holy Spirit is birthing within leaders.

▪ *Brainstorm multiple ideas.* One of the best ways to solve problems is to brainstorm multiple ideas. In the past, when a problem arose, I would search for the one right answer. This pressure would lock up my creativity as I sought the perfect solution. Now I use a whiteboard and list 15 potential answers for a dilemma.

I might write "need more leaders." We'll keep that problem on the whiteboard until we've exhausted possible solutions. Even if I feel that we've solved the problem with our third suggestion, we keep writing until we've gathered my self-imposed ideal number of 15. It's temping to quit when we've found the so-called "right idea," but I keep writing because I've learned that some great inspirations may still be waiting for us.

While listing ideas on how to find more leaders for our church, an idea came to us about a quarterly newsletter for disconnected parents. That brainchild was birthed mysteriously while trying to solve the unrelated leader problem. The ideas will come; don't give up.

▪ *Don't act on every great idea.* When you create a climate that thrives on ideas, you'll eventually get more than you can possibly use. Most of my good ideas come when I'm relaxing. In my early years of ministry, my volunteers hated my vacations because I would return rested and filled with new plans. I wasn't seasoned enough to know that every idea need not be implemented. Wisdom is selecting from among two or more good ideas.

My wife recently told me, "You've got more ideas than you have brain cells." If that's true—and I'd like to think it's not—I know I can't possibly implement all of them (that's good news for my church). I don't need to use all my ideas, and you don't, either.

Collect 'em, save 'em, and revisit 'em once a year to be reminded about them and move ahead on the crucial ones.

// 3. Testing phase

I can remember one of my seminary professors saying, "Churches are a lot like horses—they don't like to be startled or surprised. It causes wild behavior." Not only do people not like change, they especially don't like to be surprised with it. The "wild behavior" is often the result of wounded pride because a decision to change was made without an individual's input. Here are some ideas that might help you during the testing phase:

■ *Plant a loose idea with a few safe people.* Instead of springing change on everyone at once, test the idea with a few to gain valuable insight into the general reaction. This is the phase when you get to act like a secret agent, flying under the radar, and engaging with a carefully selected group.

I like to talk with people who don't post my idea on the Web page for the entire church to read and comment on. To test an idea on a friend, I might say, "Tony, I can't shake this idea, and I want to run it by you for your feedback. I haven't thought this through all the way (that's why I refer to it as a loose idea), but what would you think if we cancelled our Sunday night praise and worship program and added an extended time of singing at the end of our Wednesday night meeting? That way we'd have students and leaders out only one night of the week. (Pause.) What's your initial reaction?"

Then, I shut up and listen. After getting some feedback, I might respond by saying something like, "Obviously, I've got more thinking to do. You raised some great questions. I appreciate your insight. Instead of talking about this with anyone, will you please pray about this and let me know if you have any other thoughts, questions, or ideas?"

Most people feel honored when you trust them with a loose idea. Choose to talk with people who represent a variety ages, levels of involvement, and levels of spiritual maturity so you get a wider range of feedback.

■ *Use the term* experiment. You might say, "I've got an idea I'd like to experiment with. What if the students took more ownership in teaching the Sunday school curriculum? I think it might be a fun experiment to see how they do. What do you think?" The word *experiment* takes away some of the potential danger. So what if they blow it, right? Since it's an experiment, if it goes well you'll be the genius scientist who made the right call. If it bombs—oh, well—it was just an experiment.

■ *Don't overreact to the responses.* So you met your safe friend over coffee and you passionately presented the idea that could revolutionize the youth ministry and quicken the pace of Jesus' return. You sit there with an apprehensive smile anticipating a response of, "You're brilliant." Instead you're met with, "That's the dumbest idea I've ever heard." You get defensive and consider throwing coffee at this former friend and shouting, "Get behind me, Satan."

Testing is risky because your idea may be pulverized. It's painful to admit there have been many times when my great ideas have been met with a less-than-great response. If the reaction is pulverized, stay calm. Don't reveal your devastation. If you do, you may not get an honest response the next time. You want honesty!

Keep in mind you've only offered an idea. You're merely testing the water to see if it's hot or cold. You're not jumping in; you're gauging the temperature with your baby toe. Smile and offer thanks for the time and feedback. A negative response doesn't equate to a terrible idea. It may indicate that you need to rethink how you present it. You're likely hear the same response if you don't alter your presentation.

■ *Allow an idea to die.* A mentor of mine says, "You may love the horse, but if it's dead, it's probably time to dismount." Words of wisdom. Not all the ideas you test will be successful. That's okay. That's why you're testing them. If your personal preparation phase is going great and you're striving to fulfill God's plan for your ministry, another idea is probably waiting around the corner.

Sometimes unity is more important than implementing a change.

// 4. Question-asking phase

When you're testing an idea, spend time asking yourself questions. The people who hear about the change will immediately have some questions, so it's important that you've already asked and answered them. Here are some considerations during this phase:

■ *Identify your motive.* Some of the earliest and most important questions you can ask are personally telling:

- Why am I initiating this change?
- What's my real motivation behind the idea?
  - —Is it to make me look good?
  - —Is it to make a statement about my leadership?
  - —Is it for the ministry?
  - —Is it because another church is doing it?
  - —Is it to glorify God?

The motive question must be answered honestly before you ask other questions. Anything other than a pure-hearted answer leaves room for doubt about making any change. Because your critics will question you, be certain that your motive is pure. That way your character won't be damaged during the process.

■ *List the pros and cons.* Every change evokes positive and negative responses. These need to be addressed, so you'll have thorough information to use when you dialogue with opponents and attempt to sell the change. Thinking through all the positive reasons for the change ignites your enthusiasm. Wonderful! But if you don't consider the down side, your opposition will use it against you.

■ *Identify the obstacles.* After writing out your pros and cons, list the obstacles. Ask yourself—

- What hurdles are we going to need to clear to make the change reality?
- What physical resources need to be considered, like meeting rooms and money?
- What other resources need to be considered, like the church calendar?
- Who do I need to meet with?
- What research needs to be done?

Your list of obstacles impacts the next phase.

- *Define how to implement the change.* Think through the practical steps needed to complete this change. Your hard work will be used during the next two phases.

- *Recognize your supporters.* Once you've tested the waters, you'll probably know who supports your idea and who opposes it. Every change requires support, even if it's from a few. Identify those key people.

- *Be aware of the critics.* Whoever

said there could be change without conflict never worked in a church. Most of the arguments in youth ministry aren't about theology; they're about change. Change is often chaotic, and critics are vocal during chaos. Don't allow them to paralyze your leadership. Let your opposition motivate you to ask the tough questions.

- Am I willing to battle for this change if the battle gets ugly?
- How will the majority of students respond to this idea? Leaders? Parents? The congregation?
- What resources will I need to implement this change?
- Will my house sell quickly when I have to move to a new church?

// 5. Selling phase

This is the time for you to be a leader by publicly introducing the change. Selling an idea is typically the job of the lead youth worker, but if you're new to the church and you have a supportive relationship with your senior pastor, you might ask him to take the lead in making the announcement.

A few times during the first year at my church, I leveraged my pastor's leadership and influence. I needed to make a couple major changes, but I had no credibility with the students or families in the church. Realizing that I could only get away with leaning on him a few times, I made sure to ask for his help when making monumental changes, not only when I was afraid. Being the lead youth worker, I have learned how to communicate changes on my own whenever possible. Here are some ideas for you to consider:

■ *Discuss the obstacles and answer your critics' concerns.* Since you've already identified the obstacles and the critics, be sure to include what you've learned when you make your presentation.

I might say, "I've talked to some people about trying an experiment in which we would restructure our mid-week program to include more singing at the end of the time together. Many people have expressed excitement and support of this idea. A few have raised questions about how it will be done. Let me take a few minutes and share with you how we can make this happen with the least amount of tension." I would then present answers to the perceived obstacles and critics before they're even able to ask about them.

> Once you get to the selling phase, it's not always going to be "full steam ahead," no matter what. It's okay to occasionally kill an idea during this phase.

■ *Demonstrate what the change could be like.* Helping others embrace a change requires you to describe the future. Change isn't always pretty during the beginning stages, and it's wise to paint a picture of what awaits once the change is begun. People want to know that you have a finished product in your heart and mind that you'll lead them toward. They'll move ahead with you when they see the future and know that when they arrive the result is worth their efforts.

■ *Be positive.* I realize this sounds like a no-brainer, but if you're not extremely positive about the change, people easily sense a lack of confidence in your leadership. Your positive outlook can quiet your critics and endear those in a neutral position to embrace your idea.

■ *Admit your own fears and failures:* Humility isn't a sign of weakness while leading leaders. When I admit the mistakes I've made and what I've learned from my failures, people are more willing to cheer me on during the next phase of change. Everyone makes mistakes. Take responsibility for your past and point out how the lessons you've learned help you.

■ *Don't announce every change.* If the impact of the change will be minimal, subtly incorporate it without calling attention to it. If you want to start using a fill-in-the-blank outline when you teach, you don't need to take it through the same process you would if you want to change the entire program's format.

Take your idea through the testing stage and ask questions of yourself so you know why you're doing what you're doing. Then, be a leader and make the change.

// 6. Opposition phase

I have a friend who played professional football for several years. Now he's a youth pastor. He recently told me, "I've faced some of the toughest, meanest, nastiest athletes on the planet and none of them were as brutal as some of the people in my church. If I wanted to get beat up every week, I would have stayed in football."

This is a sad but often true statement about the people in the church. You *will* have opposition, but you're in good company: Jesus, Paul, Moses, the disciples, and just about every Christian leader who ever worked in a church. During your opposition, keep in mind these principles to ease the pain:

■ *Put out fires quickly.* Never allow vocal critics to linger and take continual shots at your change. They won't go away quietly. Go to them. Talk face-to-face about their issues.

I've had to say some difficult things to people who were vocal with their opposition. After hearing about repeated bouts of whining, I confronted Ben and said, "I'm sorry you can't support this change. While I value your concerns, they're minor in comparison to the magnitude of this change. What we're doing is bigger than any one person. This change is vital to the health of our ministry, and we're going forward. I'd like to ask you to not create division in our church by being vocally opposed."

If a critic can't support your change, ask the individual to be a mature Christian and uphold the unity of the church.

- *Take someone with you.* If the person continues to be divisive, follow the lead of Matthew 18 and take another person with you for a second face-to-face meeting. Depending on the severity of the change and the degree of opposition, you may want this additional person to be your pastor or an elder from the church. Remember, your battle shouldn't be against the saints of the church but with the Prince of Darkness (who, alas, often disguises himself as a critic of your ministry). This step is difficult, but it's vital.

- *Move on.* You'll always have opponents, but don't allow the whining minority to derail the passionate majority. Move ahead and follow God's agenda for your church and rejoice that you're not the only leader in church history who's ever been opposed.

// 7. Waiting phase

Most change won't actually happen as fast as it did in your mind. I'm no longer surprised when change is slow. The waiting phase can be tough to deal with because the idea often comes so quickly and was effectively implemented in your mind as clearly as one-two-three. Now, you're waiting...74, 75, 76, 77....

> There won't always be a distinct end to one change followed by the beginning of another one.

Relax. If you're dependent on God and you're assured it's his change, wait for him to do the impossible after you've done the possible. Think about these ideas while you wait:

- *Thank those involved.* Since you're not a lone ranger, you'll have people to thank who helped you initiate and implement the change. Use the down time to thank them. It's the right thing to do. You want those people to feel valued for their participation so they'll be supportive the next time you need to make changes. Thanked people are supportive people.

■ *Prepare for the next change.* Here the change cycle starts over. During the waiting period, go back to the principles in the personal preparation phase. That's the normal place for you to live: dependent on God, seeking his plans for your ministry, and faithfully carrying out your role in whatever he wants you to do.

■ *Don't worry about the speed.* Regardless of the number of potential changes you're considering, keep in mind that speed kills. Going too fast too soon can hurt you, so be patient. You may wait for months.

During your first two years, it's safe to implement a few ideas, not 20. Do not try to implement all the changes immediately. Be patient. You may not get to some ideas until after five or six years. That's okay.

The change process is never easy, but it does get easier the more you do it. I wish I could coach you through every change you'll make and be that safe person to hear your ideas. Obviously, that's impossible. But take comfort knowing that I, too, have cried, struggled, pleaded with God, angered people, made stupid mistakes, and occasionally made changes without much conflict. I can identify with what you're going through, and I know you can make it.

Don't fear change; embrace it. Use the change process to strengthen your faith and your leadership skills. Help others feel comfortable with change so that the next time you say, "I've got an idea…" you'll be met with support and cooperation.

The Questions at the End of the Chapter

// For group discussion

- What is your first reaction to change—negative or positive? Why?
- What's our best forum to discuss change as a group?

// For personal reflection

- Which phase of change is the most difficult for me?
- What's one change I wish I could have made but didn't?
- Why do I react to change the way I do?
- Would I be considered a flexible leader?
- Would I be considered a faith-filled leader?

// Actions to consider

- Identify a few "safe" people who you can run your ideas by.
- Begin your file that you will fill with change ideas for the future.

Go to www.dougfields.com and enter your comments under Your First 2 Years: Chapter 11

what do i do now?

defining a realistic job description for your first two years

I want to end this book by helping you create something vital to your health and longevity as a youth worker—a realistic picture of what's expected of you. All youth workers need a clear idea of how to best minister within the context of their church community.

Regardless of status—paid or volunteer, head of the youth ministry or one of the team—the best place for all youth workers to start is with a specific understanding of the expectations of their positions. If you don't know what's expected, you're doomed to fail. Expectations exist, whether spoken or not, and you need to discover them to be effective and stay healthy.

Through hundreds of restaurant meetings like you and I have had through these chapters, I've had the opportunity to discern some key steps for starting out right. They're easy to follow if you block out time to think through each one and then ask yourself some personal questions. You'll be well prepared if you're able to walk through them before starting in a youth ministry.

If you're in the middle or near the end of your first two years you can still follow these steps by asking for a review. (Read to the end of the chapter to see how.)

Discover What's Expected of You

These steps don't revolutionize the church or the world of youth ministry, but they offer youth workers a clearer picture of what's expected of them in their positions. They also give your church an accurate portrayal of who you are and what the church can expect from you. The following steps—introduced here, but in more detail beginning on page 262—have helped thousands of youth workers build a lasting foundation for youth ministry.

// Step 1—Tell

Here's who I am. I want you to know what my strengths and weaknesses and what I have to offer.

// Step 2—Ask

- What's expected of me in this position?
- Who has these expectations (the senior pastor, parents, elders)?
- How will these expectations be evaluated?
- Who oversees this position? What is his management style like?
- What does success in this position look like?

// Step 3—Present

Share the priorities you value regarding your personal growth and your family and your passion for this ministry position.

// Step 4—Identify

Reveal your ideas regarding realistic developments within the first two years. (When you've read this book you should have a picture of what's reasonable.)

// Step 5—Evaluate

Take time to pray, think, and seek God's leading. Talk with your friends, your spouse, and other appropriate people about how well you fit in the youth ministry and within the church. See if the church's expectations line up with what you'd like to see and what you believe you can accomplish with God's help.

// Step 6—Begin

Begin with attitudes and actions that will build a healthy youth ministry. Or, if necessary, begin again—move on. (See page 285.)

Typical Reactions to the Expectations Process

Don't be tempted to underestimate the power of simple, clear questions. I've heard too many horror stories of men and women who've been emotionally abused, fired, hurt, or who have left youth ministry because their blind enthusiasm matched a church's desperation for a youth worker and everyone said yes before knowing enough about one another.

I've shown this six-step process to enough people to know that you probably have one of the following reactions:

- That's too much work.
- Yeah, that makes sense.
- I've already started my job. Is it too late for all of this?
- I'm just a volunteer. The steps seem like they're for a paid position.

Here's my response to each reaction:

// That's too much work.

I'll admit that these steps seem intense, but they're not as difficult or time consuming as they might appear. Though requiring some thought, the entire exercise can be done in a few hours. Even if it took a week, the effort is worth the investment. Don't allow yourself to fall into one of the following traps:

> "Taking these steps isn't nearly as difficult as being in a job that isn't right."
> —one who knows

• An *arrogant* youth worker says, "How hard can it be to start? I came from Bible college/seminary. I can figure out where to start on my own. I don't need to do this."

• An *ignorant* youth worker says, "I love God and students, so I'll just go out and love people and let God take care of the details."

• A *stupid* youth worker says both.

Typically, arrogant, ignorant, and stupid youth workers find themselves being humbled a few years down the road, only to return to these basic, yet essential, steps.

Here's what I've found to be true: if you don't take the time to follow the first five steps (tell,

(A VOICE FROM THE TRENCHES)

I'm 23 and in my second year of youth ministry. During my senior year of college, I met a pastor who was looking for a youth minister for the first time in years because his church could now afford one full time. The church had huge facilities (they had about 700 members 20 years ago; now they were down to 80 people). The pastor had been there 10 years, spending most of his time on building repairs and beautification.

The first time I met with him, I asked for a job description. His reply was, "1 Timothy 3 is all we need!" I laughed at first, but he was serious. He said, "If stuff needs to be done, we'll do it!" I wasn't afraid of a little work, and I felt God calling me there, so my wife and I went—ready for a revival! Little did I know that my pastor could've been a perfect foreman for a construction company or a junkyard.

During my one-year tenure there, I wore my grubby clothes every day to work. The building and grounds were at the center of this pastor's ministry heart. Not people. I repeatedly asked for a *specific* job description, and he would give me the same response. So I sucked it up, supported him, and worked hard for him (while praying for direction from God).

It was a great learning experience, and God showed me a lot. When I began looking elsewhere, a specific job description was the first thing I required before going any further in the interview.

I've been a "real" youth pastor for three months now, and I look forward to coming to work every day!

—*Duane Bonner, associate minister of youth, Raleigh Heights Baptist Church, Chesapeake, Virginia*

ask, present, identify, and evaluate), you'll begin without truly understanding what's expected of you and what's realistic in your church culture. When that happens, you may end up like many of my youth ministry friends who were released for not doing what they never knew they were supposed to do because they accepted an invisible job description.

This is definitely worth your time! Don't let yourself be talked out of working through this process.

// Yeah, that makes sense.

Great! Now all you need to do is follow through. Act. If you feel unqualified and utterly dependent on God's power, you're in the right frame of leadership to begin these steps. The process makes even more sense when you've completed the steps.

// I've already started my job. Is it too late to do all of this?

It's never too late. Please find the courage to ask for a review (six-month, one-year, two-year). Then go through the steps with your supervisor. Some questions neither of you anticipated may be raised, but, in terms of your ministerial and personal health, the process is an invaluable experience. Before the review, kindly ask your supervisor to come prepared with the answers to the questions in Step 2.

// I'm just a volunteer, and the steps seem like they're for a paid position.

If you're reading this book before you commit to a volunteer position, congratulations! Either you're wise or the supervisor who gave you this book is brilliant. Either way, your church wins.

I'd like you to remove the phrase *just a volunteer* from your vocabulary. *Just* communicates a lack of worth and value that should never be used with the term *volunteer*. In my ministry, I try not to use the term *volunteer*. Everyone who helps with our ministry is *staff*. But to keep from confusion in this book, I've used *volunteer*. I love my volunteers. Effective youth ministry is impossible without them—and that's not an overstatement. Volunteers are the backbone of a healthy youth ministry. This may be the reason you've been asked to read this book.

> "Volunteers rule!"
> —a smart youth worker

If you're already a youth ministry volunteer, these are realistic steps for you to follow as well. If you're serving on a youth ministry team where you don't know what's expected of you, you'll soon burn out with frustration. If your role and the expectations of the volunteer team are clear, you may want to skim through the details of this chapter and thank the lead youth worker for doing a good job.

My Personal Experience with the Expectations Process

These six steps will save you from some of the suffering and painful consequences I know can be avoided. Clear expectations pave the way for positive first steps in ministry.

Personally, this process saved me from accepting a youth ministry job that looked appealing when viewed from a distance. Several years ago when I considered a youth ministry position I spoke with five different groups during the interview process:

- The pastor
- The pastoral staff
- A group of key (and vocal) parents
- The existing volunteers
- The existing student leaders

During my session with each group, I asked the questions from Step 2:

- What's expected of me in this position?
- Who has these expectations (the senior pastor, parents, elders)?
- How will these expectations be evaluated?
- Who oversees this position? What is his management style like?
- What does success in this position look like?

I wrote down every person's response. Later that night, after an exhausting day of interviews, I combined all the similar responses, hoping to identify a few underlying values and expectations.

Another question to ask is, "Can I punch the first student who uses the words *lock-in?*"

The results shocked me. Over 40 different expectations were presented. Only two were somewhat similar:

- Grow the group
- Create a youth ministry the students will enjoy

It hardly required discernment to realize the expectations were impossible to fulfill. Imagine trying to live up to the 40-plus articulated expectations. The job description was a set-up for failure. This church had a great building, an incredible financial package, a nice pastor, and a lot of hopes and dreams for their next youth worker. The problem was they didn't have common expectations. These weren't bad people. However, they didn't have a plan for choosing and communicating common expectations.

When expectations—even unrealistic expectations—aren't fulfilled, the youth worker looks bad, never the church. Unfortunately, this scenario isn't unusual. Thousands of youth workers accept positions with unrealistic expectations from well-meaning churches all the time. Multiple expectations are a reality, coming from everywhere and from everyone.

When you're in a paid position, everyone has expectations of you:

- The pastor
- The pastor's spouse
- Church elders
- Parents
- Volunteers
- Community leaders
- Student leaders
- Regular students
- Fringe students
- Custodians
- The pastor's pets
- Essentially, every congregational member

If you're a volunteer, the expectations may be less demanding, but they still exist. The lead youth worker, parents, other volunteers, students—all of them have an unwritten set of expectations they want you to fulfill.

Be careful not to say yes to an offer too quickly. Although a job offer can be tempting, exciting, seductive, and motivating, before you drool the words, "Sure, I'll run the youth ministry program!" or "Of course, I can be a volunteer small group leader!" work through the process of expectations.

> Because I followed Doug's advice about carefully taking a step back and evaluating what's actually expected of me as a youth pastor, I was able to make an informed decision regarding the new youth ministry position I currently hold. Because I followed Doug's steps, unknown and unspoken expectations regarding my wife's role began surfacing during the interview process. So before agreeing to the job, we asked for additional meetings with other church leaders and their spouses to dialog about the actual expectations of staff spouses. We wanted a realistic picture of what we were getting into as a family. Doug's steps, along with a lot of prayer and conversation, helped tip the scales toward the church where I serve as a youth pastor.
> —Jeff Maguire

Your goal is to create a realistic job description. Without an understandable, reasonable job description, you'll struggle with how to use your time. Ultimately, you'll have to sit through reviews that provide little encouragement and an inaccurate evaluation. It's tough to be honestly evaluated when you have little idea about what you're supposed to do.

Have I convinced you yet? Push your dessert plate aside and have the server warm up your coffee. (I'll take another dessert, though.) Let's keep talking about the evaluation process to clarify the steps a little.

Getting More Specific

// Step 1—Tell

Here's who I am. I want you to know what my strengths and weaknesses and what I have to offer.

Be realistic about yourself and don't be afraid to verbalize your strengths *and* your weaknesses. Realize that anyone in a supervisory position who's discussing a potential leadership role expects to hear a combination of the two. Personally, I'm disappointed when people don't mention weaknesses, and I'm impressed when I hear a clear grasp of both.

Here's an example of a realistic combination:

Strengths	Weaknesses
• Leadership	• Lack of experience
• Teaching	• Administration/details
• People-skills	• Conflict management

When discussing your strengths, recognize the temptation of either false pride or humility. It's tempting to brag about your gifts and abilities, proving how perfect you are for the job, even though you're not as confident as you may sound. On the other hand, when others initiate the praise, don't say, "It was nothing," because the accolades may represent a period of solid effort and leadership. My advice is to combine thankfulness with humility.

> You'll never lose with humility.

When it comes to your weaknesses, realize that people will discover them anyway! We all have limitations, and every leader is a mixture of strengths and weaknesses. Learn to accept the fact that you'll be good at some things and weak at others. As much as I want to be better, I'm still an average administrator. When you acknowledge your limitations, identify the people you need to surround yourself with (I need to be around detail people). Communicate that you're not satisfied with keeping your weaknesses weak, and that you're optimistic about learning new skills to minimize them while continuing to express your strengths.

// Step 2—Ask

- What's expected of me in this position?
- Who has these expectations (the senior pastor, parents, elders)?
- How will these expectations be evaluated?
- Who oversees this position? What is his management style like?
- What does success in this position look like?

None of these questions has one perfect response since the answers vary depending on the characteristics of the church and youth ministry position:

- Full-time youth worker
- Full-time associate with youth ministry responsibilities
- Volunteer youth worker
- Intern

Still, these questions need to be asked so that—

- You'll know what's expected
- You'll know what to do
- You'll know where to start
- You'll have a foundation for evaluation

When you fail to ask or don't get solid answers to the questions—

- Everyone will have a personal agenda for what you should be doing.
- You'll work to satisfy others' expectations.
- You'll work hard in many different directions.
- Your lack of focus will limit fruit.

If you're a church leader looking for a potential youth worker, check out "10 frequently asked questions," appendix b, page 281.

// Step 3—Present

Share the priorities you value regarding your personal growth and your family and your passion for this ministry position.

Don't be afraid to view your potential youth ministry responsibility as a marriage between you and the church. The church gets you, but you also get the church. This is the point in the process where you let the church members know what you value. You're not demanding anything; you're painting a picture of how you'd like to pursue a healthy, balanced life as a youth worker.

> Stay away from using words like *lawsuit, church split, incarceration,* and *addictions.*

This is the time for you say, "I'd like to work in an environment where my personal well-being and my family life is cared for as much as my productivity as an employee."

Some of my critics have accused me of teaching young youth workers to ask for too much. In reality, all I'm asking for is honesty. You've got to be truthful about what's important to you. If you don't talk about what you value during the interview process, you wind up in a church that doesn't value your family time or your personal life.

You'll regret skipping this step in the process. Regret grows into bitterness, and bitterness causes burnout. Be realistic about what's important to you.

You should definitely work hard for the church, but God is concerned about your family and your inner world, too. Finding balance isn't easy, but you need to pursue it if you're going to survive in youth ministry.

If you're married, find out what's expected of your spouse and express the value you place on your family time. Ask if the church has identified a number of nights that it want its ministers to be home. If not, it may communicate something about the church's leadership regarding family.

One of the many attractive elements of my church is that church leaders want me and other staff members to be at home four nights a week. That's a sign of a church that cares about family. You don't want to be blind-sided by a spouse who says, "I'm through" because you're never home. (See *Why I Left My Husband* below.)

> "Remember: you said, 'I do' to me before you said it to the church."
> —*youth worker's spouse*

If you're single, don't underestimate the power of time alone, at home, resting, being recharged. Besides being strengthened physically and spiritually, you're developing good habits if God leads you to marry in the future. You're also modeling to your students and leaders what a balanced life looks like.

No one takes as much interest in your private life as you. Even supervisors assigned to your care aren't thinking of all your personal needs. You'll have to learn to ask for what you need. The sooner you learn to do this, the happier you'll be.

Why I Left My Husband

My husband is a full-time youth director. He is extremely dedicated and spends between 50 and 70 hours a week with young people.

I think the reason he's so successful with kids is that he's always available to them, always ready to help them when they need him. That may be why the attendance has more than doubled in the past year. He knows how to talk their language. This past year he was out two and three nights a week talking with kids until midnight. He's always taking them to camps and on ski trips and overnight campouts. If he isn't with kids, he's thinking about them and preparing for his next encounter with them.

If he has any time left after that, he's speaking or attending a conference where he shares with others what God is doing through him. When it comes to youth work, my husband has always given 100 percent.

I guess that's why I left him.

There isn't much left after 100 percent.

Frankly I just couldn't compete with God. I say that because my husband always had a way of reminding me that his is God's work, and he must minister where and when God called him.

Young people today desperately need help, and God has called him to help them. When a young person needs him, he has to respond or he's letting God and the young person down.

When I did ask my husband to spend some time with the kids or me, it was always tentative. And if I became pushy about it, I was "nagging," "trying to get him out of God's work," "behaving selfishly," or I was revealing a "spiritual problem."

Honestly I've never wanted anything but God's will for my husband, but I never could get him to consider that maybe his family is part of that will.

It didn't matter how many discussions we had about his schedule—he would always end with, "Okay, I'll get out of the ministry if that's what you want." Of course I didn't want that, so we would continue as always until another discussion. You can only ask for so long. There's a limit to how long you can be ignored and put off. You threaten to leave without meaning it until you keep the threat. You consider all the unpleasant consequences until they don't seem unpleasant anymore. You decide that nothing could be more unpleasant than being alone and feeling worthless.

You finally make up your mind that you are a person with real worth as an individual. You assert your ego and join womanhood again.

That's what I did.

I wanted to be more than a housekeeper, diaper changer, and sex partner. I wanted to be free from the deep bitterness and guilt that slowly ate at my spiritual sanity. And deep inside there was something making me not only dislike my husband, but everything he did or touched.

His "I love you" became meaningless to me because he didn't act like it. His gifts were evidence to me of his guilt because he didn't spend more time with me. His sexual advances were met with a frigidity that frustrated both of us and deepened the gap between us.

All I wanted was to feel as though he really wanted to be with me. But no matter how hard he tried, I always felt like I was keeping him from something. He had a way of making me feel guilty because I had forced him to spend his valuable time with the kids and me.

Just once I wish he would have canceled something for us instead of canceling us. You don't have to believe this, but I really loved him and his ministry once. I never wanted him to work an eight-to-five job. Nor did I expect him to be home every night. I tried to believe every promise he made me, honestly hoping things would change—but they never did.

All of a sudden I woke up one day and realized that I had become a terribly bitter person. I not only resented my husband and his work, but I was beginning to despise myself. In desperation to save myself, our children—and, I guess, even my husband and his ministry—I left him.

I don't think he really believed I'd leave him. I guess I never really believed I'd leave him, either.

But I did

—Anonymous (from *Youthworker* journal, May/June 1999)

// Step 4—Identify

Reveal your ideas regarding realistic developments within the first two years. Unveil your plan about what you think you can realistically accomplish. Temper your enthusiasm. Most youth workers overestimate what they can accomplish in one year and underestimate what they can do in five years. Approach your first two years with a healthy dose of confidence and reality.

Confidence without knowledge leads to letting people down. Have you ever been with friends trying to decide what movie to see? You throw out the name of a movie you've heard is good, and you convince your friends to see it with you. Then, when it ends up being lousy, you feel foolish for getting people excited about something that didn't deliver.

Before promising the world to your church, or at least the southern hemisphere, give careful thought to this step.

// Step 5—Evaluate

Take time to pray, think, and seek God's leading. Talk with your friends, your spouse, and other appropriate people about how well you fit in the youth ministry and within the church. See if the church's expectations line up with what you'd like to see and what you believe you can accomplish with God's help.

This step is the only one that requires much time—whatever you're willing to give it. Use caution here and slow down! At this point, commit yourself to the process. It's possible you'll sense the answer during the previous steps. In your heart you might be feeling, "Yeah, this sounds good. It seems right." Wonderful! Wisdom, however, says to pull away from dialogue and honestly and prayerfully evaluate what you've been told.

Trust your feelings and allow adequate time to pray, reflect, and dialogue with significant people in your life who will ask difficult questions and offer insight from their perspectives. It's tough to tone down enthusiasm, but thousands of youth ministry vacancies exist. Finding the right fit is worth the wait.

This reflective time of evaluation may raise more questions. That's okay. This is the time to clarify the details. Don't be afraid of asking too many questions.

Consider this example: You heard the church express this expectation: "We want you to spend a lot of relational time with students." But during the next step, you expressed your desire to spend a lot of relational time developing leaders who will, in turn, care for the students in the ministry. When you explained this, the people you were speaking to nodded with enthusiasm. But which of these expectations will win? Are you going to spend a lot of time with students (their request) or a lot of time with leaders (your desire)?

You'd be foolish to think, "Oh, it doesn't matter. As long as I'm spending time with people, everything will be okay." Not true! The strategies are distinctly different. Before you say yes, make sure you know which will be your primary focus.

I can't encourage you enough to do this! Seemingly a thousand times I've asked a youth worker friend, "Did you talk about that before you started?" Most often the response is, "Yeah, I *thought* we did. Maybe I wasn't clear."

Learn from the mistakes of our youth ministry friends. Make sure you fully understand the expectations and the language of the church leaders—and that they understand it, too. Write down what was spoken.

Here's another example: The church has an expectation for you to grow the group." Ask how they define *grow*. Are they referring to numerical growth? (What number do they have in mind?) Spiritual growth? Both? Ask follow-up questions to their stated expectations. Clear communication is key to being able to effectively evaluate.

// Step 6—Begin

Begin with attitudes and actions that build healthy youth ministry. Or, if necessary, begin again—move on.

My neck is a little sore—from nonstop nodding in agreement as I read all the way through Chapter 12. I hope every new youth worker will embrace the full instruction offered here, because if you do, you're on solid ground as you explore possible places to serve God and students.

Doug writes that "thousands of youth ministry vacancies exist" and "finding the right fit is worth the wait." I couldn't agree more—jumping into a job without getting the full picture of what it's really about is unwise. But the other side is true also: Don't wait around for the perfect church to call you up—that's just as unwise!

Here's an interesting question: *Does God love students in imperfect churches and does he call leaders to serve them?* The obvious answer is "yes." Even churches with countless, disparate expectations regarding their youth ministers need and deserve leadership for their teenagers. So…if your tendency is to reject prospective churches outright, you may want to reconsider that approach. Because something as simple as proactively addressing potentially problematic issues during initial interviews can solve a ton of problems before you agree to take the position. (For example: "If I can develop a proposal that would allow us to reach our youth ministry goals—but would give me four evenings at home a week—would you support making the shift in my schedule?" Or, "Before we move further, could we assemble some core students, parents, and volunteers for several hours to see if we can build consensus regarding your expectations for the vacant position?")

Being transparent with prospective churches, asking and being asked hard questions, and analyzing the degree of convergence or divergence of vision and direction are extremely important disciplines. But those disciplines are not ends in themselves—they are *tools*. Because even after careful conversations with prospective churches (and follow-up conversations with spouses and spiritual leaders), it all comes down to you—on your knees before God.

Looking for your best ministry fit is an essential part of finding God's will. Doug has made that case better than anyone in print. But his chapter also makes it clear that, in the end, your decision needs to rest in that mystical yet concrete reality—the Call.

—*Richard Ross*

I don't know anyone who would attempt to build a house without blueprints. Directions are necessary. Now that you've got some general directions from me for youth ministry in your church, you're ready to begin by combining those directions with your enthusiasm and the picture you've received of what's expected. You should feel confident saying, "This is what I need to do to serve God in this setting."

Now that you have your ministry description, it would be beneficial to read it over and over. Can you envision yourself being fruitful in this type of service? Can you imagine getting excited about serving God in this way?

Take some time and commit your future to God. Don't succumb to the pressure to race out the door to students. Instead, drop to your knees and thank God for giving you the courage to ask the right questions, for wisdom to discern the answers, and for the faith to continue. You may have a clear picture of what the church expects, but don't lose sight of God's role in your life and ministry. You'll eventually fail if God is not part of your equation.

The rest of this chapter is developed for lead youth workers. If you're a volunteer on a youth ministry team, you may want to skip to the epilogue on page 277.

Your First Two Years: Getting to Work

I cannot present a single method to youth workers on how to begin ministry. No cookie-cutter approach exists nor a just-add-water system that works for all churches in all denominations in all cities in all cultures.

But when you've gone through the six-step evaluation process, you'll have a strong sense of where to start. Take a good look at your ministry description, identify your top priorities, and pursue them.

After reading 11 chapters, I assume you've been making notes and identifying your top priorities. Go back through the book to review all that you've read and your notes in the margins of this book so your mind is refreshed about your own priorities.

// Personal: During Your First Two Years

I wish I had statistics to give regarding the number of former youth workers who didn't give priority to their personal lives. The stats would be quite revealing— and depressing. Applause is due to the people of God who take care of their personal and inner worlds and finish the youth ministry marathon. Sadly, youth workers mostly receive praise for what they *do* and not for who they *are*.

- Develop your inner life and protect your personal life. Improve your chances of being around for many years.
- Develop a consistent habit of spending time with God in which you prepare your heart for ministry. Never underestimate the power of being connected with God on a daily basis. Schedule several days a year—entire days—to spend extended time with God.
- Clearly and consistently communicate big-picture truths. ("I want to spend time with students, develop student and volunteer leaders, and help families.")
- Develop time management skills.
- Find and cultivate at least one good friend who doesn't care about youth ministry (and your senior pastor doesn't exist).
- Take off one day per week consistently. Make it nonnegotiable.

// Relationships: During Your First Two Years

In the midst of making changes and implementing these ideas, make sure people are high on your list of priorities. In fact, regardless of where you are in your youth ministry journey, keep people as a high priority. Students, leaders, and parents should always be in your heart. Finding the balance between people and tasks will be a lifelong quest, but ministry is all about people.

- Get to know everyone in your youth group.
- Identify and confirm student leaders.
- Develop a few relationships with influential parents.
- Spend time with key church leaders, elders, and decision-makers.
- Identify the people within your community who influence students and begin making appointments to meet them (three or four a year).

// Leadership: During Your First Two Years

Leaders need other leaders to help mold and shape them. You'll do yourself a favor when you meet with a veteran youth worker and ask her to help you in your leadership position. You'll gain insight, perspective, and guidance from someone who's been where you are. Don't be shy in asking. The worst rejection won't compare to the knowledge you'll gain when you finally find the right person. Ask with humility and always honor this person's time. In addition to finding a veteran youth worker, take these beginning steps:

(A VOICE FROM THE TRENCHES)

About nine months ago, I found what seemed like the perfect church (nice facilities, good location, modern worship, et cetera). But as I interviewed with the staff, I sent my brain on vacation for two weeks of rest and relaxation. I've been in youth ministry for nine years, and I didn't ask the question I always ask—and it came back to haunt me. I didn't ask the church leaders about their *philosophy of youth ministry*. So I move my family, buy a house, get settled in, and then I learn that: (a) My pastor hates youth, (b) You can't wear shorts to church, (c) Guys who want to play in the praise band can't wear earrings, (d) Every other youth minister was raised in the church and "did it for practically nothing," (e) I'm not a pastor; I'm basically the activities director, just making sure that youth stay entertained, and, (f) I have an annual budget of $1,000—in a church with 700 people attending on Sundays. C'mon! You can't rent juggling monkeys for $1,000! In fact, we were supposed to have fundraisers, even if we don't use the money!

So please learn from my mistake and *ask the church what they think youth ministry is and their vision for it*. One good thing that's come from this is that I've gotten away from programs and focused all my energy on teaching and building relationships (vertically and horizontally). Maybe this is what God was trying to teach me.

—*Lee Brown, Crossroads Community Church, Bedford, Indiana*

- Develop a process to bring adult leaders on your youth ministry team.
- Decide on key attitudes and actions for your volunteer team.
- Develop a purpose statement for the student ministry.
- Find a parent to oversee your ministry to parents and families.
- Ask a veteran leader for the titles of two favorite books to study regarding leadership.

// Programs: During Your First Two Years

Programs come and go and, in my opinion, are way overrated. Programs are the means to an end and not the end in itself. Use programs to help you fulfill the biblical purposes and reach your target audience.

- Establish calendar dates on which you take time to evaluate.

- Evaluate all your existing programs by defining your target audience and biblical purpose.
- Pursue changes that show the biblical purposes and the target audience for each program. Get rid of dead-weight programs so you can be more effective.
- Evaluate whether your teaching is understandable and practical for students.
- Teach on the five biblical purposes: worship, evangelism, discipleship, ministry, and fellowship.

As our meal together concludes, you and the waitress look exhausted. Understandable! We discussed a lot of material. The table is messy with all our notes and diagrams. Soon you'll forget some of what we talked about. That's understandable. I want to suggest that you revisit this material in a few months or each year by paging through the book. Remind yourself about the principles you know but haven't gotten to yet.

I'd also encourage you to get a copy of this book into the hands of the other youth ministry leaders on your team. When two or more youth workers are thinking the same, a unified approach to ministry emerges. Unified leadership builds health and brings about change. You can't do it alone, but with a team you can experience success!

This book took me two years to write, as I tried to grab pockets of time in the midst of my own youth ministry schedule. And each time I sat down to write, I asked God to give me words to encourage you, ideas to help you, and insights to motivate you in the journey I know so well. As a youth pastor, my heart is filled with grace for the role you have, empathy for the hurdles you face, and excitement for your future ministry.

Thank you for being a learner. Thank you for loving Jesus and teenagers. Thank you for protecting your heart. You won't get everything right, and you won't get everything wrong, but you will get great rewards for serving faithfully. What a joy to be in the trenches together!

Keep in touch…and don't give up.

The Questions at the End of the Chapter

// For group discussion

- Do you feel like you know what's epected of you?
- If we were in Step 1 (tell), what would you list as your strenghts and weaknesses?

// For personal reflection

- Which reaction best describes me from page 257?
- What doesn't the church know about me?
- Did I say "yes" to this youth ministry position too soon? If so, is there anything I can do, now that I've read the contents of this chapter?
- What do I want to get out of my time in youth ministry?
- Where do I feel misunderstood? Or where have I misunderstood the churches expectations?

// Actions to consider

- Go through the book again and see if you underlined and/or highlighted anything that you want to reread and take action on.
- Figure out a way to make this book high-priority reading for volunteers on this youth ministry team (both current and future).
- Make a commitment to be a continual learner.

Go to www.dougfields.com and enter your comments under Your First 2 Years: Chapter 12

epilogue

I write these last words from my second office—Taco Bell—on a Sunday afternoon. My church responsibilities are over for a few hours, and I've come here to put my finishing touches on this book.

This task creates some love-hate emotions within me. Because this book has taken me so long to write, I love the fact that these are my final words…but because it's taken me so long to write, I hate the fact that I'm actually done! The rough pages of this book have been like a friend. Writing each chapter was a conversation, a delight, and a challenge to be both helpful and hopeful.

It's my hope that you've enjoyed reading it as much as I've enjoyed writing it. I've been praying this book won't be just another youth ministry book, but one that inspires volunteers to keep running and lead youth workers to keep leading.

Now that our meal is over, it's time to leave the restaurant. (I'll get the tip!)

With much appreciation for who you are and what you do,
Doug Fields

youth ministry volunteer staff commitment form
(see page 183)

After observing the youth ministry programs and reading about the commitment involved with being on this team, I have spent time in prayer, and discussed with my family the commitment involved as a volunteer leader.

I choose to commit to the following:

☐ I acknowledge the Lordship of Jesus Christ in my life and have a personal relationship with him.

☐ I am committed toward growing and maturing my relationship with God through quiet times, active attendance at church, and involvement in accountable relationships.

☐ I am committed to choices and a lifestyle that are both godly and "above reproach," knowing that my lifestyle is a model for students.

☐ I am making a commitment to the youth ministry for at least the full school year.

☐ I will attend the monthly volunteer staff meetings.

☐ I will make a committed attempt to help find at least one other adult volunteer for our growing need of leaders in the youth ministry.

☐ I understand the five biblical purposes of the church as well as the strategy of the youth ministry and commit to help fulfill the purposes and care for the students God brings in my ministry.

☐ Because I am making a significant commitment and my presence is important, I agree to be consistent and on time to the program(s) I commit myself to.

I am making a commitment to the following programs:

☐ Weekend Services Table Leader
☐ Small Group Leader
☐ Ministry Team Coordinator–Ministry: _____
☐ One-on-One Mentor

_____   _____
Signature   Date

appendix b
10 frequently asked questions

Questions 1 through 3 are directed toward church leadership/search committees
Questions 4 and 5 are directed toward lead youth workers
Questions 6 through 10 are directed toward all youth workers

1. What qualities do most churches look for in a youth worker?

It's difficult to define what most churches look for in a prospective youth worker, but when I look at youth ministry job postings, I see five dominant qualities in youth workers that seem to be attractive to most churches:

- *Young.* Churches often look specifically for youth worker candidates in their early 20s.
- *Married.* Some churches believe marriage is a sign of stability—or they've been burned by single youth workers who've had relationships with their youth group kids.
- *Likes to plan and attend activities and events.* Many churches believe that a good youth ministry keeps students busy.
- *Energetic.* I guess the reasoning is the youth worker will need a lot of energy to participate in all the planned activities!
- *Likes students.* I'm glad this was included, or it would be a pitiful list.

Unfortunately this is the type of list (i.e., pervasive thinking) that contributes to the plague of churches that constantly burn out and destroy youth workers.

If you're part of a church that's looking to hire a youth worker, I encourage you to compare the preceding list with the list that follows the next question.

2. What qualities would I look for when choosing a youth worker?

My list looks very different. If I was on a search committee, here's what I'd look for in a potential youth worker:

- *Heart for God.* If this doesn't exist, there's no use continuing.
- *Love for people.* Sound familiar? Love God and love others…
- *Leader.* When you can find a leader who also loves others, that's a hire! Sure it's nice to have some younger leaders with lots of energy—see previous list—but a good leader can still find those types to compliment the team.
- *Developer of others.* Read chapters 8 and 9 if this one doesn't make sense.
- *Communicator/teacher.* Of these five qualities, this one's the most negotiable and probably the one that's most biased toward my style of youth ministry anyway.

3. How can our church find a good youth minister and keep him/her?

Any church can hire a youth minister, but keeping one is a big issue and a big challenge. Obviously an adequate answer to this question will run deeper than a list, but since I couldn't devote an entire chapter to this question, let me give you a list and encourage you to thoroughly discuss each of these tips with the people who care about the longevity of youth workers.

- *Know the type of youth worker you're looking for.*

    Many churches enter the search process with an incomplete picture of the type of youth worker they need. It's not uncommon for the pastor, search committee, volunteers, and students to have different and/or conflicting ideas regarding the type of person who would assume leadership of the youth ministry. Before you begin the search, try hard to come to some kind of consensus.

- *Be willing to make an investment in your youth worker.*

    Since a lot of churches want "cheap labor," they often look for someone young and inexperienced who won't require much of a salary. But remember this: *If you go cheap, you'll get what you pay for.* If a church isn't willing to invest in a youth ministry position with a good salary and benefits and a budget, it'll be a high-turnover position. While money shouldn't be everything, the church needs to communicate that it desires a healthy youth ministry through what it's willing to give.

- *Post the position and pursue veterans' opinions.*

    Several youth ministry job boards advertise open youth ministry positions. If you use them, expect a lot of diverse résumés! In addition to this process, it's a good idea to contact veteran youth workers and ask the question, "Do you know of any quality youth workers out there?" You needn't add the line, "…who are looking to relocate" to your questions. Just ask for names and churches of their top-five. Then search out the addresses and send your candidates a personal letter explaining your opening. (Don't ask the veteran to do this part—that's your job!) Most good hires are found—as opposed to them looking for you.

- *Interview with integrity.*

During the interview process, be honest about what's happened in your youth ministry. No new employee likes to be caught by surprise and then mutter, "Why didn't you tell me about this?" Every church has its strengths and weaknesses—be honest about both. It's unethical to hire someone without pulling the church skeletons from under the bed. When you expose some of the pain from the past, you'll gain credibility with your new hire—and build loyalty, too.

A church recently hired a friend of mine, and two weeks after the start date, church officials told him the youth ministry was *250 percent over budget* and that he couldn't spend any money for the next nine months. Had he known this before he agreed to work at the church, he could have at least arrived with realistic expectations. Instead he's bitter at and fearful of the church leadership because they didn't tell him the truth right up front.

- *Surround your new hire with enthusiasm.*

Roll out the red carpet when your new youth worker arrives! Have some key families in the church take the new hire (and her family) to dinner. Make sure her office is ready, the computer's plugged in, the lights are on, and some encouraging notes (written from students and families) are left on her desk. You want a new hire to arrive with an "oh wow" attitude since the "oh no" of ministry is right around the corner. Plus, the first few weeks of any job are lonely. Send the message early on that you're a church that cares about its employees.

- *Resource learning.*

When a youth worker stops learning, he'll stop being an effective leader. When you make a commitment to invest in a lead youth worker, invest in his continuing education. Provide a budget that pays for him to attend conferences, seminars, and purchase books that will enhance his learning.

- *Support your youth worker's family.*

For the benefit of her husband and children, make sure your church demonstrates support for your youth minister. One of the many things I love about working at Saddleback Church is that the people there care about my family. It's written into my job description that I can't be away from home for ministry duties more than three nights a week. What's more, my children get to go to camps and attend activities at a discount, and my wife is valued for her role as my spouse, regardless of how involved she is. Bottom line: My family loves that I work at my church!

• *Provide consistent reviews.*

Every employee should have the privilege of knowing how he's doing. In the same way, the church should offer its youth minister an evaluation—based on his job description— twice a year. If you need help writing a job description, check out the Youth Specialties' book, *Youth Ministry Management Tools* (pages 349 to 353) for some coaching and examples.

• *Facilitate a mentor for this position.*

I don't advocate choosing a mentor for the lead youth worker, but I would encourage you to guide this new employee toward some gracious and caring men or women in the church who might be able to play this role in a new youth worker's life. The right mentor can add years to a youth worker's longevity!

• *Shower with praise.*

Employees rarely leave workplaces where they are valued—and this is the loudest cry I hear from youth workers! Praise must be intentional, because the longer someone works at the church, the less she will hear praise—people assume she already knows she's doing a good job. So a simple comment like, "I sure appreciate what you do with students and who you are as a person!" will always breathe fresh life into a tired and discouraged youth worker.

4. What kinds of questions should I ask during my first interview with a prospective church?

This is such an important question! Many of my fired friends have said, "I wish I would have asked better questions during my interview." The best advice I've ever read on asking questions at interviews is found in *Youth Ministry Management Tools*. (Since it's published by Youth Specialties, I'm able to provide you with these questions—but I strongly suggest that you pick up a copy of this excellent book that's filled with all sorts of helpful information on budgeting, finances, running events, preparing release forms, and other topics I didn't cover in these pages.)

Here are the crucial questions:

- If the ministry is considered successful in three months, what will that look like? In six months? In one year?
- Why did the last youth pastor leave?
- Tell me about a youth worker who didn't make it here and why.
- Tell me about a youth worker "hero" and why that person was successful.
- Are you hiring me to pastor every kid or to train and equip adults for that role?
- How are raises determined?
- What has been the youth ministry budget? How do you see that figure changing in the future? Is the youth pastor's salary included in the youth ministry budget?
- What are the church's expectations for numerical and spiritual growth?
- How often are job reviews conducted? Who conducts them? What happens to the reviews?
- Who will I report to, and how much time per week will I spend with that person/those people?
- If someone asked you about me a year from now, and you responded that I'm barely surviving in the youth ministry position, how would I be performing to make that the case?
- What's the process for determining and approving what the youth ministry does?
- What other expectations exist for the youth pastor outside the youth ministry?
- Has the staff ever had a paycheck withheld because the church was short on money?
- What happens when the church is behind on budget?
- What does a typical work week look like?

5. How do I know it's time to leave my ministry position?

There's never a good time to leave a youth ministry position when things are going great—and it feels like every day is a good time to leave when things are going badly. This is a tough one to answer without knowing all the details of an individual's ministry. One principle I've been taught is to never consider leaving when you're discouraged. When you're down, everything looks dark—and you probably know by now that many, many circumstances can get a youth worker down about the job:

- When the annual youth pastor's salary survey comes out and your pay is at the bottom.
- When you've been hurt by someone in the church.
- When you're in conflict with others.
- When your ministry seems stuck.
- When you get in trouble for something major—like not returning all the pencils to the right box.

The good news I've learned is that good youth workers are in high demand, and there are always churches looking for them. Because of this, there will typically be another church out there that pays better and looks like it's problem free.

Well, it may pay better, but don't be fooled—there are no problem-free churches or problem-free youth ministry positions! When you leave because of hurt feelings or problems and go to another church, you're just exchanging your old problems for new ones.

In addition to constant prayer and counsel, you need to ask some tough questions about your current ministry situation. As my friend Duffy Robbins writes in his book *Youth Ministry Nuts & Bolts*, you should consider five important questions before moving on:

- Have I been here long enough to reach my most effective years?
- Do I have a dream for this ministry?
- Do my spiritual gifts match the present needs of my ministry?
- Is my philosophy of ministry compatible with my church's philosophy of ministry?
- Are people willing to follow me?

In addition to Duffy's great questions, I'd add a few more:

- Has God been preparing my heart to leave through some unsettled feelings? (If you're married, your spouse should answer this question, too.)
- Am I considering a move primarily to escape my current difficulties?
- Has my church showed a consistent lack of support to me and/or the youth ministry?
- Can I continue to grow and develop here? Have I pursued all opportunities at this church to realize the full expression of my gifts?
- Is there an integrity issue at my church that violates my standards?

I'm sure you'll need to answer more questions and discern the difference between God's call and your desire to escape a tough situation. Through talking with thousands of youth workers, I do know that this decision is always a battle, and I've also learned that God can use youth workers who're working in less-than-perfect situations.

6. What should a typical year of activities look like?

While I don't believe there's any one way to do anything, I do have some rule-of-thumb options that I typically coach new leaders to consider.

In addition to your weekly program(s), I'd consider 8 to 12 activities a year as doable and healthy. I don't believe they all need to be wild, crazy, and fun in order to meet the definition of *activities*. For example, one month you might do something fun (bring your friends/evangelism) and the next month you might do a work project (ministry). I encourage you to not sponsor activities just for the sake of filling your calendar and keeping your students busy. When you plan an activity, make sure you have an answer to the question, "Why?" (See Chapter 10) Also, I would include camp experiences as two of your activities (a summer camp and either a winter camp and/or a spring-break camp). The right choice and balance of activity can really add to the health of a youth ministry.

7. How do I decide what to teach throughout the year?

When considering the big picture for a teaching plan for your ministry, the following thoughts may be helpful:

- *Teaching spiritual truths should be personal.* This means that whatever you decide to teach should spring from your passion. As teachers, we're not called to simply convey a set of truths as if we were merely dispensers of information. Instead we should communicate from the depths of our encounters with God's Spirit and his Word.

- *While teaching should be passionate, it should also possess balance.* While often the temptation is to only teach topics we know well, that will lead to imbalance and, I believe, quench our growth. So make a detailed list of the major topics you *want* to cover and those you believe you *should* cover (regardless of your knowledge and/or experience with those topics). You might consider using an academic book (e.g., *Introduction to Systematic Theology*) as a theological framework reference regarding what to teach.

- *Once you've painted the broad strokes of your teaching plan, stick with it.* But you don't need to follow it at all costs. As your ministry experiences different "seasons," you may find it necessary to adjust and rethink your current plan.

- *When you plan your topics, consider your audiences.* Students attending your entry-level program probably need to hear something different than your committed Christian students. It's important to maintain a balance between teaching what they *want* to hear ("felt needs") and what you know they *need* to hear (God's truth).

    As an example, in our entry-level programs, we teach a variety of subjects directed to both Christian and non-Christian students (our target audience). Many of our teachings focus on the basics of the faith—the life of Christ, grace, sin, the Bible, et cetera. We also teach God's truth as it relates to kids' current life-topics—sex, family, addictions, friendships, et cetera.

    During our small group time, our audience is made up of Christian students who have a developed faith. During these teaching times we either work through a book of the Bible (e.g., Genesis, Philippians, James) or teach on a biblical character (e.g., Joseph, David, Paul, Ruth).

Again, there's no "one way" to create a teaching plan. Experiment. Look through different curriculums and adapt what will fit your passion and your group. Be true to God's Word, honest about his workings in your life, understand students' needs, and teach in a way they'll understand—if you can do these things, you'll win.

8. I'm a new leader and the students don't seem to like me. They still miss the old leader. Any suggestions?

Most teenagers have had several adults coming in and out of their lives. They've learned to be cautious. Some students may be wondering if you'll be there in another year, or if you'll be like the other adults in their lives and leave them. You may need to trust me on this, but they'll give you a chance...and TIME will have to earn it. It's very normal for students to miss their previous youth worker, small group leader, teacher, et cetera. People who've impacted lives aren't easily forgotten or replaced. I suggest letting them talk freely about what they liked about the previous youth worker. This is a time for you to learn! And always speak highly of the person(s) who preceded you.

And don't do what so many adults do when they want kids to like them and be impressed by them…act like teenagers! What impresses students is when you act like *you*. Students don't need adults to act like teenagers; they need adults who are kind, caring, happy, thoughtful, loving, and tender (basically, reflecting the fruits of the Spirit). By loving God and being consistent, you'll eventually earn credibility with the students who God has entrusted to your care.

Plan to stick around, and you'll outlast your critics—and students will respond to your love and genuine care. Provide that for students, and you'll be given a chance… actually, you'll get more than a chance: You'll develop relationships with students that will impact their lives forever!

Focus on Jesus who accepts you for who you are. Allow him to work through you, and you'll soon find students accepting you, too (unfortunately, they won't be as quick to accept you as Jesus is!)

9. How do I handle a crisis at a local school (e.g., suicide, shooting)?

There's no "right way" to handle every crisis. My suggestion is that when people *outside* the church are discussing a crisis, it's probably a good time to talk about it *in* the church, too. Typically I'll cancel our regular teaching schedule and deal with the current issue. Bombings, school shootings, a local school suicide, or any crisis that becomes newsworthy is worth talking about with the backdrop of God's Word. Most students aren't hearing a biblical perspective on pain, suffering, God, or evil from their school conversations. They need to know the Bible gives direction and hope.

Times of crisis provide great opportunities to point students toward God, but don't feel like you have to have all the right answers to all the issues (especially since you don't!) Be genuine about your feelings and honest about your lack of comforting answers. I love the words in Acts 4:12, "Peter saw this as his opportunity and addressed the crowd…" Crisis is an opportunity to address your crowd. You don't need to answer every question, you just need to show students that you love them and want them to know the One who's still in control in the midst of difficult times.

10. How can I contact you to ask more youth ministry questions?

My Web site (www.dougfields.com) is filled with several frequently asked questions (FAQs). I answer a new question each week and add it to the list. Plus you can go to the First Two Years section of the Web site and interact with other learners regarding your questions. While I can't promise to answer every question, I do read every e-mail and would love to hear about your youth ministry journey and your thoughts regarding this book.

notes

resources from youth specialties www.youthspecialties.com

Ideas Library
Ideas Library on CD-ROM 2.0
Administration, Publicity, & Fundraising
Camps, Retreats, Missions, & Service Ideas
Creative Meetings, Bible Lessons, & Worship
   Ideas
Crowd Breakers & Mixers
   Discussion & Lesson Starters
Discussion & Lesson Starters 2
Drama, Skits, & Sketches
Drama, Skits, & Sketches 2
Drama, Skits, & Sketches 3
Games
Games 2
Games 3
Holiday Ideas
Special Events

Bible Curricula
Backstage Pass to the Bible Kit
Creative Bible Lessons from the Old
   Testament
Creative Bible Lessons in 1 & 2 Corinthians
Creative Bible Lessons in Galatians and
   Philippians
Creative Bible Lessons in John
Creative Bible Lessons in Romans
Creative Bible Lessons on the Life of Christ
Creative Bible Lessons on the Prophets
Creative Bible Lessons in Psalms
Wild Truth Bible Lessons
Wild Truth Bible Lessons 2
Wild Truth Bible Lessons—Pictures of God
Wild Truth Bible Lessons—Pictures of God 2
Wild Truth Bible Lessons—Dares from Jesus

Topical Curricula
Creative Junior High Programs from A to Z,
   Vol. 1 (A-M)
Creative Junior High Programs from A to Z,
   Vol. 2 (N-Z)
Girls: 10 Gutsy, God-Centered Sessions on
   Issues That Matter to Girls
Guys: 10 Fearless, Faith-Focused Sessions on
   Issues That Matter to Guys
Good Sex
The Justice Mission
Live the Life! Student Evangelism Training Kit
The Next Level Youth Leader's Kit
Roaring Lambs
So What Am I Gonna Do with My Life?
Student Leadership Training Manual
Student Underground
Talking the Walk
What Would Jesus Do? Youth Leader's Kit
Wild Truth Bible Lessons
Wild Truth Bible Lessons 2
Wild Truth Bible Lessons—Pictures of God
Wild Truth Bible Lessons—Pictures of God 2
Wild Truth Bible Lessons—Dares from Jesus

Discussion Starters
Discussion & Lesson Starters (Ideas Library)
Discussion & Lesson Starters 2 (Ideas Library)
EdgeTV
Every Picture Tells a Story
Get 'Em Talking
Keep 'Em Talking!
Good Sex Drama
Have You Ever...?
Name Your Favorite
Unfinished Sentences
What If...?
Would You Rather...?
High School TalkSheetsUpdated!
More High School TalkSheets—Updated!
High School TalkSheets from Psalms and
   Proverbs—Updated!
Junior High-Middle School TalkSheets—
   Updated!

More Junior High-Middle School
   TalkSheets—Updated!
Junior High-Middle School TalkSheets from
   Psalms and Proverbs—Updated!
Real Kids Ultimate Discussion-Starting Videos:
   Castaways
   Growing Up Fast
   Hardship & Healing
   Quick Takes
   Survivors
   Word on the Street
Small Group Qs

Drama Resources
Drama, Skits, & Sketches (Ideas Library)
Drama, Skits, & Sketches 2 (Ideas Library)
Drama, Skits, & Sketches 3 (Ideas Library)
Dramatic Pauses
Good Sex Drama
Spontaneous Melodramas
Spontaneous Melodramas 2
Super Sketches for Youth Ministry

Game Resources
Games (Ideas Library)
Games 2 (Ideas Library)
Games 3 (Ideas Library)
Junior High Game Nights
More Junior High Game Nights
Play It!
Screen Play CD-ROM

Additional Programming Resources
(also see Discussion Starters)
The Book of Uncommon Prayer
Camps, Retreats, Missions, & Service Ideas
   (Ideas Library)
Creative Meetings, Bible Lessons, & Worship
   Ideas (Ideas Library)
Crowd Breakers & Mixers (Ideas Library)
   Everyday Object Lessons
Great Fundraising Ideas for Youth Groups
More Great Fundraising Ideas for Youth
   Groups
Great Retreats for Youth Groups
Great Talk Outlines for Youth Ministry
Holiday Ideas (Ideas Library)
Incredible Questionnaires for Youth Ministry
Kickstarters
Memory Makers
Special Events (Ideas Library)
Videos That Teach
Videos That Teach 2
Worship Services for Youth Groups

Quick Question Books
Have You Ever...?
Name Your Favorite
Unfinished Sentences
What If...?
Would You Rather...?

Videos & Video Curricula
Dynamic Communicators Workshop
EdgeTV
The Justice Mission
Live the Life! Student Evangelism Training Kit
Make 'Em Laugh!
Purpose-Driven® Youth Ministry Training Kit
Real Kids Ultimate Discussion-Starting Videos:
   Castaways
   Growing Up Fast
   Hardship & Healing
   Quick Takes
   Survivors
   Word on the Street
Student Underground
Understanding Your Teenager Video
   Curriculum
Youth Ministry Outside the Lines

Especially for Junior High
Creative Junior High Programs from A to Z,
   Vol. 1 (A-M)
Creative Junior High Programs from A to Z,
   Vol. 2 (N-Z)
Junior High Game Nights
More Junior High Game Nights
Junior High-Middle School TalkSheets—
   Updated!
More Junior High-Middle School
   TalkSheets—Updated!
Junior High-Middle School TalkSheets from
   Psalms and Proverbs—Updated!
Wild Truth Journal for Junior Highers
Wild Truth Bible Lessons
Wild Truth Bible Lessons 2
Wild Truth Journal—Pictures of God
Wild Truth Bible Lessons—Pictures of God
Wild Truth Bible Lessons—Dares from Jesus
Wild Truth Journal—Dares from Jesus

Student Resources
Backstage Pass to the Bible: An All-Access
   Tour of the New Testament
Backstage Pass to the Bible: An All-Access
   Tour of the Old Testament
Grow for It! Journal through the Scriptures
So What Am I Gonna Do with My Life?
Spiritual Challenge Journal: The Next Level
Teen Devotional Bible
What (Almost) Nobody Will Tell You about Sex
What Would Jesus Do? Spiritual Challenge
   Journal

Clip Art
Youth Group Activities (print)
Clip Art Library Version 2.0 (CD-ROM)

Digital Resources
Clip Art Library Version 2.0 (CD-ROM)
Great Talk Outlines for Youth Ministry
Hot Illustrations CD-ROM
Ideas Library on CD-ROM 2.0
Screen Play
Youth Ministry Management Tools

Professional Resources
Administration, Publicity, & Fundraising (Ideas
   Library)
Dynamic Communicators Workshop
Great Talk Outlines for Youth Ministry
Help! I'm a Junior High Youth Worker!
Help! I'm a Small Church Youth Worker!
Help! I'm a Small-Group Leader!
Help! I'm a Sunday School Teacher!
Help! I'm an Urban Youth Worker!
Help! I'm a Volunteer Youth Worker!
Hot Illustrations for Youth Talks
More Hot Illustrations for Youth Talks
Still More Hot Illustrations for Youth Talks
Hot Illustrations for Youth Talks 4
How to Expand Your Youth Ministry
How to Speak to Youth...and Keep Them
   Awake at the Same Time
Junior High Ministry (Updated & Expanded)
Just Shoot Me
Make 'Em Laugh!
The Ministry of Nurture
Postmodern Youth Ministry
Purpose-Driven® Youth Ministry
Purpose-Driven® Youth Ministry Training Kit
So That's Why I Keep Doing This!
Teaching the Bible Creatively
Your First Two Years in Youth Ministry
A Youth Ministry Crash Course
Youth Ministry Management Tools
The Youth Worker's Handbook to Family
   Ministry

Academic Resources
Four Views of Youth Ministry & the Church
Starting Right
Youth Ministry That Transforms